The Waite Group

ARTIFICIAL
LIFE LAB

Rudy Rucker

Waite
Group
Press™

Publisher: Mitchell Waite
Editorial Director: Scott Calamar
Managing Editor: John Crudo
Content Editor: Heidi Brumbaugh
Technical Reviewer: Stephen Wright
Copy Editor: Kathy Caryle
Design: Ted Mader + Associates
Production: Michele Cuneo
Illustrations and Cover Design: David Povilaitis
Production Director: Julianne Ososke

Printed in the United States of America
93 94 95 96 • 10 9 8 7 6 5 4 3 2 1

Library of Congress Cataloging in Publication Data
Rucker, Rudy v. B. (Rudy von Bitter), 1946-
    Artificial life lab / by Rudy Rucker.
      p. cm.
    Includes bibliographical references and index.
    ISBN: 1-878739-48-4: $34.95
    1. Artificial intelligence--Computer simulation. 2. Biological systems--Computer simulation.
    3. Boppers (Computer file)
  I. Title.
Q336.R83 1993
003' .5--dc20   93-31742
                                  CIP

Acknowledgments

I wrote the first half of the Boppers *program while I was employed as Mathenaut in the Division of Advanced Technology at Autodesk, Inc. Many thanks to Autodesk for four fascinating years, and for granting me a license to distribute the complete program.*

Thanks to The Waite Group for taking this project on, and for giving me the encouragement and help I needed to finish it.

Thanks to San Jose State University for getting me out to California in the first place, and for giving me the leave-time to work at Autodesk and to write this book.

Thanks to my old artist friend David Povilaitis for his wonderful illustrations; and thanks to my friend and neighbor Tom Knight of Imagination Works for creating the icons for the boppers' bodies.

Special thanks to my dear family members—Sylvia, Georgia, Rudy, Jr., and Isabel—for their patience and humor during weeks and months of writing and computer hacking.

And, finally, thank God it's done!

—Rudy Rucker, San Jose State University, August 23, 1993

Dear Reader:

What is a book? Is it perpetually fated to be inky words on a paper page? Or can a book simply be something that inspires—feeding your head with ideas and creativity regardless of the medium? The latter, I believe. That's why I'm always pushing our books to a higher plane; using new technology to reinvent the medium.

I wrote my first book in 1973, Projects in Sights, Sounds, and Sensations. I like to think of it as our first multimedia book. In the years since then, I've learned that people want to experience information, not just passively absorb it—they want interactive MTV in a book. With this in mind, I started my own publishing company and published Master C, a book/disk package that turned the PC into a C language instructor. Then we branched out to computer graphics with Fractal Creations, which included a color poster, 3-D glasses, and a totally rad fractal generator. Ever since, we've included disks and other goodies with most of our books. Virtual Reality Creations is bundled with 3-D Fresnel viewing goggles and Walkthroughs and Flybys CD comes with a multimedia CD-ROM. We've made complex multimedia accessible for any PC user with Ray Tracing Creations, Multimedia Creations, Making Movies on Your PC, Image Lab, and three books on Fractals.

The Waite Group continues to publish innovative multimedia books on cutting-edge topics, and of course the programming books that make up our heritage. Being a programmer myself, I appreciate clear guidance through a tricky OS, so our books come bundled with disks and CDs loaded with code, utilities and custom controls.

By 1993, The Waite Group will have published 135 books. Our next step is to develop a new type of book, an interactive, multimedia experience involving the reader on many levels. With this new book, you'll be trained by a computer-based instructor with infinite patience, run a simulation to visualize the topic, play a game that shows you different aspects of the subject, interact with others on-line, and have instant access to a large database on the subject. For traditionalists, there will be a full-color, paper-based book.

In the meantime, they've wired the White House for hi-tech; the information super highway has been proposed; and computers, communication, entertainment, and information are becoming inseparable. To travel in this Digital Age you'll need guidebooks. The Waite Group offers such guidance for the most important software—your mind.

We hope you enjoy this book. For a color catalog, just fill out and send in the Reader Report Card at the back of the book. You can reach me on CIS as 75146,3515, MCI mail as mwaite, and usenet as mitch@well.sf.ca.us.

Mitchell Waite

Mitchell Waite
Publisher

About the Author

Novelist, scientist, and cult hero Rudy Rucker has emerged as a key figure in the cyberpunk culture that has developed at this century's close. Two of his best-known novels are the award-winning cyberpunk science-fiction classics SOFTWARE and WETWARE. A professor of mathematics and computer science at San Jose State University, Dr. Rucker is also the co-author of two software packages, CA LAB: RUDY RUCKER'S CELLULAR AUTOMATA LABORATORY and JAMES GLEICK'S CHAOS: THE SOFTWARE. Rucker published such non-fiction books on mathematics as THE FOURTH DIMENSION and MIND TOOLS. He recently co-edited MONDO 2000: A USER'S GUIDE TO THE NEW EDGE with R.U. Sirius and Queen Mu.

Contents

Preface

What is life? Gnarl, sex, and death.

What is artificial life? Computer programs that act that way.

How do you tweak such a program? You let it evolve.

The first three chapters of Artificial Life Lab *flesh out the meaning of these remarks, while filling in the theory and background of artificial life. The remaining four chapters are devoted to an exploration of one particular artificial life program, the* Boppers *program for Windows 3.1 which is included with this book. I've had a lot of fun working with the book and the program, and I hope that you will too. But be warned—the experience may change the way you look at life!*

Read This Before Leaping In

You are probably eager to begin running *Boppers* immediately, but please take a moment to read this important information before attempting to install and run the program. You will find installation information in Chapter 4, *Installation and Quick Start,* and Chapters 5, *The Boppers and Their World,* and 6, *Boppers User's Guide,* provide detailed information on running the program.

MINIMUM REQUIREMENTS

A 3.5-inch program disk containing *Boppers* is located on the back flap of this book. To run this program, your IBM PC-compatible computer *must* have:

- Windows 3.1

- At least 4MB or more RAM

- At least 1.5MB available on a hard disk

MAKE A WORK DISK

It is recommended that you make a copy of the *Boppers* disk. Use the copy as a work disk to protect the original program files from accidental damage. You can use the DOS diskcopy command to copy the contents to a blank, formatted 1.44MB disk. If you are running Windows, either exit Windows or click on the MS-DOS Prompt icon. At the DOS prompt type:

```
diskcopy a: a:          (ENTER)
```
[If your 3.5-inch disk drive is designated B:, type `diskcopy b: b:` instead.]

Follow the on-screen instructions. The bundled *Boppers* disk is considered the SOURCE diskette, and the blank disk is the TARGET diskette. Once copied, use this newly created work disk during the installation, and store the original disk.

COPY BOPPERS TO THE HARD DISK

Use DOS commands to copy the program to your hard disk. To copy *Boppers* to the C: drive, insert the newly created work disk in the disk drive and type:

```
c:                      (ENTER)
```
[Switches DOS to the hard disk; you can replace C: with another drive designation]

```
cd\                     (ENTER)
```
[Switches to the hard disk's root directory]

```
md boppers              (ENTER)
```
[Creates a directory on the hard disk called BOPPERS]

```
copy a:*.* c:\boppers   (ENTER)
```
[Copies the files to the new directory; if you're 3.5-inch drive is B:, type `copy b:*.* c:\boppers` instead.]

SET UP BOPPERS IN WINDOWS

After copying *Boppers* to the hard disk, you must set up Windows so that it recognizes the new program. You'll need to return to Windows, so if you are not already running Windows, type:

```
win                     (ENTER)
```

If you have been running MS-DOS from within Windows, type:

```
exit                    (ENTER)
```

Once Windows is running, click on the program group where you'd like to locate *Boppers;* don't forget, you can always move the program later by dragging the *Boppers* icon into another program group.

Click on the Program Manager's **File** option at the top left part of the screen, then click on **New**. The Program Item Properties dialog box appears. You can use the

Browse option to locate the BOPPERS.EXE file in the BOPPERS directory, or you can type in the appropriate information.

If you are typing the information, for **Description**, type Boppers. For the **Command Line**, type `c:\boppers\boppers.exe`; if you installed *Boppers* in a directory other than C:\BOPPERS, type in the proper drive and directory. For the **Working Directory**, type `c:\boppers`; if you installed *Boppers* in a different directory, change this line accordingly, too.

HELP!

If you encounter problems while installing *Boppers,* technical assistance may be obtained from Waite Group Press through these channels:

- Phone: (415) 924-1724, extension 133
- CompuServe: 75120,1705
- Mail: 200 Tamal Plaza; Corte Madera, CA 94925

PART ONE: THEORY

1

Life
and
A-Life

Artificial life is the study of how to create man-made systems that behave as if they were alive. The purpose of this study is to get a better understanding of how life works.

It is important to study life because the most interesting things in the world are the things that are alive. Living things grow into beautiful shapes and develop graceful behavior. They eat, they mate, they compete, and over the generations they evolve.

In the planetary sense, societies and entire ecologies can be thought of as living organisms. In an even more abstract sense, our thoughts themselves can be regarded as benignly parasitic information viruses that hop from mind to mind. Life is all around us, and it would be valuable to have a better understanding of how it works.

Investigators of the brand-new field of artificial life, or *a-life,* are beginning to tinker with home-brewed simulations of life. A-life can be studied for its scientific aspects, for its aesthetic pleasures, or as a source of insight into real living systems.

In the practical realm, artificial life provides new methods of chemical synthesis, self-improving techniques for controlling complex systems, and ways to automatically generate optimally tweaked computer programs. In the future, artificial life will play a key role in robotics, in virtual reality, and in the retrieval of information from unmanageably huge data bases.

One can go about creating a-life by building robots or by tailoring biochemical reactions—and we'll talk about these options later in this chapter. But the most inexpensive way to experiment with a-life is to use computer programs. *Artificial Life Lab* and the accompanying *Boppers* program are primarily devoted to exploring ways of creating computer-based a-life.

What are some of the essential characteristics of life that we want our a-life programs to have? We want programs that are visually attractive, that move about, that interact with their environment, that breed, and that evolve.

Three characteristics of living systems will guide our quest:

- Gnarl
- Sex
- Death

This chapter includes sections on Gnarl, Sex, and Death, followed by three sections on *noncomputer* a-life. And from Chapter 2, *Computer A-Life,* on, we'll focus on *computer* forms of artificial life.

GNARL

The original meaning of "gnarl" was simply "a knot in the wood of a tree." In California surfer slang, "gnarly" came to describe complicated, rapidly changing surf conditions. And then, by extension, "gnarly" came to mean anything that included a lot of surprisingly intricate detail.

Living things are gnarly in that they inevitably do things that are much more complex than one might have expected. The grain of an oak burl is of course gnarly in the traditional sense of the word, but the life cycle of a jellyfish is gnarly in the modern sense. The wild three-dimensional paths that a hummingbird sweeps out are kind of gnarly, and, if the truth be told, your ears are gnarly as well.

A simple rule of thumb for creating artificial life on the computer is that the program should produce output that looks gnarly. "Gnarly" is, of course, not the word that most research scientists use. Instead, they speak of life as being *chaotic* or *complex*. Chaos as a scientific concept became popular in the 1980s. Chaos can be defined to mean *complicated but not random.*

The surf at the shore of an ocean beach is chaotic. The patterns of the water are clearly very complicated. But, and this is the key point, they are *not random*. The patterns the waves move in are, from moment to moment, predictable by the laws of fluid motion. Waves don't just pop in and out of existence. Water moves according to well understood physical laws.

People might think waves are random because the computation which the water (viewed as an analog computer) performs is many orders of magnitude larger than anything today's digital computers can simulate. For practical purposes, the waves are unpredictable, but they are really chaotic rather than random.

As it turns out, you don't need a system as complicated as the ocean to generate unpredictable chaos. Over the last couple of decades, scientists have discovered that sometimes a very simple rule can produce output that looks, at least superficially, as complicated as physical chaos. Computer simulations of chaos can be obtained either by running one algorithm many many times (as with the famous Mandelbrot Set), or by setting up an arena in which multiple instances of a single algorithm can interact (as with computer a-life).

Some chaotic systems explode into a full-blown random-looking grunge, while others settle into the gnarly, warped patterns known as chaotic attractors. A computer screen filled with what looks like a seething flea circus can be a chaotic system, but the chaotic images you see on T-shirts and calendars are pictures of chaos as well. Like all other kinds of systems, chaotic systems can range from having a lesser or a greater amount of disorder. The less disorderly kinds of chaos are often called *chaotic attractors*.

To return to the surf example, you might notice that the waves near a rock tend every so often to fall into a certain kind of surge pattern. This recurrent surge pattern would be a chaotic attractor. In the same way, chaotic computer simulations will occasionally tighten in on characteristic rhythms and clusters that act as chaotic attractors.

But if there is a storm, the waves may be completely out of control and choppy and patternless. This is full-blown chaos. As disorderliness is increased, a chaotic system can range from being nearly periodic, up through the fractal region of the strange attractors, on up into impenetrable messiness.

Recently some scientists have started using the new word *complexity* for a certain type of chaos. A system is *complex* if it is a chaotic system that is not too disorderly. The notions of chaos and complexity come from looking at a wide range of systems—mathematical, physical, chemical, biological, sociological, and economic. In each domain, the systems that arise can be classified into a spectrum of disorderliness.

At the ordered end we have constancy and a complete lack of surprise. One step up from that is periodic behavior in which the same sequence repeats itself over and over again—as in the structure of a crystal. At the disordered end of the spectrum is full randomness. One notch down from full randomness is the zone of the gnarl.

Table 1-1 shows how the disorderliness spectrum looks for various fields.

Amount of Disorder

Field	None	Low	Gnarly	High
Math	Constant	Periodic	Chaotic	Random
Matter	Vacuum	Crystal	Liquid	Gas
Pattern	Blank	Checkers	Fractal	Dither
Flow	Still	Smooth	Turbulent	Seething

Table 1-1 Spectrums of disorderliness for various fields

As an example of the disorderliness spectrum in mathematics, let's look at some different kinds of mathematical functions, where a *function* is a rule or a method that takes input numbers and gives back other numbers as output. If f is a function then for each input number x, f assigns an output number f(x). A function f is often drawn as a graph of the equation y = f(x), as shown in Figure 1-1.

The most orderly kind of mathematical function is a constant function, such as an f for which f(x) is always two. The graph of such a function is nothing but a horizontal line.

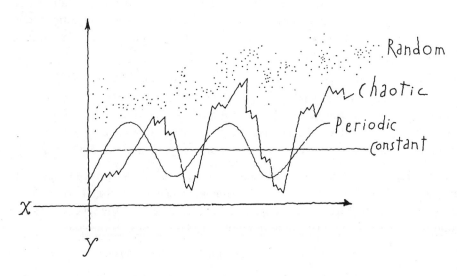

Figure 1-1 Order and disorder in mathematics

At the next level of disorder, we might look at a function f for which f(x) varies periodically with the value of x. The sine function sin(x) is an example of such a function.

The gnarly zone of mathematics is chaos. Chaotic functions have finitely complicated definitions, but somewhat unpredictable patterns. A chaotic function may range from being nearly periodic to being a smeared-out mess.

A truly random mathematical function is a smeared-out mess that has no underlying rhyme or reason to it. A typical random function has a graph that breaks into a cloud of dots. Formally, something is truly random if it admits to no finite definition at all. An old question in the philosophy of science ponders whether anything in the universe truly is random in this sense of being *infinitely complicated*. It may be the whole universe itself is simply a chaotic system whose finite underlying explanation happens to lie beyond our ability to understand.

Before going on to talk about the disorder spectrums of Matter, Pattern, and Flow, let's pause to zoom in on the appearance of the mathematical field's disorderliness spectrum within the gnarly zone of chaos. This zoom is shown in Table 2-1.

Amount of Disorderliness

Field	Less	More	Critical	High
Chaos	Quasiperiodic	Attractor	Complex	Pseudorandom

Table 1-2 Spectrum of disorderliness for the chaos field

The most orderly kind of chaos is "quasiperiodic," or nearly periodic. Something like this might be a periodic function that has a slight, unpredictable drift. Next comes the "attractor" zone in which chaotic systems generate easily visible structures. Next comes a "critical" zone of transition that is the domain of complexity and is the true home of the gnarl. And at the high end of disorder are "pseudorandom" chaotic systems, whose output is empirically indistinguishable from true randomness—unless you happen to be told that the algorithm is generating the chaos.

Now let's get back to the other three fields from Table 1-1: Matter, Pattern, and Flow.

In classical (pre-quantum) physics, a vacuum is the simplest, most orderly kind of matter: nothing is going on. A crystalline solid is orderly in a predictable, periodic way. In a liquid the particles are still loosely linked together; but in a gas, the particles break free and bounce around in a seemingly random way. In classical physics, the trajectories of gas particles can, in principle, be predicted from their starting positions—

much like the bouncing balls of an idealized billiard table—so a classical gas is really a pseudorandom chaotic system rather than a truly random system. Here, again, chaotic means "very complicated but having a finite underlying algorithm."

In any case, the gnarly, complex zone of matter would be identified with the liquid phase, rather than the pseudorandom or perhaps truly random gas phase. The critical point where a heated liquid turns into steam would be a zone of particular gnarliness and interest.

In terms of patterns, the most orderly kind of pattern is a blank one, with the next step up being something like a checkerboard, as shown in Figure 1-2. Fractals are famous for being patterns that are regular yet irregular. The most simply defined fractals (such as the famous Mandelbrot Set) are complex and chaotic patterns that are obtained by carrying out many iterations of some simple formula. The most disorderly kind of pattern is a random dusting of pixels, such as is sometimes used in the random dither effects that are used to create color shadings and grayscale textures. Fractals exemplify gnarl in a very clear form.

The flow of water is a rich source of examples of degrees of disorder. The most orderly state of water is, of course, for it to be standing still. If one lets water run rather slowly down a channel, the water moves smoothly, with perhaps a regular pattern of ripples in it. As more water is put into a channel, eddies and whirlpools appear—this is what is known as turbulence. If a massive amount of water is poured down a steep channel, smaller and smaller eddies cascade off the larger ones, ultimately leading to an essentially random state in which the water is seething. Here the gnarly region is where the flow has begun to break up into eddies with a few smaller eddies, without yet having turned into random churning.

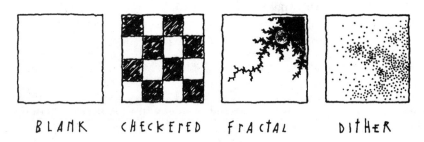

BLANK   CHECKERED   FrACtAL   DItHER

Figure 1-2 Order and disorder in patterns

In every case, the gnarly zone is to be found somewhere at the transition between order and disorder. Simply looking around at the world makes it seem reasonable to believe that this is the level of orderliness to be expected from living things. Living things are orderly, but not too orderly; chaotic, but not too chaotic. Life is gnarly, and a-life should be gnarly too.

SEX

In saying that life includes gnarl, sex, and death, the flashy word "sex" stands for four distinct things:

- Having a body that is grown from genes

- Reproduction

- Mating

- Random genetic changes

Let's discuss these four sex topics one at a time.

Genomes and Phenomes

Genes are seeds for growing the body. All known life forms have a genetic basis. That is, all multicellular living things can be grown from eggs or seeds. And even single-celled creatures are patterned according to the genetic information in their cell nuclei. In living things, the genes are squiggles of DNA molecules that somehow contain a kind of program for constructing the living organism's entire body. In addition, the genes also contain instructions that determine much of the organism's repertoire of behavior.

A single, complete set of genes is known as a *genome*, and an organism's body and its behavior are known as the organism's *phenome*. What a creature looks like and acts like is its phenome; it's the part of the creature that *shows*, as indicated in Figure 1-3. (The word "phenome" comes from the Greek word for "to show." Think of the word "phenomenon.")

Modern researches into the genetic basis of life have established that each living creature starts with a genome. The genome acts as a set of instructions that are used to grow the creature's phenome.

It is conceivable that somewhere in the universe there may be things with phenomes that we would call living that are *not* grown from genomes. These geneless aliens might be like clouds, or like tornados. But all the kinds of things that we ordinarily think of as being alive are based on genomes, so it is reasonable to base our investigations of a-life on systems having a genetic basis.

Given that we are going to be looking at computer-based a-life in this book, it is very appropriate to work with a-life forms whose phenomes grows out of their genomes. In terms of a computer, you can think of the genome as the program and the phenome as the output. As illustrated in Figure 1-4, a computer a-life creature has a genome which is a string of bits (a bit being the minimal piece of binary information, a zero or a one), and its phenome includes the creature's graphic appearance on the computer's screen. Keep in mind that the phenome also includes *behavior*, so the way in which the creature's appearance changes and reacts to other creatures is part of its phenome as well.

Figure 1-3 Genomes are codes that grow phenomes

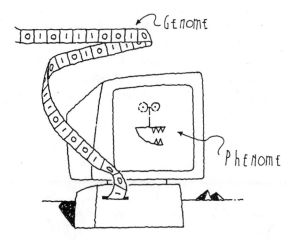

Figure 1-4 A computer program is the genome that grows the phenome that is the computer display

Reproduction

The big win in growing your phenome from a small genome is that this makes it easy for you to grow copies of yourself. Instead of having to copy your large and complicated phenome as a whole, you need only make a copy of your relatively small genome, and then let the copied genome grow its own phenome—as illustrated in Figure 1-5. Eventually, the newly grown phenome should look just like you. Although this kind of reproduction is a solitary activity, it is still a kind of sex, and is practiced by such lowly creatures as the amoeba.

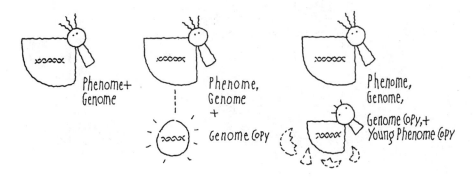

Figure 1-5 A phenome reproduces by copying its genome

As it happens, the genome copying ability is built right into DNA because of the celebrated fact that DNA has the form of a *double helix* which is made of two complementary strands of protein. Each strand encodes the entire information of the genome. In order to reproduce itself, as shown in Figure 1-6, a DNA double helix first unzips itself to produce two separate strands of half-DNA, each of which is a long, linked protein chain of molecules called *bases*. The bases are readily available in the fluid of any living cell, and now each half-DNA strand gathers unto itself enough bases to make a copy of its complementary half-DNA

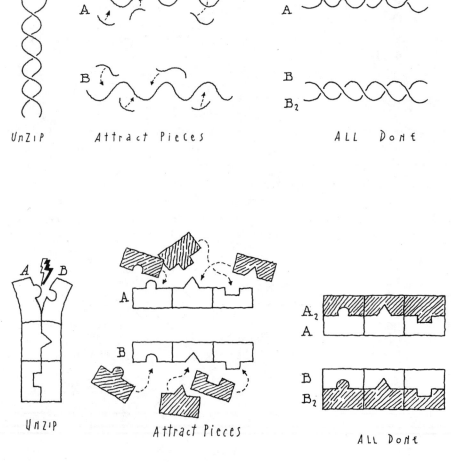

Figure 1-6 Two representations of DNA reproducing itself

strand. The new half-DNA strands are assembled in position, already twined around the old strands, so the net result is that the original DNA genome has turned itself into two. It has successfully reproduced; it has made a copy of itself.

This process is illustrated in two different ways in Figure 1-6. In the first illustration, the DNA strands are spiral curves and the bases are short curve segments. In the second illustration, the bases are drawn like jigsaw puzzle pieces with the property that each kind of base can be paired up with only one other kind of base.

In most a-life worlds, reproduction is something that is done in a simple mechanical way, as shown in Figure 1-7. The bitstring or sequence of bits that encodes a creature's program is copied into a new memory location by the "world" program, and then both creature programs are run concurrently so that two phenotypes can appear.

Mating

Most living creatures reproduce in pairs, with the offspring's genome containing a combination of the parents' genomes. Rather than being a random shuffling of the bases in the parents' DNA, genomes are normally mated by a process known as *crossover*, as illustrated in Figure 1-8.

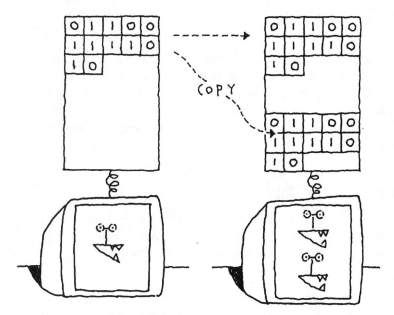

Figure 1-7 An a-life creature reproducing itself

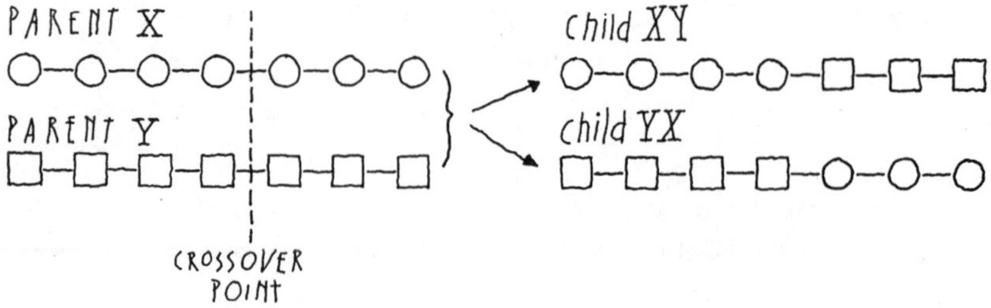

Figure 1-8 Genome crossover

To simplify the picture, we leave out any DNA-like details of genome reproduction, and simply represent the two parent genomes as a chain of circles and a chain of squares, both chains of the same length. In the crossover process, a crossover point is chosen and the two genomes are broken at the crossover point. The broken genomes can now be joined together and mated in two possible ways. In real life, only one of the possible matings is chosen as the genome seed of the new organism.

In computer a-life, we often allow *both* of the newly mated genomes to survive. In fact, the most common form of computer a-life reproduction is to replace the two original parent programs by the two new crossed-over programs. That is to say, two a-life parents often "breed in place."

In a world where several species exist, sometimes one species' genome can incorporate some information from the genome of a creature from another species! Although rare, this does seem to occur in the real world. It is said that snippets of our DNA are identical to bits of modern cat DNA. (Gag me with a hairball!) The *Boppers* program includes a version of this breeding method under the name *exogamy*.

Mutation, Transposition, and Zapping

Mating is a major source of genetic diversity in living things, but genomes can also have their information changed by such randomizing methods as mutation, transposition, and zapping. While mating acts on pairs of genomes, randomization methods act on one genome at a time.

For familiar wetware life forms like ourselves, mutations are caused by things like poisons and cosmic rays. Some mutations are lethal, but many of them make no visible difference at all. Now and then a particular mutation, or

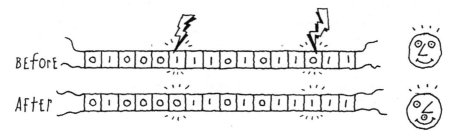

Figure 1-9 Two mutations in an a-life genome

accumulation of mutations, will cause the phenome to suddenly show a drastically new kind of appearance and behavior. Perhaps genius, perhaps a harelip, perhaps beauty, perhaps idiocy.

In the a-life context, where we typically think of the genome as a sequence of zeroes and ones, a mutation amounts to picking a site and flipping the bit: from zero to one, or from one to zero—as shown in Figure 1-9.

The idea in Figure 1-9 is that a genome is drawn as a string of zeroes and ones. The picture on the top shows a genome that is just about to be hit by two mutation rays, and the bottom picture shows how the genome looks after the mutation. Note that the left mutation ray changes a one to zero, while the right mutation changes a zero to a one.

Besides mutation, there are several other forms of genome randomization, some of which are still being discovered in the real world and are as yet poorly understood.

One interesting genome changer is known as *transposition*. In transposition, two swatches of some genomes are swapped, as illustrated in Figure 1-10.

Another genome randomizer that we'll use is something we'll call *zapping*, whereby every now and then *all* of some single creature's genome bits are randomized. In the

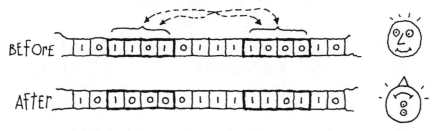

Figure 1-10 A-life transposition

real world, zapping is not a viable method of genetic variation, as it will almost certainly produce a creature that dies instantly. But in the more forgiving arena of a-life, zapping can be useful.

In the natural world, species typically have very large populations and big genomes. Here the effects of mating—sexual reproduction—are the primary sources of genetic diversity. But in the small populations and short genomes of a-life experiments, it is dangerously easy for all the creatures to end up with the same genome. And if you crossover two identical genomes, the offspring are identical to the parents, and no diversity arises! As a practical matter, random genome variation is quite important for artificial life simulations.

DEATH

What would life be like if there were no death? Very crowded or very stagnant. In imagining a fictional situation like *no death*, it's always a challenge to keep a consistent mental scenario. But let's try! Suppose that Death forgot about Earth starting in the Age of the Dinosaurs. What would today's Earth be like?

There would still be lots of dinosaurs around, which might be nice. But if they had been reproducing for all of this time, the dinosaurs and their contemporaries would be piled many hundreds of meters deep all over Earth's surface. Every kind of twisted and deformed dinosaur mutation would be plentiful as well. One might expect that they would have eaten all the plants, but of course there would be no death for plants either, so there would be huge jungles of plants under the mounds of dinosaurs, with all of the dinos taking turns squirming down to get a bite. The oceans would be gill to gill with sea life, and then some. It might be reminiscent of Heironymus Bosch's painting of the Earth before Noah's flood.

Would mammals and humans have evolved in such a world? Probably not. Although there would be many of the oddball creatures around that were our precursors, in the vast welter of life there would be no way for them to select themselves out, get together, and tighten up their genomes.

Math Alert

Actually, if death had ended during the Age of the Dinosaurs, the dinosaurs on Earth's surface would by now be piled a lot higher than "hundreds of meters deep." In fact, while lying awake last night, I calculated that the immortal dinosaurs would fill all known space! To make it easier, I worked my example out in terms of people instead of dinosaurs. If one immortal couple had emerged in 5,800 B.C., their immortal descendants would now fill all space. For those who like playing with numbers, here's my calculation.

Suppose that each person, on the average, produces a new person every thirty years. So if nobody dies, but everyone keeps on breeding, then the number of people will double every thirty years. If you start with exactly two immortals, there will be 2 to the nth power immortals after 30 n years. One estimate is that the universe is the same size as a cube that is ten billion (or ten to the 10th) light-years per edge. A light-year is about ten trillion kilometers, or ten to the 16th meters, so the universe is a cube ten to the 26th meters per edge. Cubing ten to the 26th gives ten to the 3 * 26th, or ten to the 78th. Suppose that a person takes up a cubic meter of space. How many years would be needed to fill the universe with ten to the 78th immortal people? Well, for what value of n is 2 to the nth power bigger than ten to the 78th? A commonly used computer science fact is that two to the 10th, known as a K, is almost equal to a thousand, which is ten cubed. Now ten to the 78th is ten to the 3 * 26th, which is one thousand to the 26th, which is about one K to the 26th, which is two to the 10 * 26th, which is two to the 260th. That means it would take 260 generations for the immortal farmers to fill up the universe. At 30 years per generation, that makes 7,800 years. In 5800 B.C. people were giving up being hunter-gatherers and were learning to farm. By comparison, Sumeria flourished in 4000 B.C. and the Early Period of Ancient Egypt was 3000 B.C. So if two of those early farmers had mastered immortality, the whole universe would be stuffed with their descendants!

An alternative vision of a death-free Earth is a world in which birth stops as well. What kind of world would that lead to? Totally boring. It would be nothing but the same old creatures stomping the same old environment forever. Kind of like the job market looks to a young person starting out!

Meaningless proliferation or utter stagnancy are the only alternatives to death. Although death is individually terrible, it is wonderful for the evolution of new kinds of life.

Evolution is possible whenever one has (1) reproduction, (2) genome variation, and (3) natural selection. We've already talked about reproduction and the way in which mating and mutation cause genome variation—so that children are not necessarily just like their parents. Natural selection is where death comes in: not every creature is able to reproduce itself before it dies. The creatures that do reproduce have genomes which are selected by the natural process of competing to stay alive and to bear children that survive.

What this means in terms of computer a-life is that one ordinarily has some maximum number of memory slots for a creature's genomes. One lets the phenomes of the creatures compete for a while and then uses some kind of fitness function to decide which creatures are the most successful. The most successful creatures are reproduced onto the existing memory slots, and the genomes of the least successful creatures are erased, as indicated in Figure 1-11.

Nature has a very simple way of determining a creature's fitness: it manages to reproduce before death or it doesn't. Assigning a fitness level to competing a-life phenomes is a more artificial process. Various kinds of fitness functions can be chosen on the basis of what kinds of creatures one wants to see evolve. In most of the *Boppers* experiments, the fitness is based on the creatures' ability to find and eat positively weighted food cells while eating as little negatively weighted food as possible.

So far in this chapter, we've talked about life in terms of three general concepts: gnarl, sex, and death. In Chapter 2, *Computer A-Life,* we're going to start looking at how to find computer programs that are gnarly, that breed, and that compete to stay alive. But before going into computer a-life, we'll look at some other approaches to artificial life. The next three sections examine artificial life in the fields of biochemistry, robotics, and culture.

BIOLOGICAL A-LIFE

The amazing part about real life is that it keeps itself going on its own. If anyone could build a tiny, self-guiding, flying robot he or she would be a hero of science. But a fly can build flies just by eating garbage. Biological life is a self-organizing process, an endless round that's been chorusing along for hundreds of millions of years. In this section, we first talk about Frankenstein, and then we talk about modern biochemistry.

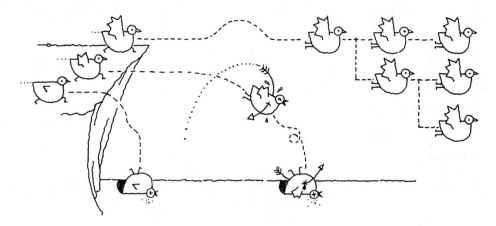

Figure 1-11 Survival of the fittest

Frankenstein

The most famous fictional character who tries to create life is Victor Frankenstein, the protagonist of Mary Shelley's 1818 novel, *Frankenstein or, The Modern Prometheus*.

Most of us know about Frankenstein from the movie versions of the story. In the movie version, Dr. Frankenstein creates a living man by sewing together parts of dead bodies and galvanizing the result with electricity from a thunderstorm. The original version is quite different.

In Mary Shelley's novel, Victor Frankenstein is a student with a deep interest in chemistry. He becomes curious about what causes life, and he pursues this question by closely examining how things die and decay—the idea being that if you can understand how life leaves matter, you can understand how to put it back in. Victor spends days and nights in "vaults and charnel-houses," until finally he believes he has learned how to bring dead flesh back to life. He sets to work building the Frankenstein monster:

> *In a solitary chamber ... I kept my workshop of filthy creation: my eyeballs were starting from their sockets in attending to the details of my employment. The dissecting room and the slaughter-house furnished many of my materials; and often did my human nature turn with loathing from my occupation.... Who shall conceive the horrors of my secret toil, as I dabbled among the unhallowed damps of the grave, or tortured the living animal to animate the lifeless clay?*

Finally Dr. Frankenstein reaches his goal:

> *It was on a dreary night of November, that I beheld the accomplishment of my toils. With an anxiety that almost amounted to agony, I collected the instruments of life around me, that I might infuse a spark of being into the lifeless thing that lay at my feet. It was already one in the morning; the rain pattered dismally against the panes, and my candle was nearly burnt out, when, by the glimmer of the half-extinguished light, I saw the dull yellow eye of the creature open; it breathed hard, and a convulsive motion agitated its limbs.... The beauty of the dream vanished, and breathless horror and disgust filled my heart.*

The creepy, slithery aspect of *Frankenstein* stems from the fact that Mary Shelley situated Victor Frankenstein's a-life researches at the tail-end of life, at the part where a living creature's life dissolves back into a random mush of chemicals. In point of fact, this is really *not* a good way to understand life—the processes of decay are not readily reversible.

BIOCHEMISTRY

Contemporary a-life biochemists focus on the way in which life keeps itself going. Organic life is a process, a skein of biochemical reactions that is in some ways like a parallel three-dimensional computation. The computation being carried out by a living body stops when the body dies, and the component parts of the body immediately begin decomposing. Unless you're Victor Frankenstein, there is no way to kick-start the reaction back into viability. It's as if turning off a computer would make its chips fall apart.

Is there any hope of scientists being able to assemble and start up a living biological system?

Chemists have studied complicated systems of reactions that tend to perpetuate themselves. These kinds of reactions are called *autocatalytic* or *self-exciting*. Once an autocatalytic reaction gets started , it produces by-products which pull more and more molecules into the reaction. Often such a reaction will have a cyclical nature, in that it goes through the same sequence of steps over and over.

The cycle of photosynthesis is a very complicated example of an autocatalytic reaction. One of the simpler examples of an autocatalytic chemical reaction is known as the *Belusov-Zhabotinsky reaction* in honor of the two Soviet scientists who discovered it. In the Belusov-Zhabotinsky reaction, a certain acidic solution is placed in a flat glass dish with a sprinkling of palladium crystals. The active ingredient of litmus paper is added so that it is possible to see which regions of the solution are more or less acidic. In a few minutes, the dish fills with scroll-shaped waves of color which spiral around and around in a regular, but not quite predictable, manner.

There seems to be something universal about the Belusov-Zhabotinsky reaction, in that there are many other systems which behave in a similar way: generating endlessly spiralling scrolls. It is fairly easy to set up a computer simulation that shows something like the Belusov-Zhabotinsky reaction. The *Boppers* program includes such a simulation. If you have *Boppers* running, you can use the File menu's Open popup's Open Params selection to enter the Open dialog and load the ZHABOBUG.BL parameter file. A screen dump of a version of this file appears in Figure 1-12.

In addition to trying to understand the chemical reactions that take place in living things, biochemists have investigated ways of creating the chemicals used by life. In the famous 1952 Miller-Urey experiment, two scientists sealed a glass retort filled with such simple chemicals as water, methane, and hydrogen. The

Figure 1-12 A Belusov-Zhabotinsky pattern in *Boppers*

sealed vessel was equipped with electrodes that repeatedly fired off sparks—the vessel was intended to simulate primeval Earth with its lightning storms. After a week, it was found that a variety of amino acids had spontaneously formed inside the vessel. Amino acids are the building blocks of protein and of DNA—of our phenomes and of our genomes, so the Miller-Urey experiment represented an impressive first step toward understanding how life on Earth emerged.

Biochemists have pushed this kind of thing much further in the last decades. It is now possible to design artificial strands of RNA which are capable of self-replicating when placed into a solution of amino acids. One can even set a kind of RNA evolution into motion. In one recent experiment, a solution was filled with a random assortment of self-replicating RNA along with amino acids for the RNA to build with. Some of the molecules tended to stick to the sides of the beaker. The solution was then poured out, with the molecules that stuck to the sides of the vessel being retained. A fresh food supply of amino acids was added and the cycle was repeated numerous times. The evolutionary result? RNA that adheres very firmly to the sides of the beaker.

Genetic engineers are improving methods to tinker with the DNA of living cells to make organisms that are in some part artificial. Most commercially sold insulin is created by gene-tailored cells. The word *wetware* is sometimes used to stand for the information in the genome of a biological cell. Wetware is like software, but it's in a watery living environment. The era of wetware programming has only just begun.

ROBOTS

In this section we compare science fiction dreams of robots to robots as they actually exist today. We also talk a bit about how computer science techniques may help us get from today's realities to tomorrow's dreams.

Science Fiction Robots

Science fiction is filled with robots that act as if they were alive. Existing robots already possess such life-like characteristics as sensitivity to the environment, movement, complexity, and integration of parts. But what about reproduction? Could you have robots that build other robots?

The idea is perhaps surprising at first, but there's nothing logically wrong with it. As long as a robot has an exact blueprint of how it is constructed, it can assemble the parts for child robots, and it can use a copying machine to give each child its own blueprint so that the process can continue, as illustrated in Figure 1-13. For a robot, the blueprint is its genome, and its body and behavior are its phenome. In practice, the robots would not use paper blueprints, but would instead use CAD/CAM (computer aided design and manufacturing) files.

Boppers, included with this book, takes its name from the futuristic robots introduced in my science fiction novels *Software* and *Wetware.* In *Software,* some robots are sent to the Moon where they build factories to make robot parts. They compete with each other for the right to use the parts (natural selection), and then they get together in pairs (sex) to build new robots onto which parts of the parents' programs are placed (self-reproduction). Soon they rebel against human rule, and begin calling themselves *boppers.* Some of them travel to Earth to eat some human brains—just to get the information out of the tissues, you understand.

In *Wetware,* the boppers take up genetic engineering and learn how to code bopper genomes into fertilized human eggs, which can then be force-grown to adult size in less than a month. The humans built the boppers, but now the boppers are building people—or something *like* people. The irate humans kill most of the boppers at the end of *Wetware,* but the bopper genomes are still available and I think they'll be back one of these days in a third book.

Real Robots

After such heady science fiction dreams, it's discouraging to look at today's actual robots. These machines still lack in adaptability, which is the ability to function well in unfamiliar environments. They can't walk and/or chew gum at the same time.

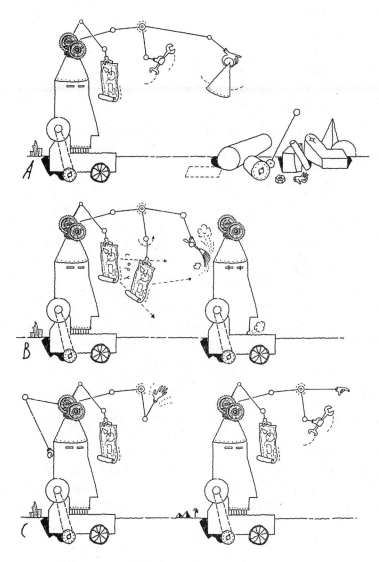

Figure 1-13 A Robot that reproduces by (a) using a blueprint to (b) copy itself, and then (c) giving the new robot a copy of the blueprint

The architecture for most experimental robots is something like this: you put a bunch of devices in a wheeled garbage can, wire the devices together, and hope that the system can converge on a stable and interesting kind of behavior.

What kind of devices go in the can? Wheels and pincers with exquisitely controllable motors, TV cameras, sonar pingers, microphones, a sound synthesizer, and some computer microprocessors.

The phenome is the computation and behavior of the whole system—it's what the robot does. The robot's genome is its blueprint, with all the interconnections and the switch settings on the devices in the wheeled garbage can, and if any of those devices happens to be a computer memory chip, then the information on the chip is part of the genome as well.

Traditionally, we have imagined robots as having one central processing unit, just as we have one central brain. But, in point of fact, a lot of our information processing is done in our nerve ganglia, and some contemporary roboticists are interested in giving a separate processor to each of a robot's devices.

This robot design technique is known as *subsumption architecture*. Each of an artificial ant's legs, for instance, might know now to make walking motions on its own, and the legs might communicate with each other in an effort to get into synch. Just such an ant (named Attila) was designed by Rodney Brooks of M.I.T. Brooks wants his robots to be cheap and widely available.

Another interesting robot is being designed by Marc Pauline of the art group known as Survival Research Laboratories. Pauline and his group stage large, dadaistic spectacles in which hand-built robots interact with each other. Pauline is working on some new robots he calls Swarmers. His idea is to have the Swarmers radio-aware of each other's position and chase each other. The idea is to try and find good settings so the Swarmers exhibit maximally chaotic behavior.

In practice, developing designs and software for these machines is what is known as an *intractable problem*. It is very hard to predict how the different components will interact, so one has to actually try each new configuration to see how it works. And commonly, changes are being made to the hardware and to the software at the same time, so the space of possible solutions is vast. In Chapter 3, *Genetic Algorithms,* we'll talk about how the a-life *genetic algorithm* approach can be used on this kind of problem.

Telerobotics

For many applications, the user might not need a fully autonomous robot. A remotely operated hand used to handle dangerous materials is like a robot, in that it is a complicated machine which imitates human motions. But a remote hand does not necessarily need to have much of an internal brain, particularly if all it has to do is to copy the motions of your real hand. A device like a remote robot hand is called a *telerobot*.

Radioactive waste is sometimes cleaned up by using telerobots that have video cameras and two robotic arms. The operator of such a telerobot sees what it sees on a video screen, and moves his or her hands within a mechanical harness that sends signals to the hands of the telerobot.

There are indications that, in the coming decades, telerobotics is going to be a much more important field than pure robotics. People want *amplifications* of themselves more than they want *servants*. A telerobot projects an individual's power. Telerobots would be useful for exploration, travel, and sheer voyeurism, and could become a sought-after high-end consumer product.

Even if telerobots are more commercially important than self-guiding robots, there is still a need for self-guiding robots. Why? Because when you're using a telerobot, you don't want to have to watch the machine every second so that the machine doesn't do something like get run over by a car, nor do you want to worry about the very fine motions of the machine. You want, for instance, to be able to say "walk toward that object" without having to put your legs into a harness and emulate mechanical walking motions—and this means that, just like a true robot, the telerobot will have to know how to move around pretty much on its own.

Evolving Robots

Artificial life is very likely to be a good way to evolve better and better robots. In order to make the evolution happen faster, it would be nice to be able to do it as a computer simulation—as opposed to building dozens of competing prototype models.

My most recent novel about robots, *The Hacker and the Ants*, is based on the idea of evolving robots by testing your designs out in virtual reality—in, that is, a highly realistic computer simulation with some of the laws of physics built into it.

You might, for instance, take a CAD model of a house, and try a wide range of possible robots in this house without having to bear the huge expense of building prototypes. Because changing a model would have no hardware expense, it would be feasible to try many different designs and thus more rapidly converge on an optimal design.

There is an interesting relationship between a-life, virtual reality, robotics, and telerobotics. These four areas fit neatly into Table 1-3, which is based on two distinctions. First, is the device being run by a computer program or by a human mind; and second, is the device a physical machine or a simulated machine?

Technology	Mind	Body
Artificial Life	Computer	Simulated
Virtual Reality	Human	Simulated
Robotics	Computer	Physical
Telerobotics	Human	Physical

Table 1-3: Four Kinds of Computer Science

Artificial life deals with creatures whose brains are computer programs, and these creatures have simulated bodies that interact in a computer-simulated world. In virtual reality, the world and the bodies are still computer-simulated, but at least some of the creatures in the world are now being directly controlled by human users. In robotics, we deal with real physical machines in the real world that are run by computer programs, while in telerobotics we are looking at real physical machines that are run by human minds. Come to think of it, a human's ordinary life in his or her body could be thought of as an example of telerobotics: a human mind is running a physical body!

Memes

In the wider context of the history of ideas, one can observe that certain kinds of fads, techniques, or religious beliefs behave in some ways like autonomous creatures that live and reproduce. The biologist Richard Dawkins calls these thought-creatures *memes*.

Self-replicating memes can be brutally simple. Here's one:

The Laws of Wealth:

Law I: Begin giving 10% of your income to the person who teaches you the Laws of Wealth.

Law II: Teach the Laws of Wealth to ten people!

The Laws of Wealth meme is the classic Ponzi pyramid scheme. Here's another self-replicating idea system:

System X:

Law I: Anyone who does not believe System X will burn in hell;

Law II: It is your duty to save others from suffering.

Of System X, Douglas Hofstadter remarks, "Without being impious, one may suggest that this mechanism has played some small role in the spread of Christianity."

Most thought memes use a much less direct method of self-reproduction. Being host to a meme-complex such as, say, *the use of language* can confer such wide survival advantages that those infected with the meme flourish. There are many such memes with obvious survival value: the tricks of farming, the craft of pottery, the arcana of mathematics — all are beneficial mind-viruses that live in human information space.

Memes that confer no obvious survival value are more puzzling. Things like tunes and fashions hop from one mind to another with bewildering speed. Staying up to date with current ideas is a higher-order meme which probably does have some survival value. Knowing about a-life, for instance, is very likely to increase your employability as well as your sexual attractiveness!

NOTES AND REFERENCES

- There are two very comprehensive anthologies of technical and semi-technical papers on artificial life: *Artificial Life,* edited by C. Langton, Addison-Wesley, 1989, and *Artificial Life II,* edited by C. Langton, C. Taylor, J. Farmer, and S. Rasmussen, Addison-Wesley, 1992. These books are anthologies of papers presented at the first two conferences on artificial life, which were held at Los Alamos, New Mexico, in 1987, and at Santa Fe, New Mexico, in 1990. A third a-life conference was held in Santa Fe in 1992, and a volume of papers from this conference will be published soon.

  A less technical book on a-life is Steven Levy's, *Artificial Life: The Quest for a New Creation*, Pantheon Books, 1992. Another popular source of information about a-life is Stephen Prata's *Artificial Life Playhouse*, The Waite Group, 1993.

- The classic popular book on chaos theory is James Gleick's, *Chaos: Making a New Science,* Viking, 1987. There is a useful companion program for DOS written by Rudy Rucker, Josh Gordon, and John Walker: it is *James Gleick's Chaos: The Software,* Autodesk, 1990.

- Someone might object to my claim that *ocean waves are not random* by saying that the quantum uncertainties of atomic motions make the waves random. Well, okay, that's actually true. But most chaos theorists believe that the waves would look just as random even if perfect classical physics held and there were no quantum uncertainties at all!

- John Rennie's article, "DNA's New Twists," in *Scientific American,* March 1993, pp. 122–132, contains a discussion of transposition and some of the other methods of genome variation being currently investigated.

- One of the first accounts of the Belusov-Zhabotinsky reaction can be found in Arthur Winfree's article, "Rotating Chemical Reactions," *Scientific American,* June, 1974, pp. 82–95.

  The Miller-Urey experiment was first announced in S.L. Miller and H.C. Urey's article "Organic Compound Synthesis on the Primitive Earth," *Science* 130 (1959), p. 245.

  The RNA evolution experiment is described in Gerald Joyce's article, "Directed Molecular Evolution," *Scientific American*, December, 1992. A good quote about wetware appears in *MONDO 2000: A User's Guide to the New Edge*, edited by R.U. Sirius, Queen Mu, and Rudy Rucker for HarperCollins, 1992. The quote is from the bioengineer Max Yukawa: "Suppose you think of an organism as being like a computer graphic that is generated from some program. Or think of an oak tree as being the output of a program that was contained inside the acorn. The genetic program is in the DNA molecule. Your software is the abstract information pattern behind your genetic code, but your actual wetware is the physical DNA in a cell."

- Attila the ant appeared on the cover of *Scientific American* in December, 1991, in connection with the article "Silicon Babies," by Paul Wallach.

- Richard Dawkins talks about memes in his book *The Selfish Gene,* Oxford University Press, 1976. This book is mainly about the idea that an organism is a genome's way of reproducing itself—a bit as if we were big robots being driven around by DNA. The memes take further advantage of us. As Dawkins puts it: "Just as genes propagate themselves in the gene pool by leaping from body to body via sperms or eggs, so memes propagate themselves in the meme pool by leaping from brain to brain.... When you plant a fertile meme in my mind you literally parasitize my brain, turning it into a vehicle for the meme's propagation in just the way that a virus may parasitize the genetic mechanism of a host cell."

  System X appears in the chapter "On Viral Sentences and Self-Replicating Structures," in Douglas Hofstadter's *Metamagical Themas*, Basic Books, 1985.

2

Computer
A-Life

In the first chapter we talked about life, a-life, and their relationships to biochemistry, robotics, and culture. In this chapter we get down to the nitty-gritty: artificial life on the computer.

We begin with a discussion of how computers work, and then go on to talk about computer viruses. Next we introduce the idealized computers known as Turing machines, and then show how Turing machines can be placed into artificial bug worlds to create a gnarly new form of computer a-life known as the *turmite*.

The chapter ends with sections on other forms of computer a-life shown by the *Boppers* program, including the *boids*, who flock around in lovely, shifting groupings; and the hypnotic *cellular automata*, which come close to simulating the metabolisms of living things.

INSIDE THE MACHINE

Ordinary computers all have the same basic design: memory and a processor. Computer memory is thought of as being like a very long single-column list of memory slots, with an address assigned to each slot. In visualizing the long column-like list of computer memory slots, we draw a ladder-like shape as shown in Figure 2-1.

The values of the addresses run from top to bottom, from one on through the thousands, and on down from there into the millions. When you add memory to your

Figure 2-1 The memory slots

computer, you are increasing the value of the largest possible address your machine can handle; that is, you are making the ladder longer.

The computer memory slots are so-called *words* that consist of 16 or 32 bits of information, where a *bit* is a single zero or one. Here "word" does not mean "meaningful language unit," it simply means a particular fixed number of bits. In our ladder-like picture of memory, we think of each rung as holding a word of memory.

When the computer is running, the processor repeatedly interprets words of memory as commands. Which words? The processor uses a movable marker called the *instruction pointer* to keep track of which word of memory the processor is currently interpreting. According to which word the processor encounters, it can:

- Jump the instruction pointer to a new position

- Read from memory

- Carry out Boolean or arithmetical operations

- Write to memory

In the rest of this section, we'll say a bit about each of these four kinds of instructions, followed by remarks on input and output and a brief comment on timesharing.

The material in this section may be too computer intense for some readers, and it is not all that crucial for what follows in the rest of the book. So feel free to skip the rest of this section if it's not your cup of tea.

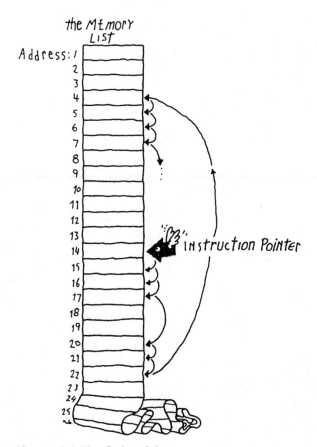

Figure 2-2 The flight of the instruction pointer

Moving the Instruction Pointer

Often the instruction pointer simply moves ahead in standard word-sized steps, one rung to the next, but every now and then it jumps forward or backward, as illustrated in Figure 2-2. The net effect is a kind of dance of computation.

If you have some familiarity with programming, you will probably know that jumps in the instruction pointer's position can be caused by if-then-else statements, by loops, and by function calls, as indicated in the more detailed Figure 2-3.

Where does the instruction pointer live? Not in the memory ribbon, as this is what is being read from and written to. No, the instruction pointer lives in a special memory

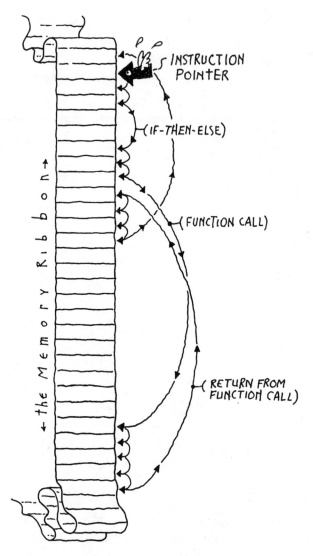

Figure 2-3 The flight of the instruction pointer—detailed version

slot known as a *register* that is on the processor itself. Although we like to visualize the instruction pointer as something that moves up and down the memory ribbon, the instruction pointer is really just an *address* that changes from step to step.

A processor also has registers it uses to keep track of other useful addresses, a register it uses for a loop counter, several registers that it uses to store words of data from memory, and so on, making about 20 registers in all.

Reading Data

Just as the processor keeps track of an address called the instruction pointer, it keeps track of an address that we may as well call the *data read pointer*. The processor reads the information found at the address indicated by the data read pointer. What does it do with this information? It saves it in a register called an *accumulator*, as shown in Figure 2-4.

One initially surprising feature of standard computer design is that there is no inherent distinction between program and data. This combined-program-and-data design is often known as the *von Neumann architecture*, in honor of the mathematician John von Neumann who did much to promote the creation of the first digital computers in the late 1940s.

In the von Neumann architecture, both program and data are simply patterns of bits which are laid down in the memory. Whatever bits are at the instruction pointer are interpreted as program instructions for the processor. When the processor needs to

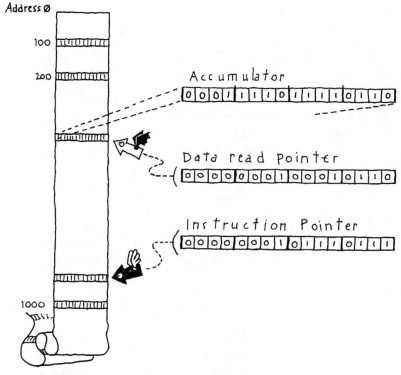

Figure 2-4 Reading data

read data bits, it can reach out to any memory position desired, using the data read pointer to keep track of where to read.

Logic and Arithmetic

When the processor carries out logic and arithmetic operations, it is doing what we traditionally think of as *computing*. Rather than acting directly on the memory, the logic and arithmetic instructions act on words of data that have been placed into registers during the data reading steps. When the processor executes a logic and arithmetic instruction, it alters the bits in a register, often by mashing them together with the bits from another register. More specifically, logic and arithmetic instructions may copy register values among each other, perform binary additions of register values, shift an individual register's bits to the right or the left, compare register values, and more.

How does the processor know how to do things like carry out instructions to add numbers and shift bits? This is really a two-part question. First of all, the processor needs to understand that a certain sequence of bits *means* something like "compare two registers," and second, the processor needs to know how to do things like add.

The first part is handled by a tiny program, known as *microcode*, that is coded right into the processor. Microcode interprets strings of bits as instructions to do things with the registers.

The second part—the actual execution of shifts, additions, and so on—is handled by specialized circuitry on the chip. Adding, for instance, is handled by a little maze of logic gates that can do things like add two bits together. The physical logic of the etched-in circuitry sews all of this together into tiny adding machines, multipliers, shifters, and the like.

Writing Data

This step is simply the reverse of the read data step. The processor copies the contents of one of its registers to the location addressed by the processor's *data write pointer* register.

Even though there is no intrinsic difference between instructions and data, most computer programs do keep code and data in separate segments of the memory. This makes it possible for the programs to behave in a predictable and stable way. Commonly, there are three segments used: the data segment, the code segment, and the stack segment, as shown in Figure 2-5. The instructions that the

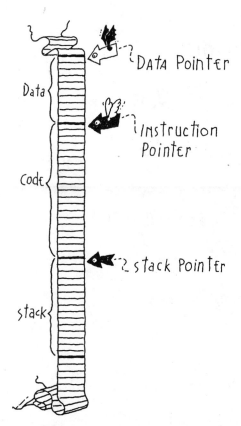

Figure 2-5 Typical memory segmentation

program is to execute are placed in the code segment, the data that the program is to operate on is placed in the data segment, and the stack segment is used by the processor as a scratch pad when it runs out of room in its registers for short-term memory.

So now we've pretty well described the four kinds of instructions a computer carries out. Keep in mind that the computer does not need to cycle strictly through doing move, read, logico-artithmetic, and write operations—in that order. Often it will do a whole string of reads at once, or go through a long period of just moving and doing logic and arithmetic.

Input and Output

What about input and output? Input and output are ways of directly putting data into the memory and getting it back out, as suggested by Figure 2-6. Input devices can place a few bits or even a long patch of bits directly into the memory ribbon. A key-

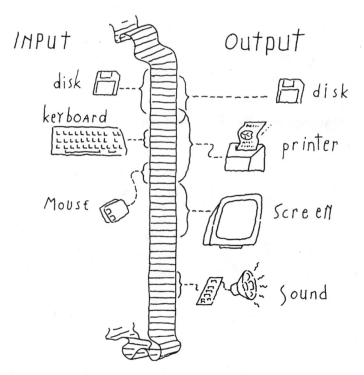

Figure 2-6 Input and output

board feeds in perhaps 32 bits of data with each keypress, while a disk drive can load in millions of bits at a time. Each time you move your mouse, the mouse puts something like a 32-bit description of its most recent move into the computer memory.

Output devices convert bits into audible or visible displays. A vanilla text screen might show 16 bits of data with each character, while a graphics screen can display millions of bits at once. You can print out your text or graphics screens, or you can write their information onto a disk. A sound card converts swatches of bits into audible noises.

Timesharing

Our description so far makes it sound as if a computer can only do one thing at a time. How is it that computers often seem to be doing several things at once? The answer is simple: the machine allocates successive time-slices to a series of

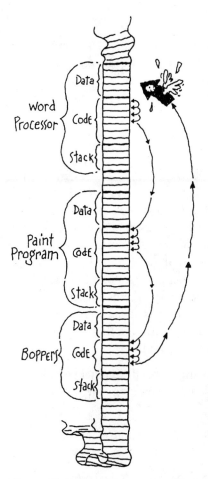

Figure 2-7 One processor working on three programs

tasks, and rapidly cycles around and around this task loop, giving the illusion that all the tasks are being worked on at once. Therefore, if in Windows you have three windows open, say, one with a word-processor, one with a paint program, and one with the *Boppers* program, the computer can keep working on the three in turn, as illustrated in Figure 2-7.

VIRUSES AND WORMS

Now we check out the "untamed" computer a-life forms called viruses and worms, as well as artificial life workers' attempts to domesticate these forms.

Computer Viruses

Computer viruses are the most notorious forms of computer a-life. The most common computer viruses are parasitic pieces of code that live by attaching themselves to executable programs—also known as *executables* or *apps*. In the MS-DOS world, executables are the programs that *do something* if you enter their name at the DOS prompt; they normally have the file extension .EXE or .COM. When you run a virus-infected executable on your computer, some or all of the other executables on your machine will be infected by the virus as well.

In addition to copying themselves from executable to executable, most viruses also have a way of signalling the user that his or her machine is infected. The "gotcha" signal of a virus can range from something as lightweight as a message saying, "KODEZ KIDZ RULE!" to something as extreme as a command to erase the hard disk, complete with a string of follow-up commands to make sure the erasure goes through. A virus may send out this signal every time it runs or, more commonly, it may silently spread for a while before signalling the user. Sometimes a virus is designed to send out its signal only when some trigger condition occurs. A trigger condition might be that the virus has already replicated, say, ten times, or that a certain date has arrived, or perhaps even that a certain employee's name has been removed from a company's payroll.

The gotcha refinements are the easy part; the tricky thing about computer viruses is getting them to self-replicate. How do viruses do it? A typical virus works like this:

1. The virus searches the computer's disk drives for a host program, that is, for an executable program to infect.

2. If the virus finds a good host, it copies the host from disk into the computer memory, and searches the host code for the first occurrence of some common instruction—let's call this the *infection site instruction*.

3. The virus replaces the infection site instruction by a *jump* command that, when interpreted by the processor the next time the host program runs, will move the instruction pointer down to the end of the existing host code.

4. The virus adds a bit-for-bit copy of its code to the end of the host program.

5. At the very end of the newly expanded host program the virus now writes the missing infection site instruction followed by a jump command that will send control back to the spot right after the original infection site instruction.

6. Now the virus saves the infected host back to disk with the same name as before.

7. The virus is free to deliver a gotcha message as well.

Figure 2-8 shows how the host code looks before and after being infected by the virus.

It requires a certain amount of low cunning to figure out a good infection site instruction, how to get the memory address of the end of a program, how to jump back from there to the infection site, and so on. There are a handful of computer programmers who enjoy working out newer and better viruses. Most computer professionals share a healthy dislike for these people. Virus writers are like the graffiti taggers who clutter every available surface with their stupid names. Taggers are not to be confused with the skilled and creative individuals who create lovely wall-sized graffiti pieces, and far less are they to be confused with legitimate artists trying to create new and visionary worlds. By the same token, virus writers should not be confused with productive computer hackers or a-life scientists.

Generally, the best way to catch a virus is to use pirated software. People who write viruses tend to associate with the same people who are involved in breaking copy protection and selling dirt-cheap copies of expensive software. Some even take the odd moral stance that putting viruses into pirated software makes it okay to sell this software, because the pirate's customers don't actually get long-term usable copies of the stolen software they seek to illegally buy.

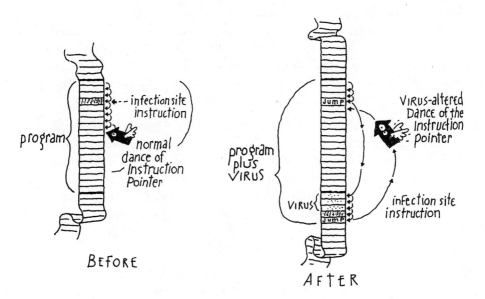

Figure 2-8 Infection by a computer virus

Worms

A *computer worm* is a self-contained computer program that, like a virus, repro-duces itself. The difference is that a worm does not spread by infecting host exe-cutable programs. Instead a worm manages to start running on its own, and copies itself to new memory locations. Some worms send copies of themselves to other users over electronic mail—sort of like self-perpetuating chain letters.

The most famous worm to date was the *Internet worm* of November, 1988. The Internet is a computer network that connects many universities and research institutions together, enabling scientists to exchange large pieces of computer code. The Internet worm, written by Robert Morris, Jr., was allegedly designed to go to every node on the Internet and report back in—to provide a kind of map of the Internet. But the worm got out of control, and reproduced itself so wildly that many systems staggered to a halt as they tried to time-share their processing power among hundreds or thousands of local copies of the worm. Somewhat disturbingly, Morris' father is a government expert on computer security. In May, 1990, Morris was sentenced to a ten thousand dollar fine and four hundred hours of community service.

A-Life Investigations

Several a-life researchers have worked with worlds of creatures that are similar to self-reproducing computer worms. In each case, the scientist sets up a *virtual computer* that runs as a simulation inside a real computer. The codes used in these worm worlds are made-up artificial computer codes rather than the actual machine codes that are really used by the computer's chips, so there is no dan-ger at all of these toy worms breaking loose and wreaking havoc.

In a typical worm world, there will be a memory arena filled with randomly generated computer instructions. This random start is sometimes spoken of as a *primordial soup*, in analogy to the planetary seas in which organic life evolved. Scattered in the world's primordial soup will be dozens or scores of instruction pointers—the pointers are the a-life creatures of this world. One by one, each pointer is allowed to interpret the instruction at its current location and to act on it. A pointer's action might be to copy an instruction from one part of the arena to the other, or to move itself to a different memory location.

The worm world's pointers are also allowed to split; this is how the creatures reproduce. When a pointer reproduces it also tries to copy some words of memory to the location of the new pointer, so the child pointer will behave like the parent. When a pointer splits, it may be that the code at the location of the child pointer is not quite the same as the code at the parent pointer, even if the parent code has tried to copy itself accurately. This introduces an element of genome variability.

As time goes by, the world fills up to some maximum capacity, and the older pointers are systematically killed off. A pointer also may die if it runs across a meaningless instruction. In this way an element of natural selection arises. Given the combination of reproduction, genome variation, and natural selection, evolution can occur.

Two of the best-known worm worlds are Kee Dewdney's *Core Wars* and Tom Ray's *Tierra*. Ray, who was a pure biologist before getting drawn into a-life, excels at making up colorful scenarios to describe what his worms are doing. He talks of parasites, hyper-parasites, and even speaks of his creatures as "having sex with the dead." But in and of themselves, worm world programs are not—at least to my eye—very compelling. They don't give you much of anything to look at: they're not *gnarly* enough.

Has there been any scientific a-life work with computer viruses? Not that I know of. The problem is that most a-life workers have very strong negative feelings about viruses—as the reader may have noticed from my previous comments on viruses! A-life workers tend to dislike viruses not only because all the viruses we've seen have been destructive, but also because viruses get a disproportionate amount of media attention—attention that might otherwise be focused on the positive and constructive kinds of a-life that have already been discovered.

But it may conceivably be that in the future some a-life workers will start creating viruses that have *beneficial* effects, such as making your computer run faster, or making your operating system more intelligent. Alternatively, future viruses might deliver commercial "gotcha" messages for companies that help fund the worldwide computer network!

TURING MACHINES

In this section, we talk about the definition of Turing machines, give some examples, and then briefly mention some facts about them. The "Notes and References" section for this chapter includes some material about Alan Turing.

Definition

In 1936, the British mathematician Alan Turing formulated what seems to be the simplest possible description of a computer. This idealized device, now known as a *Turing machine*, consists of a *tape* of memory cells plus a moving processor called a *head*. Figure 2-9 shows a Turing machine with, just for fun, a propeller to hold up the Turing machine's head.

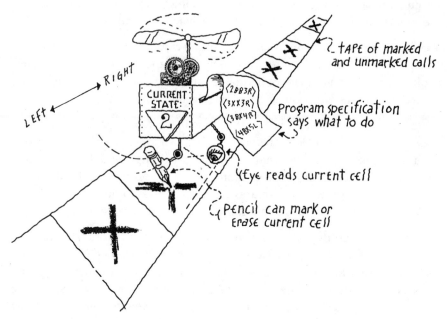

Figure 2-9 A Turing machine

As the propeller suggests, the Turing machine is not meant to be a practical design for a physical computer; it is rather an idealized kind of computer that is easy to think about. But for the moment let's think of it as a physical machine.

Rather than keeping an instruction pointer in a register, the Turing machine physically moves its head up and down the memory tape. Instead of being able to move its position (or instruction pointer) through arbitrarily large leaps, a Turing machine can typically only move one cell per computation cycle. We can think of the two possible motions as being called "L" and "R" for "move one cell to the left" and "move one cell to the right."

The processor head of a Turing machine has only a small amount of internal register memory. Rather than having hundreds of register bits and zillions of possible states, a typical Turing machine might have a range of, say, 12 states, or maybe 100 states. In general, we'll think of our Turing machines as having the N states 1,2,...,N.

Another difference between Turing machines and standard computers is that a Turing machine does not read and write entire words of memory at a time. In the simplest version, a Turing machine just reads and writes one bit at a time from its tape. Thus, rather than being a ribbon of words, the Turing memory tape is thought of as a string of cells each of which is either blank or marked. We symbolize the blank state as B, and the marked state as X.

Just as a regular computer processor has microcode that tells the processor how to react to what it finds in memory, a Turing machine has a little program that tells it what to do with its tape. We can think of a Turing machine program as a finite list of five-symbol instructions. Each of these quintuples has the form **<present state, read color, write color, new state, move direction>**. Let's say a bit about each of these five.

- **present state** is a current internal state that the head might be in. The head acts differently depending on what state it's in. As we said before, an N-state Turing machine can be in any of the states **1,...,N**.

- **Read color** describes the contents of a cell the Turing head might be positioned at. If the tape cells can only be marked or unmarked, the only possible read colors are B and X.

- **Write color** specifies a color for the Turing head to write into the current cell. In the simplest case this again is B or X. If the write color is B, this means that the head will erase the mark in the cell if there is one; if the write color is X, the head will ensure that the cell is marked. Marking a cell several times has the same effect as marking it once.

- **New state** specifies a new internal state for the Turing head to go into. The changing values of the head's state can serve as short-term memory that helps the head remember what it is currently doing.

- **Move direction** specifies a direction for the head to move. In the simplest case the possible move directions are L and R.

Consider, for instance, an instruction quintuple of the form **<1BX2R>**. The number 1 means this instruction applies when the machine is in state 1, and the letter B means that the instruction applies when the machine's head is located at a blank cell. The letter X means that when the instruction is applied, the current cell is to be marked. The number 2 means that when the instruction is applied, the machine is put into state 2. The letter R means that when the instruction is applied, the head of the machine is moved one cell to the right. More concisely, **<1BX2R>** means: *if* you are in state 1 and you see a blank cell (this takes care of the 1B part), *then* mark the cell, go into state 2, and move one cell to the right (this takes care of the "X2R" part).

A Turing machine's program is a set of instruction quintuples. The quintuples have the effect of taking pairs of the form **<current state, read color>** as input, and assigning triples of the form **<write color, new state, move direction>** as output.

It is required that a Turing machine's program can't have two different quintuples starting with the same two symbols, for if that were to happen, you wouldn't know which quintuple to apply. That is, you can't have, for instance, both <1BX2R> and <10X3R> in a Turing machine's program because if you did, then you wouldn't be able to decide which quintuple to obey if you were in state 1 looking at a blank cell.

Although you can't have *more than one* applicable quintuple, you can sometimes have *no* applicable quintuple. That is, it is permissible for there to be some combinations of current state and read color which cannot be found as the first two members of any of the quintuples in the program. When a Turing machine can't find a relevant quintuple, it turns itself off. A Turing machine that stops like this is said to *halt*.

Sometimes we want to avoid the possibility of having a Turing machine run out of instructions, and give the machine a *complete program*, meaning that every possible pair `<current state, read color>` appears as one of the program's quintuples. A Turing machine like this never runs out of instructions, so it never halts.

Operation

To run a Turing machine, you put it into state 1, and then set it down on a tape which may or may not have marks on it. The computation cycle of a Turing machine consists of the following six steps, which are repeated forever, or until the machine halts:

- `Read`. Read the value of the current cell to determine the `read color`.

- `Consult Program`. Look through the program for a quintuple that starts with the correct pair `<current state, read color>`. If there is no such quintuple, then halt. Otherwise get the new values of `write color, new state,` and `move direction` from the quintuple.

- `Update State`. Set the *current* `state` to `new state`.

- `Write`. Change the marking of the current cell to `write color`.

- `Move`. Shift your position as specified by `move direction`.

- `Loop`. Return to the `Read` step.

As a first example of a Turing machine, let's look at a machine called *Marker* whose program holds only one instruction: { <1BX2R> }. Let's put Marker into state 1 and set it down on a cell on an endless blank tape. In the Read step, the Marker machine looks at the current cell and realizes that it's a blank, or B, cell.

In the Consult Program step, Marker looks for a quintuple that starts with its current state 1 followed by the symbol B for the current cell color; that is, it looks for a quintuple that starts <1B>. As it happens, the only quintuple Marker has is <1B2R>, which does indeed start out in the desired way. The machine uses this quintuple to decide that its write color is X, its new state is 1, and its move direction is R.

In the Update State step, Marker sets its current state to the new state 1 (actually the same as the old state).

In the Write step, Marker puts a mark in the current cell, changing it from B to X.

In the Move step, Marker shifts one cell to the right.

And in the Loop step, Marker cycles back to the Read step. In the new Read step, Marker looks at the new cell and realizes it's a blank.

Can you see what the resulting behavior of the machine named Marker will be when you place it on a blank tape? Marker will end up endlessly putting marks into blank cells while moving off to the right.

But what if the tape you set Marker down on happens to already have a marked cell on it? If Marker encounters this cell, it will have to halt during an execution of the Consult Program step. This is because Marker does not have any instructions that start with the pair <1X>, which symbolizes being in state 1 and looking at a marked cell.

If you wanted to make sure that Marker never halts, you could give it an instruction for dealing with marked cells. You might, for instance, think of a Turing Machine called *Flipper*, whose program looks like this: { <1BX1R, 1XB1R> }. Flipper moves endlessly to the right, putting marks in blank cells, and erasing the marks in marked cells!

Let's look at some more Turing machines: *AddOne*, *AddThree*, and *Doubler*. These three machines each have the property of representing mathematical functions. That is, we can think of each of these machines as being like a function that turns input numbers into output numbers.

An input number k is presented to a Turing machine in the form of a tape with k marked cells in a row. The machine is put into state 1 and is set down on the left-most marked cell. If the machine runs for a while and then halts, leaving a string of j marked cells in a row, then we say that the machine has computed j as the output.

We want AddOne to turn k marked cells into k+1 marked cells and halt; AddThree is supposed to turn k marked cells into k+3 marked cells and halt; and Doubler is to turn k marked cells into k+k marked cells and halt. Programs for the three appear in Listing 2-1.

Listing 2-1 Three Turing machine programs with comments

```
AddOne:
{
   <1XX1R>,        //move right past the marked cells
   <1BX2R>         //make a mark and move right in a new state
}
AddThree:
{
   <1XXR1>,        //move right past the marked cells
   <1BXR2>,        //make a mark and move right in a new state
   <2BXR3>,        //make a mark and move right in a new state
   <2BXR4>         //make a mark and move right in a new state
}
Doubler:
{
   <1XB2R>,        //erase the leftmost mark and move right
   <2XX2R>,        //move right past marked cells
   <2BB3R>,        //skip a blank cell and move right
   <3XX3R>,        //move right past marked cells
   <3BX4R>,        //mark a blank cell and move right
   <4BX5L>,        //mark a blank cell and move left
   <5XX5L>,        //move left past the marked cells
   <5BB6L>,        //skip a blank cell and move left
   <6XX6L>,        //move left past marked cells
   <6BB1R>,        //move right and return to starting state
}
```

If we start AddOne in state 1 at the left end of a string of k marked cells, where k is greater than zero, then the machine will repeatedly use the <1XX1R> quintuple until it reaches a blank cell. Then the <1BX2R> quintuple is used and the blank cell is marked. If there were no more than k marks on the tape to begin with, the AddOne machine will next have a combined state and read color of <2B>. None of its instructions start with <2B>, so it will now halt. The net result is that k marks were changed to k+1 marks. Note, that if k had been zero at the start, then AddOne would have started on a blank tape. In this case, it would have applied the <1BX2R> instruction right away to make a single mark and then halt.

The AddThree machine is similar to the AddOne machine, except that it does include an instruction that starts with <2B>: the instruction <2BXR3>. It next needs a quintuple that starts with <3B>, and it has one: <3BXR4>. As there is no instruction starting with <4B>, the machine now halts. If you start AddThree in state 1 at the left end of a row of k marked cells, it converts the tape to show k+3 marked cells and then halts.

Doubler is a little more complicated than AddOne and AddThree. Doubler peels off marked cells from the left and marks pairs of cells at the right. Once all the original cells are gone, Doubler will be in state **1** looking at read color **B**, and there are no Doubler quintuples that start with **<1B>**, so it will halt. A step by step picture of Doubler computing two plus two to get four appears in Figure 2-10.

In looking at Figure 2-10, you should interpret the triangle as the Turing machine's head, and the number inside the triangle as the machine's current state. The intended

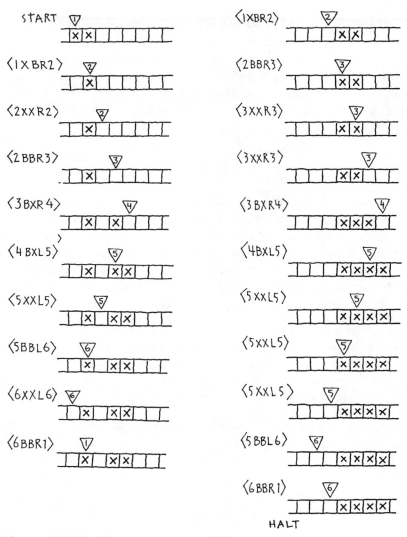

Figure 2-10 Doubler computes two plus two

order is that you first read all the way down the left-hand column of pictures and then read down the right-hand column. The listed quintuples are the ones that are applied to move from one picture to the next.

In looking at Figure 2-10, you can note that the order in which the quintuples are used has no real relation to the order in which they are listed in the presentation of the Doubler program. Turing machine "programs" are *not* like computer language programs that have their commands listed in the intended execution order. In a Turing machine program, you simply use the first command that applies.

As we saw above with the example of Marker, not every Turing machine has to halt. As another example of a non-halting Turing machine, consider adding the quintuple `<1BB1R>` to Doubler; for instance, we would get a machine called, let us say, ReDoubler. If you start ReDoubler out on a tape with two marks, ReDoubler goes though cycle after cycle of doubling—first turning two marks into four, then turning the four into eight, then turning the eight into 16, on and on forever.

Theory

Unlike a von Neumann style computer, a Turing machine only has access to one memory location at a time—while a von Neumann computer is free to use separate pointers to pick out separate locations to read and to write. Another seeming limitation of the Turing machine is that it is required to cycle over and over through the same lockstep loop of **read, consult program, update state, write, move**. Nevertheless, Alan Turing was able to prove that anything that can be computed at all can be computed by a Turing machine.

How would you go about using a Turing machine as a computer? The idea is to code your *input* as a series of blank cells and marked cells that you put onto a tape. Put your Turing machine into state 1 and set it down with its head resting on the left-most marked cell. And then you let the machine run until it halts. The pattern that remains on the tape after halting is the *output*.

Every computation that can be done by a digital computer can also be done by an appropriately complicated Turing machine. The details of the proof are not simple, but the basic idea is that, just like a Turing machine, all a microprocessor does is read from memory, write to memory, move, and change its internal state. Because Turing machines are quite simple to describe, it is easier to prove things about Turing machines than to prove things about arbitrarily complicated computers.

How complicated does a Turing machine have to be to be as powerful as an arbitrary computer? Turing discovered a design for a so-called *universal Turing machine* which uses less than a hundred states. The universal Turing machine can emulate the action of any computer program. The existence of such a Turing machine shows that a computing device can be very simple and yet be able to emulate all other computations.

Using a subtle, self-referential argument, Turing was next able to use his notion of a universal Turing machine to prove that there is in general no way to predict in advance what a given Turing machine T will do, even when you are given all the quintuples of the T's program. It turns out that just about *any* reasonable class of questions about Turing machines is unsolvable!

That is, there's no uniform way to predict if a machine will ever print out an X, no uniform way to predict if a machine will ever enter state 3, no uniform way to predict if a machine will ever get stuck in a repeating cycle, and so on. These questions are all *unsolvable*.

Come again? "Unsolvability" here means the absence of a computer program. The *unsolvability* of a question of the form "Does a Turing machine T have property P?" means that there is no computer program that can take Turing machine programs (in the form of coded-up sets of quintuples) as input and always give back correct "T has property P" or "T does not have property P" answers as output. Sometimes, for a specific machine, it's easy to tell what it will do; but in general, the only way to predict what an arbitrary Turing machine will do is to watch it run.

Suppose, for instance, that you are interested in finding out if machine T ever enters state 3. You start T up and watch it run for a long time. You watch and watch, and T is still doing different things, but T still hasn't entered state 3. Can you say with certainty that T will never enter state 3? Turing proves that, in general, you cannot. It may even happen that you end up watching T forever, always waiting for 3 to come in, never sure that it won't come in, even though it never really does come in.

Turing's proofs of the unsolvability of various questions about Turing machines depend on the *universality* of Turing machines—on the fact, that is, that any kind of computer program can be emulated by a Turing machine. Without covering the details of Turing's proofs, here, suffice it to say that they depend on a sophisticated kind of self-reference; on the fact that a universal Turing machine can emulate its own behavior.

It is the universality of Turing machines that makes them good candidates for a-life creatures. On the one hand Turing machines are quite simply describable. It's not hard to imagine coding a Turing machine's program as a bitstring genome. But because they can emulate any kind of computation, Turing machines can give very complicated behavior. They can be very gnarly.

Any individual Turing machine is completely deterministic and predictable. Yet Turing's unsolvability results show that there is no good way to pick out certain kinds of machines short of letting them run. If you want to find out what a bunch of Turing machines are like, you have to turn them loose and let them live. This is very reminiscent of life itself. If you want to know which seeds in your packet are good, you have to plant them and watch what they do.

BUG WORLDS

Computer a-life simulations work by building a virtual world in which little computer programs can move about, compete, and evolve. In the case of the toy worm worlds, the virtual world is a simulated one-dimensional swatch of computer memory. But it is more common for computer a-life experiments to use a two- or even three-dimensional virtual world. Just as the one-dimensional worlds are often generically known as *worm worlds*, the two-dimensional and three-dimensional worlds are commonly called *bug worlds*.

In a worm world simulation, the world is made up of computer instructions, some of which are also part of individual worms. But in a bug world, the bugs are thought of as having an identity separate from the world. Each bug is a data structure, while the shared world is an arena in which information is posted.

What kinds of data does an individual bug have? A bug will commonly keep track of its personal ID number, its position, and some kind of score value that tracks how well the bug is doing compared to its fellows. A bug may also keep track of such additional data as its mood (or *state*), its velocity, its colony membership, and the ID numbers of its predators and its prey. A bug's data may also include lookup tables and/or the names of functions that the bug uses for computing such things as how it moves and how its score is changed.

What kind of information appears in the shared bug world? So that the bugs can interact, there will always be a moving marker or a growing trail corresponding to each bug's changing position: that is, the bugs post their current and some of their past positions to the world, using some characteristic markings so the bugs can tell each other apart, as suggested in Figure 2-11. In addition, the world may also maintain some markings of its own—markings that the bugs may perhaps interpret as food, poison, or walls.

The bugs go through a cycle like this:

1. Move

2. Get input information from the world

3. Compute output, new position, and new score

4. Post output information to the world

Note that these four steps are analogous to the four kinds of instructions computer processors perform.

What kind of input information do the bugs take in? Computationally, the cheapest thing is to have the bugs simply look at what is in the world at their present location. In most cases, the world of the bugs is broken up into individual cells, which means the simplest way for a bug to get input is to *look at the contents of the cell it is just moving into.* Alternatively, we can let a bug look at *several neighboring cells* with each move.

If your bug population is not too great, and your computer is reasonably powerful, you can be more generous with computational resources. You can give the bugs something like *vision*—that is, you can allow each bug to compute the distance and direction of each of the other bugs, perhaps figuring out which of the other bugs is closest as well.

Let's turn now to the third step of a bug world simulation: the part where the bug computes its output, its change in score and, above all, its new position.

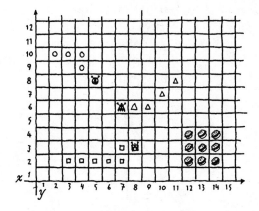

$\bullet$ – is a bug at $\langle 5, 8 \rangle$ with a trail of 4 cells

$\bullet$ – is a bug at $\langle 7, 6 \rangle$ with a trail of 4 cells

$\bullet$ – is a bug at $\langle 8, 3 \rangle$ with a trail of 6 cells

$\bullet$ – is food markings

Figure 2-11 Three bugs making marks in their bug world

For the purposes of discussion, let's think of a world that is a two-dimensional array of cells. In such a world, a bug's position can be thought of as an ordered pair `<x,y>`. If a bug's prior position was the pair `<oldx,oldy>`, we say that the bug is moving with a *velocity* `<vx, vy>`, where `<vx=x-oldx>`, and `<vy=y-oldy>`.

In ordinary language, "velocity" is often taken to mean much the same thing as "speed," but here and in the following sections, we want to think of velocity as a *vector* quantity. This mathematical way of looking at things views velocity as being both a *speed* and a *direction*. Moving three pixels per step to the right is different from moving three pixels per step upward. In two-dimensional space, we express vector velocity as a pair of numbers, and in three-dimensional space, velocities are written as triples of numbers.

The most common way to manage a bug's motion is to compute its new position `<newx, newy>`, by *first* computing its new velocity `<newx, newy>`, and by *then* defining `newx = x + newvx`, and `newy = y + newvy`, as shown in Figure 2-12. That is, we normally compute a bug's new position by first computing the bug's new velocity and by then adding the new velocity vector to the bug's current position.

The virtue of the velocity-based approach is that it makes it easier to think in terms of how the bug might think if it were alive: "turn right a little, now turn left a lot, now turn around...." Keeping track of the velocity also enables us to think of the bug as having momentum, which makes its motions seem that much more realistic. A third consideration is that if a bug's motions are calculated from its velocity, a bug's behavior will not be greatly affected by

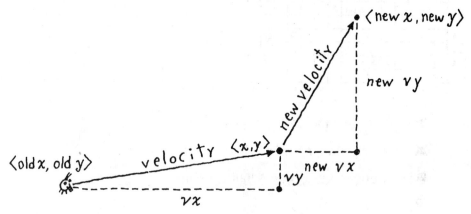

Figure 2-12 A bug moves

which direction it happens to start out moving in. The motions of the bugs in their world will be more nearly *isotropic* (meaning that if you turn your computer screen on its side the patterns you see will be more or less the same).

So how do various computer a-life bug world programs go about updating their bugs' velocities? The simplest approach of all was used by Michael Palmiter, who wrote a program called *Simulated Evolution* in which each bug uses a weighted randomizer to decide how far to turn. At each step, Palmiter calls a bug that tends to turn very little a "cruiser" and he calls a bug that turns a lot a "twirler."

Direction

	0	1	2	3	4	5
Change in X	2	1	−1	−2	−1	1
Change in Y	0	2	2	0	−2	−2

Table 2-1 A six-direction windrose

To be more specific, Palmiter's bugs move in six different directions labelled 0 through 5, as shown in Table 2-1 and Figure 2-13. Table 2-1 is called a *windrose*, because in German "windrose" means "compass card," that is, the paper under a compass needle that has the cardinal directions drawn on it.

The bugs keep track of their current velocity simply by remembering their current direction_number. A bug can turn any amount from zero through five by adding a turn_number to its current direction_number—and by then subtracting six if the result is bigger than five. Symbolically:

```
new_direction_number = (direction_number + turn_number) MODULO 6.
```

(Here "MODULO 6" means that if a number is bigger than six, you replace it by the remainder you get if you divide it by six. Thus, nine means MODULO 6 is three, because nine divided by six gives a quotient of one and a remainder of *three*.)

Therefore, a turn of three means turning 180 degrees, and turning three steps from direction five gives direction eight, which means MODULO 6 is direction two—the opposite of direction five, as can be seen from Figure 2-13.

As mentioned above, Palmiter's bugs compute their new velocities by using a weighted randomizer to pick which turn to add to the current direction to give the new direction. *Weighted randomizer* means something like a game spinner with different sized "pie slices" for different numbers. The numbers chosen are random, yet some of

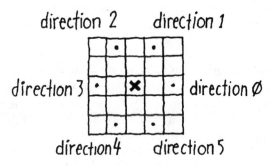

Figure 2-13 Six directions on a rectangular grid

the numbers are likelier than others. More precisely, each of Palmiter's bugs has a genome which assigns a probability P(i) to each of the possible turns i, with the stipulation that each P(i) lies between zero and one, and the sum of the six P(i)s is equal to one. A bug that has a very high P(0), for instance, will not be likely to turn at all—these are Palmiter's "cruisers." A bug with, on the other hand, a very high value of P(2), will tend to turn sharply—these bugs are Palmiter's "twirlers."

Maxis, Inc., of Orinda, California has created several bug worlds, notably *SimAnt* and *SimLife*. Let's focus on *SimLife*, whose creatures are known as *orgots* rather than just plain bugs. The *SimLife* orgots seem to use a combination of preprogrammed motion, weighted randomizer motion, and sniffing motion.

Preprogrammed motion refers to an instruction of the form "move along a uniform zigzag path," or "move along an expanding spiral." *SimLife* includes several kinds of preprogrammed motion, and allows the orgots' genes to decide which, if any, of these motions to use. *Weighted randomizer motion* means the kind of genome-determined turns that were just described relative to Palmiter's bugs. *Sniffing motion* means the kind of motion where a bug tests all of its nearest neighbor cells and moves towards certain kinds of cells and away from certain other kinds of cells, as shown in Figure 2-14.

The kinds of bug motions described so far are reasonably efficient at finding food, but they are not very interesting to look at, nor are they creative motions that the bugs themselves evolve to do.

A preprogrammed motion, after all, is simply something that the programmer has imposed on the bug as if it were a wind-up toy. There is no surprise here, no chaos, no gnarl. This is the low end of the spectrum of disorder.

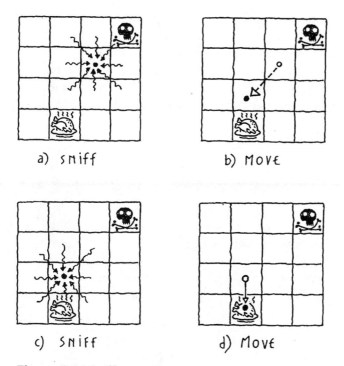

a) sniff   b) MOVE

c) SNiff   d) Move

Figure 2-14 Sniffing motion

The motion of a weighted randomizer, on the other hand, is something that can be refined by evolving better values for the weights. But in the end, it is still random motion—which is at the *high* end of the disorder spectrum.

Sniffing is effective if there is plenty to sniff, but it degenerates into random-looking motion in a sparse environment where a bug is often not in the immediate neighborhood of any cells with positive or negative weight.

In order to get gnarly bug motions, we need for the bugs to be performing computations more sophisticated than following a pattern or flipping a coin. Some a-life workers have experimented with giving each bug a neural net, others have tried endowing each bug with a small LISP program. My choice has been to make the turmites of my *Boppers* program act like Turing machines.

TURMITES

A *turmite* is a computer a-life creature which emulates a Turing machine. Instead of placing the turmites on a one-dimensional tape, we set them loose on a two-dimensional array: the pixels of a computer screen! We beef up the Turing instructions to allow turmites to move up and down as well as left and right. All the turmites work in the same space at once, and the result is a gloriously gnarly screen filled with computation. If you have *Boppers* installed, you can choose the File menu's Open popup's Open Params selection to enter the Open dialog and load the TURMITE.BL parameter file to see two-dimensional turmites in action.

I first heard of turmites through the investigations of Greg Turk. Turk, then a graduate student at the University of North Carolina, had the idea of using two-dimensional Turing machines to draw patterns on a computer screen. He wrote A.K. Dewdney, then editor of the "Computer Recreations" column at *Scientific American*, about his experiments.

Dewdney reports that, casting about for a name for Turk's creatures, he thought, "Well, they're Turing machines studied by Turk, so they should be *tur*-something. And they're like little insects, or *mites*, so I'll call them *tur-mites*! And that sounds like *termites*!" With the kind permission of Turk and Dewdney, I'm going to leave out the hyphen, and call them *turmites*.

At this point I should explain more clearly what is meant by a *two-dimensional Turing machine*. As already mentioned, the simplest kind of two-dimensional turmite can move *up* and *down* as well as right and left. We could write programs for such machines using quintuples that allow the *move direction* symbols U and D along with L and R.

But instead of doing it this way, we prefer to think in terms of the Turing machine's head as having a *direction* as well as a *state*. The head changes position by adding a *turn* to its *direction* and then moving in that direction. This means that each turmite has a program consisting of quintuples of the form **<present state, read color, write color, new state, turn>**. We start the turmites out in some initial direction, and their motions are determined from then on by the turns and, which is important, a windrose table.

Suppose, for instance, that we are interested in two-dimensional Turing machines that move in four directions: right, up, left, and down. These directions can be thought of as the indices 0, 1, 2, and 3 into a four-direction windrose table shown in Table 2-2. We assume that each Turing machine has a direction at all times, and that at the end of each cycle, each machine moves a step in its current direction. A picture of the four-direction windrose appears at the top of Figure 2-15.

Direction

	0	1	2	3
Change in X	1	0	−1	0
Change in Y	0	1	0	−1

Table 2-2 A four-direction windrose

We talk about changing direction in terms of **turn**. A turn of k will always mean to turn k steps counterclockwise around the windrose or, in terms of numbers, to add k to the current direction modulo the total number of possible directions. If you use a four-direction windrose, there will be four possible turns: 0, 1, 2, and 3. We can think of these turns as none, left, right, and about-face. The effects of these four turns on the four possible directions are shown in Table 2-3, and an illustration of how the turn is added to the direction appears in Figure 2-15.

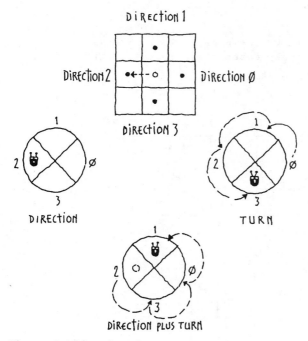

Figure 2-15 In a four-direction windrose, two plus three is one

Direction

	0	1	2	3
Turn 0 (None)	0	1	2	3
Turn 1 (Left)	1	2	3	0
Turn 2 (About-Face)	2	3	0	1
Turn 3 (Right)	3	0	1	2

Table 2-3 Adding turns to directions

A simple example of a turn-specified Turing machine is specified in Listing 2-2 and illustrated in Figure 2-16.

Listing 2-2 A two-dimensional Turing machine in <current state, read color, write color, new state, turn> format

```
Stairs =
{
  <1BX23>,       //make a mark, enter state 2, turn right
  <2BX11>        //make a mark, enter state 1, turn left
}
```

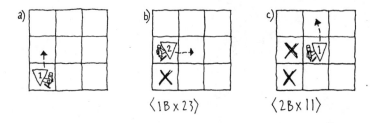

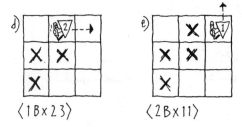

Figure 2-16 The stairs turmite

Stairs draws a zigzag line right and up forever, as illustrated in Figure 2-16. The idea here is to start out with the Stairs turmite on an empty array of cells. The turmite starts in state 1, and with an upward pointing direction. At each step of Figure 2-16, we write information about the turmite in the position where its head is located. The information we write is a number to represent the turmite's state, and an arrow to indicate the turmite's current direction.

Turmites exhibit various classes of behavior, some of which are depicted in Figure 2-17.

Moving up along the spectrum from order to disorder, there are numerous different kinds of turmites.

- *Polygon turmites* get stuck in one region, racing around a small pattern like a line or triangle or square.

- *Rail turmites* move along in one direction laying down a pattern like railroad tracks or like a dotted line.

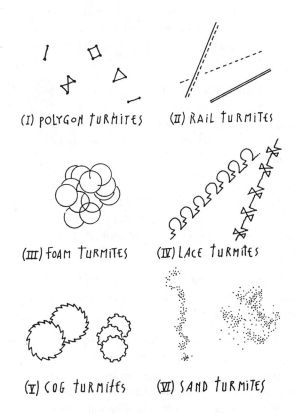

(I) POLYGON TURMITES   (II) RAIL TURMITES

(III) FOAM TURMITES   (IV) LACE TURMITES

(V) COG TURMITES   (VI) SAND TURMITES

Figure 2-17 Some types of turmites

- *Foam turmites* that repeatedly move around in a tight circles, run into the start of the circle, turn and start a new circle, forming a foamy mass of circles.

- *Lace turmites* move in one direction and lay down a pattern like a lacy border.

- *Cog turmites* are to the foam turmites as the lace turmites are to the rail turmites—meaning that the cog turmites move around in repetitively embroidered lacy circles to draw patterns like piles of machine cogs.

- *Sand turmites* dither about in messy chaos.

The lace, foam, and cog turmites are the ones in the gnarly zone. If you happen to be looking at TURMITE.BL and *don't* see all of these types, try using the File Randomize Genes selection to randomize the Turing programs of the turmites. All of the types are fairly common.

The Boppers Turmites

There's a lot of detailed information about the *Boppers* turmites in Chapter 5, *The Boppers and Their World,* but here let's just quickly mention some of the differences between these turmites and the standard two-dimensional Turing machines discussed in the last section.

The most significant difference between the *Boppers* turmites and true Turing machines is that the *Boppers* turmites do not get to move around in an unbounded space of cells. One reason Turing machines can perform such complicated calculations is that there is no limit whatsoever to the amount of tape they are allowed to use to write on.

In a certain sense, ordinary computers also have unlimited memory storage—for if necessary you can always copy parts of your program and data off to disks, and have the machine ask for these disks when it needs them. But in practice nobody ever does this—instead you equip your computer with enough RAM memory to comfortably run your applications.

The world that the *Boppers* turmites live in is of a certain finite size related to the number of pixels on the video display of the system running the program. For a standard VGA display, the size happens to be 648 by 432 cells.

When in "Wrapped" mode, *Boppers* avoids having the turmites bump into edges by treating the space as if it were wrapped around in both dimensions like a torus. But then you get the problem that the turmites keep circling around their world to come back to the same cells. In order that the *Boppers* world does not get completely covered with turmite markings, the older turmite marks are erased after a certain amount of time.

Another difference between the *Boppers* turmites and standard two-dimensional Turing machines is that rather than merely distinguishing between marked and unmarked cells, the turmites of the *Boppers* program distinguish among different colors with which a cell might be marked. So it is possible for a turmite to act like a lace turmite when it is near one color of cell, but to act like a sand turmite when it is near some other color.

We store the information from the *Boppers* turmites' quintuples in an alternate format known as *lookup tables*.

Boppers tries to evolve its turmites' lookup tables in such a way that, over time, they get better at spending time near the favorable colors and rushing away from the unfavorable colors. A good strategy for a turmite might be, for instance, to act like a rail turmite when it hits a negatively weighted color, and to act like a cog turmite when it hits a positively weighted color.

Boppers works with a whole range of turmite windroses, that is, directional lookup tables. One of the windroses that gives the best action is the 12-direction windrose, which is used by TURMITE.BL and is shown in Table 2-4. A picture of this appears in Figure 2-18.

Direction

	0	1	2	3	4	5	6	7	8	9	10	11
Change in X	2	2	1	0	–1	–2	–2	–2	–1	0	1	2
Change in Y	0	1	2	2	2	1	0	–1	–2	–2	–2	–1

Table 2-4 A 12-direction windrose

Note that some windroses allow a *Boppers* turmite to jump right over several cells of its two-dimensional tape, rather than having to move only to a nearest neighbor cell

Figure 2-18 The 12-direction windrose

each time. On the other hand, a *Boppers* turmite is still not allowed to make arbitrarily large jumps (like a computer's processor), and is limited to the combined x and y moves that appear in the windrose it uses.

A *Boppers* improvement over standard two-dimensional Turing machines is that the *Boppers* turmites can be *three*-dimensional as well as two-dimensional. This means that the turmites can move around putting marks in the cells of a three-dimensional space. When the system is using a VGA display, this space will have 648 by 432 by 432 cells. The three-dimensional windroses are described in the ESCHER subsection of Chapter 7, *Examples*.

What about states? *Boppers* is designed so that its turmites can have a total number of states between one and a hundred. (The number of states is called "IQ" on the Controls menu's Individuals Dialog.) In general, the more states a turmite can use, the more complicated is its motion, although some turmites are efficient enough to get very complex motions out of only a few states.

When people first learn about Turing machines and turmites, they often have difficulty understanding what an internal state variable is good for. One way of thinking of it is to imagine the state as a *mood*, so that a turmite might be thought of as being alarmed, bored, in a feeding frenzy, and so on—all according to which state it is in. Another way of thinking about the turmites' states is to note that the internal states can serve as short-term memory, so that a felicitously designed turmite can base its behavior on what it has encountered during its last few moves.

In the *Boppers* program, we will frequently look at turmites that we let run for a long time. It would be visually boring if any of these turmites were to halt (i.e., to come to a stop and not even *try* to draw anything anymore). In a-life, we are typically more interested in computing processes which go on and on until some external Grim Reaper pulls their plug. A-life is hard enough without having your creatures commit suicide!

Therefore, the *Boppers* turmites all have programs that are *complete* in the sense that for every possible pair `<current state, read color>` there will be a quintuple that starts with that pair. We are not sacrificing any generality here, as the class of non-halting Turing machines is in fact as computationally rich as the full class of all Turing machines.

The key thing to keep in mind about the *Boppers* turmites is that each of these creatures is a compact, possibly universal computer. With luck and proper training, your turmites can learn almost anything!

BOIDS

Boids were invented by Craig Reynolds in 1989. His goal was to produce computer a-life creatures that flock together like birds. He briefly considered calling his creatures *birdoids*, and then opted for the simpler word *boids*.

Like a turmite, at each step a boid updates its velocity vector and then moves along this vector to its new position. But the way in which a boid computes its new velocity vector is quite different from a turmite's method.

The main difference between boids and turmites is that a boid is aware of the positions and velocities of all the other boppers in its world, and it uses this information in computing its new velocity. This is quite different from the turmites, who base their new velocity computation on (1) the color of the single pixel immediately under their head and (2) their internal state. The turmites' use of internal state variables to some extent makes up for their extreme nearsightedness.

Simple boids do not have an internal state, and always react the same to the same situation. If you put a single boid alone into an empty unwalled world, the boid will do nothing but fly straight ahead at a fixed velocity, for the situation the boid sees at every step remains the same.

But once you have several boids in your world, the number of possible situations becomes very large—each boid reacts differently according to the positions and velocities of all the other boids. In most configurations, the boids swoop about on a chaotic feedback loop with exquisitely beautiful dynamics.

Another difference between the boids and the turmites is that the boids' velocities are continuously varying vectors, rather than the discrete (`deltax, deltay`) windrose vectors used by the turmites.

Boid Vectors

A vector is a position-independent arrow that has a direction and a length. The fact that a vector is *position-independent* means that if you draw several arrows of the same length and direction, then these arrows are simply different pictures of the same vector, in the same way that distinct pairs of objects are different instances of the number two. A vector is an abstraction of the idea of moving a certain distance in a certain direction.

For computational purposes, vectors are expressed as pairs or triples of numbers. Vectors are added by adding the respective components to each other. *Geometrically,*

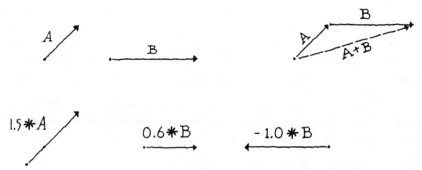

Figure 2-19 Vector addition and multiplication by scalars

vector addition is the same as putting the tail of one vector at the head of the other, and letting the resultant displacement vector be the sum, as shown in Figure 2-19.

A vector can be multiplied by an ordinary number, which is called a *scalar* in this context to distinguish it from a vector, as is also shown in Figure 2-19. Computationally, each of the vector's components is multiplied by the scaler. Geometrically, multiplication by a scalar has the effect of stretching or shrinking a vector. Multiplying a vector by a negative scalar reverses its direction.

For each vector V, one can find a unit-length vector U that points in the same direction—simply draw a picture of the vector and measure out a unit length along it. When thinking about boids, you may find it useful to think of each boid's velocity V as having the form s * U, where s is a scalar quantity and U is a unit direction vector, as shown in Figure 2-20. We speak of s as the *speed* and of U as the *tangent vector*. Changing the value of s corresponds to speeding up or slowing down, while changing the direction of U corresponds to turning. Generally, a boid will try to change its tangent vector and its speed gradually. This corresponds to the idea that a boid should act as if it has *inertia*. Flying

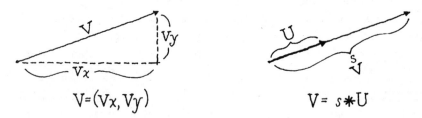

Figure 2-20 The velocity vector as components, and as speed times a unit direction vector

objects do not make sharp right-angled turns; they turn by changing their tangent vector a little bit at a time.

The boid computation works by updating the values of the speed and the tangent vector and by then setting the new position equal to the old position plus the speed times the tangent vector. In terms of components, if the old position is (x, y, z) and the tangent vector is (ux, uy, uz) and the speed is s, then the new position will be $(x + s * ux, y + s * uy, z + s * uz)$.

The Reynolds Algorithm

Once we have set up the machinery to make the boids move about by changing their speed and their tangent vectors, the boids are capable of what Reynolds calls *geometric flight*.

Now let's look at the Reynolds' algorithm. In his own words:

> To build a simulated flock, we start with a boid model that supports geometric flight. We add behaviors that correspond to the opposing forces of collision avoidance and the urge to join the flock. Stated briefly as rules ... the behaviors that lead to simulated flocking are
>
> 1. Collision Avoidance: avoid collisions with nearby flockmates.
>
> 2. Velocity Matching: attempt to match velocity with nearby flockmates.
>
> 3. Flock Centering: attempt to stay close to nearby flockmates.

Now for a few words on each of these behaviors.

1. Collision Avoidance. Each boid keeps track of some optimal cruising distance that it would like to maintain between itself and its nearest flockmates. If a boid's nearest visible neighbor is at a distance less than this cruising distance, then the boid is in danger of colliding with its neighbor. The boid avoids the collision by slowing down if the too-near neighbor is in front of the boid, and by speeding up if the too-near neighbor is behind the boid, as illustrated in the first part of Figure 2-21.

As well as trying not to get too *close* to the nearest neighbor boid, a boid also tries not to get too *far* from the nearest visible boid. That is, if you're a boid and the nearest visible neighbor boid is farther than the optimal cruise distance, you speed up if that boid's in front of you, and slow down if it's behind you, as shown in the second part of Figure 2-21.

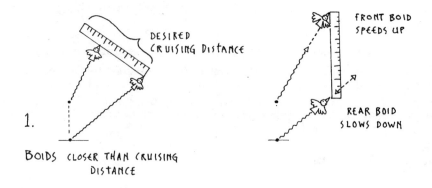

1.

BOIDS CLOSER THAN CRUISING
DISTANCE

2. BOIDS FARTHER THAN CRUISING DISTANCE

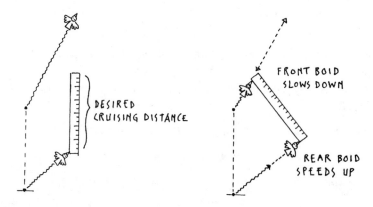

Figure 2-21 Boids try to maintain cruising distance by their speeds

Note that these adjustments to cruising distance are done solely by changing the boids' speeds, rather than by changing their tangent vectors. The phrases "in front of" and "behind" for boids are used in the sense illustrated in Figure 2-22.

2. Velocity Matching. Each boid tries to fly parallel to its nearest neighbor. This is done by adjusting the boid's tangent vector to match the tangent vector of its nearest neighbor. This does not change the boid's speed.

3. Flock Centering. Each boid tries to be surrounded by other boids on every side. This is done by having each boid compute the average position or *centroid* of the other boids, and to try and move toward the centroid. To do this, a boid

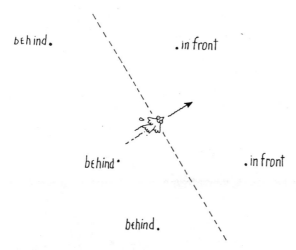

Figure 2-22 What boids mean by "in front" and "behind"

computes the unit vector that points toward the centroid, and then turns its own tangent vector to match this unit vector. This does not change the boid's speed.

The Boppers Boids

Counting the inertial drive to coast, a boid really combines *four* different behaviors: coast, avoid collisions, copy the nearest neighbor's velocity, and fly toward the center of the flock. Avoiding collisions is done by adjusting the speed alone, while the other three behaviors involve adjusting the boid's tangent vector. Cruising tells the boid to leave its tangent vector alone, copying tells it to set its tangent vector equal to the nearest neighbor's tangent vector, and centering tells the boid to set its tangent vector equal to the unit vector pointing toward the centroid of the flock. How does a boid set its tangent vector to satisfy these three conflicting drives?

The trick *Boppers* uses is to have the boid average the three directional drives out. Suppose, for instance, that a boid's current direction is Tan, that the direction of its nearest neighbor is Copy, and that the unit vector pointing toward the weighted centroid of the flock is Center. In this case, the boid's new unit direction vector NewTan will be computed to be the unit vector that has the same direction as the *Sum* vector computed as the vector sum **(Tan + Copy + Center)**, as shown in Figure 2-23.

In looking at Figure 2-23, note that in Part 1 of the figure, the Center vector is a unit length vector drawn in the direction of the line that leads from the boid's position to the position of the centroid. Part 2 of the figure, shows how the three unit vectors are

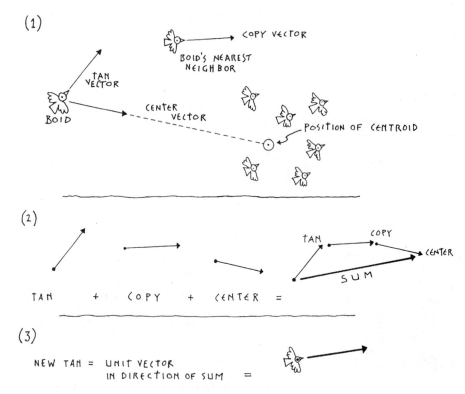

Figure 2-23 Updating a boid's unit direction vector

added together by putting them head to tail to get the resultant Sum vector. In Part 3 of the figure, the Sum vector is adjusted to be of unit length, and this is taken to be the NewTan vector.

In practice, a boid might want to emphasize one of the three behaviors at the expense of the others, so we allow each boid to keep track of two personal variables called `CopyWeight` and `CenterWeight`, and we actually compute `NewTan` as the unit vector with the same direction as the `Weighted Sum` vector computed as (Tan+(CopyWeight x Copy) + (CenterWeight x Center)). `CenterWeight` and `CopyWeight` are constrained to lie between 0.0 and 1.0.

As well as having a **CopyWeight** and a **CenterWeight** variable, each boid's flocking behavior is influenced by the following personal variables as well: **Acceleration, MaxSpeed,** and **VisionAngle**.

A boid's **Acceleration** variable has to do with how rapidly the boid changes its speed during collision avoidance. The boid speeds up by multiplying its speed by its acceleration, and it slows down by dividing its speed by its acceleration. The boid's **MaxSpeed** variable sets an upper bound on how fast it is allowed to go.

A boid's **VisionAngle** controls which of the other boids can be candidates for being the boid's nearest neighbor. When a boid computes the centroid of the flock, it uses *all* of the other boids' coordinates, but when it tries to pick out which boid is its nearest neighbor, it only considers those boids whose positions place them within the boid's cone of vision, as shown in Figure 2-24. A boid's VisionAngle can range from 1 degree to 360 degrees.

The fact that a boid has a limited angle of vision means that avoiding collisions is less straightforward than previously described. A boid avoids collisions not with the absolutely nearest boid, but with *the nearest boid that lies within its VisionAngle*. This is a slight distinction, but it has the effect of making boids move in a more lifelike fashion. Because a boid cannot usually see a boid that is directly behind it, there will sometimes be an effect of a boid overtaking a target boid and startling the target boid into activity when the pursuing boid suddenly gets into the target boid's cone of vision.

Two additional behaviors we have not mentioned yet are that in *Boppers*, the boids veer away from walls, and they attack or flee boids of other colors depending on whether these boid colonies are perceived as prey or as predators. In addition, the *Boppers* boids have the option of reacting to the *two* closest boids rather than to only the *single* closest boid.

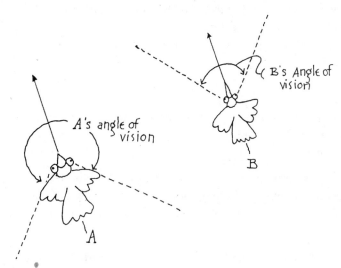

Figure 2-24 Boid vision—A sees B, but B doesn't see A

How are the boid variables set? Like the turmites' lookup tables, the boid variables are set from the genetic information of the boid. Over time, the genetic information is allowed to evolve. The coding is such that each *Boppers* boid has 18 bytes worth of genetic information, which is a total of 144 bits. You might say that each boid has a personality that's coded as a gross of bits.

Chapter 5, *The Boppers and Their World,* includes more, and gorier, details on the exact way in which *Boppers* implements the rather complex boids algorithm. But for now we can sum up by saying that flocking behavior arises if a group of a-life creatures are programmed to coast around a virtual world with the requirements that they try and stay at a *constant cruising distance* from each other, try to *fly parallel* to their nearest neighbors, and try and *head toward the center* of the flock.

Some use of flocking algorithms has been made in generating special effects for movies. In the movie *Arachnophobia*, for instance, there is a scene in which hundreds of spiders are swarming down a wall. These spiders were added to the film by computer graphics animation at the Industrial Light and Magic company of George Lucas. Rather than programming each of the hundreds of spiders' motions individually, the computer animation used a variation of the flocking algorithm in which several of the spiders were designated as *leaders* that the others tried to follow. By moving the leaders about by hand, the ILM animators were able to get the mass of spiders to move in the desired direction.

Of course in a pure flocking algorithm there are no leaders, which is one of the most interesting things about it. The overall motion of the flock of boids is an example of what a-life workers call *emergent behavior*. In emergent behavior, the individual creature's algorithms work in synergy to produce a global effect that might not have been expected simply on the basis of the individuals.

TURBOIDS

The turmites have internal states, but a simple boid does not. On the other hand, a boid can see where all the other boppers are, but a turmite can only see what's right under its head.

A turboid is a bopper that shares the strengths of both turmites and boids. Turboids can see all the other boppers, and they compute an internal state. The *Boppers* program includes four types of turboids: the wolf, the beaver, the dog, and the owl turboids.

Behaviorally, the wolves swoop around like boids, but they enter turmite mode to chew up whatever valuable food they encounter. The beavers like to group together and build large turmite-like patterns, although now and then they fly around like boids to find a more comfortable spot. The dogs are like boids that keep pausing to sniff around and mark their trails; they leave irregular, brambly paths. The owls are boids that think a great deal about what they are doing, and they tend to make more wiggly paths than do the boids. A little more detail on the four algorithms appears in the following text.

The wolf turboid decides at each update whether to act like a turmite or a boid. In effect, this means that the wolf simply has two internal states: the boid state and the turmite state. If the wolf's score level has increased over the last update, it spends the next update acting like a turmite. Otherwise, it spends the next update acting like a boid. The motive here is that turmites tend to stay in one place, so if you are in a region where the food is increasing your score, you do well to act like a turmite. If the food in the present region is nonexistent or of negative value, the wolf acts like a boid and moves on.

Like a wolf turboid, a beaver turboid uses a single pair of states to decide whether to act like a turmite or a boid. But the decision is made in a more complicated way. Basically, a beaver prefers to act like a turmite. But if a predator bopper is too close to it, it acts like a boid to fly away. In addition, if the nearest other bopper is a prey bopper that is relatively far away, the beaver acts like a boid and flies toward the prey.

A dog turboid keeps track of an internal state at all times. As with a turmite, this state can range through as many as a hundred values. The dog uses this state plus information about which boppers are closest to it to decide what its new state will be. It then uses a lookup table on the state to decide whether it should now act like a turmite or a boid.

An owl turboid acts like a boid all the time, but like a dog keeps track of an internal state that can range through as many as one hundred values. With each step, the owl changes its boid variables using a lookup table based on the current situation and its current state.

More detail on the four turboid algorithms appears in Chapter 5, *The Boppers and Their World*. In writing the *Boppers* program, I was very pleased to come up with the turboid algorithms, as they give behaviors with a truly awesome amount of gnarl.

There is no ironclad reason why these four *particular* kinds of turboid algorithms ended up being included—it's simply that I tried a variety of turmite/boid fusions, and these four gave the most interesting behavior. You might say that the turboids arose through a higher-order evolutionary process which took place in my *Boppers*-possessed brain.

CELLULAR AUTOMATA

Cellular automata, known as *CAs* for short, represent a kind of computer architecture quite different from the "von Neumann" architecture of the computations we've talked about so far. Cellular automata are like self-generating computer graphics movies, or like image-processing routines that operate on a whole rectangle of pixels at the same time.

Working cellular automata into the *Boppers* program was natural because CAs provide some interesting examples of a-life quite different from the main "bug world" approach of *Boppers*. In addition, the interactions between boppers and CAs provide a nice model of the interaction between living creatures and the world. Ordinary serial computations are like the actions of creatures *in a world*, but a CA is like *the world itself*.

Formally, cellular automata are defined as a *spatial array* of cells, where each cell holds a digital state number. The cells' states are updated in *parallel*. In addition, we require that the method of updating the cells' states is *local* and *homogeneous*.

In the next four subsections, we say a bit about each of these four aspects of CAs, and in the two subsections after that we discuss examples of how CAs can be used for simulating physics and a-life.

But first—why are computer scientists interested in such an odd kind of computation? There are two reasons which will be discussed here: CAs are good models of physics, and CAs support the emergence of lifelike patterns.

A less obvious reason for studying CAs is that CAs are a kind of computation that our machines like to do. CAs are native to the world of the computer. Your principal interface with the computer is what you see on the screen: a rectangular raster of pixels. The raster is updated in hardware approximately thirty times a second. If we think of the pixel display as being like a cellular automaton, we can imagine the computer to be acting on the contents of the pixel display directly—rather than acting on bytes in the memory ribbon. Thinking this way makes the screen world seem more real.

Another suggestive aspect of CAs is that they wholeheartedly embrace the idea of a space that is divided up into discrete cells. Some programs behave as if the creatures in computer a-life worlds have continuously varying positions, but this is not really the case. Computer a-life creatures hop about from cell to cell. This is especially true for the turmites; the whole essence of the turmites is that they live on a plane that is broken up into discrete little cells.

A Space of Cells

A CA's array of computations can be of any dimensionality—like a line, like a plane, or like a space of cells, or even like a four-dimensional hypercube—but here we'll limit our attention to two-dimensional CAs. Each of the CAs we'll look at is a computation that takes place in a rectangular grid of cells as shown in Figure 2-25. In some CAs we look at, the cells' discrete state numbers range from zero to 255. Some other of our CAs are content to use only two states: zero and one.

The world, like a CA, is something that is spread out in space. The world does not really break up into discrete little cells, but we can certainly imagine overlaying a cellular coordinate grid onto the world. If the grid cells are small enough, we might imagine that what's happening in any given cell at any given time can be specified by a digital state number which codes up such things as, for instance, temperature and pressure.

Parallel Computation

So that we can observe our CA computations in action, each cell has an internal state that is visible to the user as a color. The fact that a CA is a *parallel* computation is shown by having all of the cells in the CA seem to change at once.

The world is everywhere, and with each tick of time, the whole world changes—all at once. If we think of the world as a computation that is distributed over a grid of cells, it is indeed a computation that is parallel rather than serial.

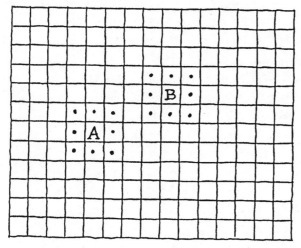

Figure 2-25 Two cells with their nearest neighbors

Ideally, we might imagine having a separate dedicated microprocessor for each cell of the CA, with all the processors running at the same speed. But in practice, the CAs you see in the *Boppers* program are going to be run by a single micro-processor: the chip in your computer. *Boppers* simulates CA parallelism by using an update buffer to store the new values while they are being computed. Once all the new values are ready, they are rapidly blasted to the CA arena you see on the screen.

Local Neighborhoods

Saying a CA computation is *local* means that the cells only look at nearby cells. In the rules we look at, each cell will look at its eight nearest neighbors: the four that touch at a corner as well as the four that touch on an edge. Two examples of these cell neighborhoods appear in Figure 2-25.

In the world, the next state of a small region is affected only by its immediate neighborhood. This fact is enshrined as a physical principle: *there is no action at a distance*. In standard physics, one object can act on another only by sending some intermediary particle or force field through the intervening space so as to come into the target particle's immediate neighborhood.

Homogeneity of Law

Saying that a CA computation is *homogeneous* means that each cell of a CA updates itself in the same way: each cell looks at its own state and the states of its nearest neighbors and performs some simple logical operations to determine its new state. Each cell, might, for instance, set its new state to the average of values of its eight closest neighbors.

All physical observations to date confirm the physical principle of homogeneity: that each region of spacetime evolves according to the same natural laws. This means that if we do think of the world as being like a huge CA, then each "cell" of the universal CA updates itself according to the same rule.

CAs for Physics

In this section we'll talk about the three physics-inspired CA rules in *Boppers:* the Melt rule, the Rug rule, and the Vote rule.

Melt

The Melt CA rule, which is included in *Boppers,* is modelled on the physical concept of *diffusion.* The spread of perfume obeys a rule like Melt, as does the spread of heat through a piece of metal. The Melt rule allows cell values to range from zero through 255, and with each update, each cell's value is replaced by the average of its eight nearest neighbors. If we think of the cell value as being, say, a perfume concentration or a temperature, then Melt is a good way of simulating diffusion.

It is particularly interesting to run Melt with the boppers active. Here you will see the trails of the boppers leaving clouds of color which diffuse through the space of the CA. If the CA is set to a large size, the effect is particularly interesting.

Rug

The Rug CA rule is a slight variation on the Melt rule. In the Rug rule, the cell values range from zero to 255 as before. But when a cell is updated, its value is set to the average of the cell's eight nearest neighbors *plus one.* If the resulting value is 256 or higher, you subtract 256 from it, thus wrapping it around to zero or some other low value.

Rug produces an effect which has been compared to *boiling.* If all of a cell's neighbors are at the maximum value of 255, then that cell's new value will be 256, which gets wrapped down to zero. At the next generation, the presence of this zero-valued cell will lower the values of that cell's nearest neighbors. The process is analogous to the way in which a hot enough region of water gives up some heat by forming a bubble of steam. The water right around the steam bubble cools off for a moment.

Vote

The Vote CA rule displays a process akin to physical *weathering*—meaning the process by which jagged features of the world get smoothed off over time. Vote is a rule which allows only two different cell values: zero and one. Each cell takes a majority vote among itself and its eight nearest neighbors. That is, the sum is taken over a three by three block consisting of nine cells. If the majority is for zero, then the cell goes to zero, otherwise the cell goes to one. But hold on, it's not *quite* that simple. CA experimentation reveals that Vote yields a more interesting and dynamic rule if near-ties are awarded to the loser. That is, if there are five votes for zero and four votes for one, the cell goes to one; and if there are four votes for zero and five votes for one, the cell goes to zero, as shown in Table 2-5.

Sum Over Nine Cells

	0	1	2	3	4	5	6	7	8	9
New Cell Value	0	0	0	0	1	0	1	1	1	1

Table 2-5 The CA vote rule

CAs for A-Life

Some CAs act like completely artificial non-physics-like universes in which life of a sort may emerge. When I first saw rapidly running cellular automata at Boston University in 1985, one of the scientists working with them said something that struck me as very exciting: "I feel like Leuwenhook after discovering the microscope. There are so many new worlds for us to explore!"

In the following sections we look at five kinds of a-life CA rules included with *Boppers*.

Life

The most famous CA of all is John Horton Conway's game of Life. In Life, each cell has a value of zero or one. Each cell takes the sum of its eight nearest neighbors, getting a neighborhood sum value that can range from zero to eight. If a cell is in state zero, then it goes into state one if it has a neighborhood sum of exactly three. If a cell is in state one, then it remains in state one if its neighborhood sum is two or three. In all other cases, a cell's new value is zero. These rules are summarized in Table 2-6.

Sum Over Eight Cells

	0	1	2	3	4	5	6	7	8
New Cell Value If Cell Is 0	0	0	0	1	0	0	0	0	0
New Cell Value If Cell Is 1	0	0	1	1	0	0	0	0	0

Table 2-6 The CA life rule

The Life CA rule is remarkable for the way in which a random soup of pixels can lead to a variety of self-perpetuating structures. One such structure that you may notice is the Life *glider*, a small pattern of turned-on pixels which moves about at 45 degree angles.

Brain

Another very rich, but less well-known rule is Brian Silverman's Brain rule. In Brain, each cell has a value of zero, one, or two. These states are often thought of as being ready, firing, and resting states, respectively. The cells update themselves by computing how many of their eight nearest neighbors are in state one. This is the *firing eight sum*. If a cell is in the ready state, it goes into the firing state if its firing eight sum is exactly two. A firing cell always becomes a resting cell, and a resting cell always becomes a ready cell. These rules are summarized in Table 2-7.

Firing Sum Over Eight Cells

	0	1	2	3	4	5	6	7	8
New Cell Value If Cell Is 0	0	0	1	0	0	0	0	0	0
New Cell Value If Cell Is 1	2	2	2	2	2	2	2	2	2
New Cell Value If Cell Is 2	0	0	0	0	0	0	0	0	0

Table 2-7 The CA brain rule

Brain consists of patterns that move around horizontally and vertically, often with interesting little things flying off of big things. You may occasionally see a small pattern that moves at 45 degree angles. This pattern is known as the Brain *butterfly*, and is analogous to the Life glider.

Faders

The Faders rule is a kind of cross between the Life and the Brain rules. Like Life, a Faders cell which is in state one is allowed to stay in state one if it has the right number of neighbors in state one. Like Brain, a cell that does not stay in state one enters a resting state rather than going straight back to state zero. Unlike Brain, Faders uses 32 resting states instead of just one resting state. The Faders resting states are all the even numbers from 2 to 64.

The Faders rule is partially displayed in Table 2-8.

Firing Sum Over Eight Cells

	0	1	2	3	4	5	6	7	8
New Cell Value If Cell Is 0	0	0	1	0	0	0	0	0	0
New Cell Value If Cell Is 1	2	2	1	2	2	2	2	2	2
New Cell Value If Cell Is 2	4	4	4	4	4	4	4	4	4
New Cell Value If Cell Is 4	6	6	6	6	6	6	6	6	6
New Cell Value If Cell Is 62	64	64	64	64	64	64	64	64	64
New Cell Value If Cell Is 64	0	0	0	0	0	0	0	0	0

Table 2-8 The CA Faders rule

When the Faders CA patch is seeded with random pixels, it takes about 30 cycles for the crud to clear away. What you may notice is that inside the crud there will be some little right-angled three-pixel fader eggs like the ones shown in Figure 2-26. Each pixel in a fader egg is in state one, and the pixels around it are in other states.

As long as the pixels around a fader egg are not in state zero, the fader egg persists. Each pixel in the fader egg has exactly two neighbors in state one, which allows each pixel to stay in state one. And as long as the pixels around the fader egg are not in state zero, they do not get changed to state one.

Once the crud around a fader egg melts away to zero, the fader egg starts to grow, turning some of its state zero neighbors to state one.

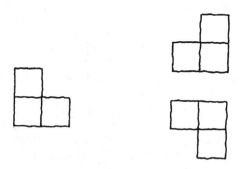

Figure 2-26 Fader eggs

Ranch

The Ranch rule is an attempt at a CA ecology. Ranch actually runs three rules at once: the Vote rule, the Life rule, and the Brain rule. Ranch uses the Vote rule to divide the CA world up into two different regions. In one of these regions, the Life rule is applied, and in the other region, the Brain rule is used. Looking at this world, you might think of the active cells as being like living creatures that swim about in the dark water using the Brain rule, and occasionally crawl on to the bright land and lay eggs which obey the Life rule. When Vote erodes an edge to uncover a Life egg, it hatches live Brain cells in the water.

Zhabotinsky

The Zhabotinsky rule displays lifelike behavior at a larger scale. No matter what starting pattern you give the Zhabotinsky rule, the rule will eventually create a pattern of scrolls that grow endlessly out from themselves. These patterns are reminiscent of lima beans, of fetuses, and of the cross-sections of mushroom caps. The Zhabotinsky rule is a remarkable example of order arising from randomness. Without analyzing the details of this version of the Zhabotinsky rule, which is also known as the Hodgepodge rule, the Zhabotinsky rule allows the cells to be in a limited number of different states, and works like the CA Rug rule. It replaces each cell by an average of its neighbors plus something, with the stipulation that when a cell's value passes the maximum state value it lingers in that state for a generation and then drops down to zero. Lingering in the maximum state brings the cells' waves of excitation into synch.

The Lambda Rule

The last CA rule type in *Boppers* is the so-called Lambda rule, which is really a huge number of different rules. The inspiration for the Lambda rule is neither physics nor a-life. The Lambda rule was inspired by the theories of chaos and complexity.

In the *Boppers* implementation, each instance of the Lambda rule allows the cells to be in one of 16 different states. Each cell computes how many of its eight nearest neighbors is in an odd state; this is viewed as the cell's *firing eight sum*, and can range from zero to nine. The cell's new state is obtained by consulting a lookup table that has a new state value for each combination of firing eight sum and cell state.

Each time you start a Lambda CA rule, a lookup table is created for the rule. The lookup table is filled with random numbers subject to the specification (1) that all the numbers lie within the specified state range, and the specification (2) that only some fixed percentage of the numbers can be nonzero. This percentage of nonzero entries is known as the lookup table's *lambda* parameter.

For a low value of lambda, most of the entries in the lookup table will be zero, and the CA is likely to die out. For a high value of lambda, most of the lookup table entries are nonzero, and the CA is likely to go into a seething activity that looks like visual static on a television. The gnarly transition between rules that die out and rules that seethe is somewhere in between, at the medium lambda values.

Looking for cool new random Lambda, CAs can become a kind of compulsive addiction not unlike playing a slot machine. If you want to rapidly keep trying new Lambda rules, the key combination (CONTROL)-(D) will keep randomizing the lookup table. What you are more or less hoping to see when you do this is a pattern of gliders that crawl around and bump into each other, kind of like patterns in Brain. What you don't want to see is a pattern that dies out or that just becomes almost solid. You are, as is usual in a-life researches, seeking gnarl at the interface between order and disorder.

NOTES AND REFERENCES

- Eight bits are known as a *byte*, and, according to Eric Raymond's highly entertaining *The New Hacker's Dictionary*, MIT Press, 1991, larking hackers occasionally refer to four bits as a *nybble*, 16 bits as a *playte*, and 32 bits as a *dynner*. The Intel 8086 and 80386SX processors use playte-sized words, whereas the 80386DX and 80486 chips use dynners. Be warned that this usage is "rare and extremely silly."

But while we're at it, what would be some good names for larger computer word sizes? Mainframes use 64-bit words already, so how about a *tayble* for 64 bits? And, moving onward, 128 bit *ynns*, 256 bit *chaynes*, 512 bit *wyrlds*, and K-sized *univyrses*? Maybe you can think of better names yourself!

Math Alert

The original Intel 8086 16-bit processor had 14 registers, with room for 16 bits in each register, making a total of 224 bits of register memory on the processor. If you think of putting zeroes and ones randomly into those 224 slots, you get two to the 224th power different states that a processor could be in—where the state of the processor completely describes its current status. Two to the 224th power is about two to the 230th, which is two to the 10 * 23 power. Because two to the 10th is, once again, a K, or 1,024, which is practically a thousand, two to the 10 * 23 is about a thousand to the 23rd, or ten to the 3 * 23, which is ten to the 69th power. That's a lot. The theoretical study of Turing machines shows that you can do any computation with a processor that only has a hundred (or fewer) states, but these kinds of processors run much slower.

- Several chapters on Core Wars can be found in A.K. Dewdney's two anthologies of his *Scientific American* columns: *The Armchair Universe* and *The Magic Machine*, published in paperback by Freeman in 1988 and 1990, respectively, with a third volume due out in Fall, 1993. Dewdney left *Scientific American* to publish his own magazine for recreational programming, *Algorithm*. *Algorithm* is now defunct, but back issues are available from P.O. Box 29237, Westmount Postal Outlet, 785 Wonderland Road, London, Ontario, CANADA N6K 1M6. Dewdney continues as a professor of computer science at the University of Western Ontario.

- Thomas Ray's *Tierra* program is described in his paper, "An Approach to the Synthesis of Life," in the *Artificial Life II* anthology. Information about getting a copy of Ray's program can be obtained by e-mailing him on the Internet at ray@hip.atr.co.jp.

- Alan Turing originally defined his machines in a 1936 paper called "On Computable Numbers...." This paper is reprinted in Martin Davis, ed., *The Undecidable*, Raven Press, 1965. In the paper, Turing focuses on using his machines to generate endless strings of digits. That is, he is primarily interested in Turing machines that do *not* halt, but instead generate the endless decimal expansion of a real number. He defines a computable real number to be a number whose digits can be printed by a Turing machine. It is interesting to read Turing's own definition of his machine in this quote (lightly edited by me) from his 1936 paper:

> *We may compare a man in the process of computing a real number to a machine which is only capable of a finite number of conditions q1, q2, ..., qR, which will be called* internal states. *The machine is supplied with a* tape *(the analogue of paper) running through it, and divided into sections (called* squares*) each capable of bearing a symbol. At any moment there is just one square, say bearing the symbol S, which is "in the machine." We may call this square the* scanned square. *The symbol on the scanned square may be called the* scanned symbol. *The scanned symbol is the only one of which the machine is, so to speak, directly aware. However, by altering its internal state the machine can effectively remember some of the symbols which it has "seen" previously. The possible behavior of the machine at any moment is determined by the internal state q and the scanned symbol S. This pair < q, S > will be called the* configuration: *thus the configuration determines the possible behavior of the machine. In some of the configurations in which the scanned square is blank the machine writes down a new symbol on the scanned square: in other configurations it erases the scanned symbol. The machine may also change the square which is being*

scanned, but only by shifting it one place to the right or left. In addition to any of these operations the internal state may be changed. Some of the symbols written down will form the sequence of figures which is the decimal of the real number which is being computed. The others are just rough notes to "assist the memory."

There is more information on Turing machines in my book, *Mind Tools*, Houghton Mifflin, 1987. A good technical treatment of Turing machines can be found in Marvin Minsky's, *Computation: Finite and Infinite Machines*, Prentice-Hall, 1967.

Turing's life was quite interesting: in the Second World War he led a British team that broke the Enigma code being used by Germany. Turing was gay, and when he reported having been robbed by a male prostitute, the British courts sentenced Turing to estrogen treatments to reduce his sex drive. Depressed by these treatments, Turing committed suicide by injecting poison into an apple and eating it. He was also a chemist, and he was the first to speculate that Belusov-Zhabotinsky-style reactions, like the ones discussed in the "Biochemistry" subsection of Chapter 1, *Life and A-Life,* might be responsible for the spots and stripes of animals' skins. A good biography of Turing is Andrew Hodges, *Alan Turing, The Enigma*. There is also an interesting play about Turing by Hugh Whitmore called *Breaking the Code*, Amber Lane Press, 1987.

- Michael Palmiter's *Simulated Evolution* bug world was first described in A.K. Dewdney's "Computer Recreations" column for *Scientific American*, May, 1989, which was reprinted in Dewdney's anthology, *The Magic Machine*. .

  The Maxis *SimLife* program was mostly written, I'm proud to say, by Ken Karakotsios, who once took a class on Cellular Automata at San Jose State from me. Before being infected by the a-life meme, Karakotsios was a chip designer for Apple. Karakotsios has also written a CA simulator for the Macintosh called *CA Sim*.

- A.K. Dewdney's "Computer Recreations" column on Greg Turk's turmites appeared in the September, 1989, *Scientific American*. As of spring 1993, Turk is on a post-doc grant doing computer graphics at Stanford University. The artificial life pioneer Christopher Langton worked for a time with some turmite-like creatures he called vants. The vants are essentially turmites that have only one internal state and move in only four directions. Some footage of Langton's vants appears in the fascinating *Artificial Life II Video Proceedings*, published by Addison-Wesley in 1992.

- Craig Reynolds first demonstrated his boids in a computer-generated video called *Stanley and Louise* that he made for Symbolics, Inc. The video, which concerns a girl fish that falls in love with a boy boid, was first shown at the annual SIGGRAPH computer graphics meeting in 1987, and is reproduced in the *Artificial Life II Video Proceedings*. Reynolds' paper "Flocks, Herds, and Schools: A Distributed Behavioral Model," appeared in the July, 1987, issue of *Computer Graphics* as part of the acm SIGGRAPH '87 proceedings.

- One other type of bug world a-life creatures that should be mentioned are the *Braitenberg vehicles*. They are two-dimensional boids that react to various movable "light sources" as well as to each others' motions. Braitenberg has written a brilliant book about his vehicles in which he imagines adding successively greater capabilities to them. Valentino Braitenberg, *Vehicles: Experiments in Synthetic Psychology*, MIT Press, 1984.

- At least one scientist, named Edward Fredkin, strongly believes that the world really *is* a CA. An interesting profile of Fredkin appears in Robert Wright's, *Three Scientists and Their Gods*, Times Books, 1988.

The most complete popular treatment of cellular automata is Rudy Rucker and John Walker's, *CA Lab: Rudy Rucker's Cellular Automata Laboratory*, Autodesk,1989. *CA Lab* includes a book-like manual, and two DOS software packages for running CAs. Autodesk is in the process of changing the name of *CA Lab* to prevent confusion with the products of an east coast company called Computer Associates, and they may in fact discontinue *CA Lab* entirely. Get it while you can. Another good book on CAs is Tommaso Toffoli and Norman Margolus' *Cellular Automata Machines*, MIT Press, 1987.

The Brain CA rule first appeared in Brian Silverman's *The Phanton Fishtank*, Logo Computer Systems, 1987. This package includes software for running CAs on an Apple II.

The Ranch rule is described in Rudy Rucker's article, "Symbiotic Programming" in *Complex Systems,* 1989, pp. 79–90, and the Faders rule first appears in *CA Lab*. The version of the Zhabotinsky CA rule we use was invented by M. Gerhardt and H. Schuster, and is discussed in the "Hodgepodge Reactions" chapter of Dewdney's *The Magic Machine* anthology.

The notion of the continuum of Lambda CA rules comes from Christopher Langton, and is discussed in his essay, "Life at the Edge of Chaos," which appears in the *Artificial Life II* anthology.

- The *Artificial Life II* anthology, along with most of the other books we've mentioned, plus the *Artificial Life II Video Proceedings*, Tom Ray's *Tierra*, Michael Palmiter's *Simulated Evolution*, Ken Karakotsios' *SimLife* and *Cell Sim* programs, and Walker and Rucker's *CA Lab* are all available by mail order from Media Magic, P.O.Box 598, Nicasio, CA 94946, Phone: (415) 662-2426—write or phone Media Magic for an interesting catalog that includes just about all the available a-life books, programs, and videos.

3

Genetic
Algorithms

Many tasks come down to the problem of searching out a good solution from a large, but well-defined, space of possibilities. Say, for instance, that you are playing the stock market. Which stocks do you sell and which do you buy? The possibilities are fixed, but you need to find a way to choose.

Or suppose that you are arranging a factory's schedule for ordering raw materials and shipping products. Here again, the possibilities are definite, but there's the complicating matter of the dependencies between what you order and what you ship.

Even planning a personal shopping trip involves choosing a solution from a big space of possibilities. Where should you go first, when should you break for lunch, how much money should you bring, and so on. Over and over, we have to make interrelated choices from vast sets of possibilities.

In many situations, the computer search techniques known as *genetic algorithms* provide an efficient and automatic way of looking for a good solution.

The techniques used by genetic algorithms are inspired by the techniques that nature uses in picking genomes from the huge set of all possible gene strings: fitness-proportional reproduction, sex, and mutation.

The genetic algorithm approach to a scientific problem is, in short, to create a computer simulation of the problem and to then try and let the solution *evolve*. The idea is to create a sort of arena inside the computer where various proposed algorithms can compete and breed.

In this chapter, we'll first look at some examples of the type of search problems which genetic algorithms are used for, and then we'll look at the details of one standard approach to using a genetic algorithm. After that comes a discussion of the relationship between genetic algorithms and artificial life.

SEARCH PROBLEMS

In a *search problem*, you are presented with a *solution space* of possibilities from which you are supposed to choose. You are also supplied with a procedure known as a *fitness function* that lets you compute the numerical *score* for any proposed solution you care to consider. Your *goal* is to pick a high-scoring solution as rapidly as you can. Let's discuss the three parts of this definition.

Theoretically, a search problem's solution space can be as simple as a line segment or a plane—maybe you are supposed to find a good value for some particular number or for some pair of numbers. But in practice, the search problems that computer scientists work with have solution spaces that are like fractally branching bramble bushes.

More pointedly, a typical search problem's solution space is akin to a Borgesian library of all the possible 200-page books that might be printed using the letters of the English language. And if even one letter is changed in a book, it can mean something completely different and the fitness function is liable to assign it a totally different score. This is why real-world search problems are so hard!

But for the moment, let's *do* think of a solution space that is like a line or like a plane—so that we can draw some pictures of fitness functions, as in Figure 3-1 and Figure 3-2.

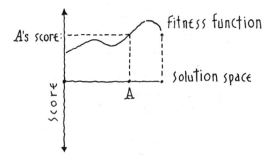

Figure 3-1 A smooth fitness landscape over a one-dimensional solution space

In Figure 3-1, the solution space is a line segment, and the fitness function is the curved graph above the line. The idea is that for each point in the solution space, the score at that point is the vertical height up to the curve that represents the fitness function.

An example of the type of search problem depicted in Figure 3-1 might be if, for example, you were trying to find the sale price that would position a product for the biggest financial gain. In this case, the vertical axis would represent the profit and the horizontal axis would represent the sale price. The shape of the fitness function suggests that if the price is very low or very high the profit will be low. The fact that the fitness function has two bumps might represent the fact that there are two distinct sale prices that position the product for relatively high profits. It might be, for instance, that at the lower price the product is perceived as a good value, and at the higher price, the product is perceived as having excellent quality. Because the profit is greater for the right-hand bump, you would want to pick the sale price that corresponds to the position on the horizontal axis right under this bump.

In Figure 3-2, the solution space is a square, and the fitness function is the curved surface above the square. For each point in the solution space, the score at that point is the vertical height up to the surface that represents the fitness function. A search problem like this might arise if you were trying to maximize the gain obtained by setting two independent variables—corresponding to the two axes of the square.

Maybe, for instance, you are trying to decide what mix of volume and treble settings you should set your car stereo speakers to. The vertical axis might represent your listening pleasure (perhaps on a subjective scale of one to ten), the horizontal axis might represent the bass setting, and the axis that runs perpendicular to the page might represent the treble setting. The fact that the fitness function has a single bump in the middle represents the fact that you will have the greatest listening pleasure if both bass and treble are set to mid-range.

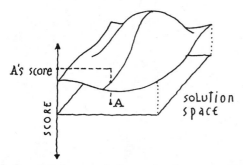

Figure 3-2 A smooth fitness landscape over a two-dimensional solution space

Note that the surface drawn in Figure 3-2 looks a bit like a landscape with hills and valleys. As we'll see in just a moment, fitness functions are usually *not* this smooth and well behaved. But a picture like Figure 3-2 does suggest a useful analogy: the fitness function can be thought of as a landscape, and in this landscape the *goal* of the search problem is to climb to the top of the highest hill.

Figure 3-2 makes finding the highest point look too easy, for you feel like you can just *look* at a picture like Figure 3-2 and *see* where the highest spike is. But in reality, you can't see these fitness landscapes all at once. The problem is that actually *calculating* the fitness function for any proposed solution point can take quite a bit of time.

Put a bit differently, rather than being *outside* the fitness landscape looking *at it*, you are down *inside* the fitness landscape walking around *in it*.

On a real, physical landscape we can in fact find hilltops even if we can't see very far. One technique might be to repeatedly find the altitudes of four nearby points and then move to the highest of these nearby points. One might, for instance, always look at points a hundred meters away in each of the primary compass directions. If you find that you are overshooting a peak, you might next switch to looking at points only ten meters away, and then to points only one meter away. Ultimately, you will narrow down on the top of a hill.

The kind of technique just outlined is known as *hill climbing*. The hill-climbing method is to keep looking for better solutions that are *near* the best solutions you've found so far.

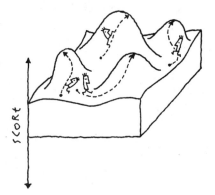

Figure 3-3 Hill-climbing multiple peaks

One problem with hill climbing is that you may not climb the highest hill. If you start out on the slope of a small hill, you may end up on the peak of that hill while completely overlooking a much higher hill nearby. You can try and compensate for this by doing repeated runs of the hill-climbing algorithm, starting from different points in the solution space, as shown in Figure 3-3.

Many, or even *most*, of the fitness functions we encounter in the a-life field turn out to be very unsmooth. Typical a-life fitness functions tend, in fact, to be fractal and chaotic, with zillions of unexpected jumps up and down, as suggested in Figure 3-4. The whole fitness landscape is marked with unexpected sharp peaks, and even these peaks are jagged masses of finer and finer spires. In this kind of landscape, two solutions that are very near to each other may have radically different fitness scores.

Another peculiar feature of the search problems we encounter in a-life and other branches of computer science is that the solution spaces for these problems are *discrete*, rather than continuous. Say, for instance, that you are looking for the best

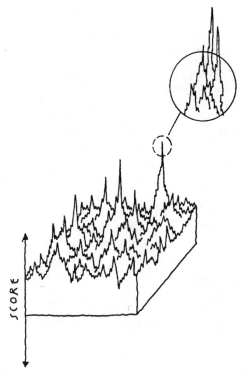

Figure 3-4 A fractal-like fitness landscape over a two-dimensional solution space

possible string of four zeroes and ones—according to some fitness function's notion of "best." If you are looking at the string 0110, for example, and there is no other four-bit string that is *very* near to this string, any string that is not the same as 0110 has to differ by at least one bit. The closest neighboring strings to 0110 might be said to be those strings obtained by changing a single bit: 1110, 0010, 0100, and 0111. Yet each of these "closest" strings differs from 0110 by 25 percent!

In terms of the bitstring that defines a turmite's lookup tables, it is conceivable that changing a single bit might completely change the behavior of the turmite. Look back, for instance, at the Marker Turing machine of Chapter 2, *Computer A-Life*, whose Turing machine program consisted of the single quintuple `<1BXR1>`. Suppose that the second 1 were to be changed to 2, making the quintuple `<1BXR2>`. If you put this Broken Marker machine into state 1 and set it down on a blank tape, it will mark one cell, enter state two, move one cell to the right, and then halt—because it doesn't have any instruction that starts with the pair `<2B>`.

Even though there is unsmoothness and discreteness, computer search problems can still use something like the hill-climbing idea of *looking for better solutions that are suggested by the best solutions found so far*. This is, in fact, the idea that underlies genetic algorithms: keep trying out new bitstrings that are in some way based on the best bitstrings you've already found.

Before going into the details of genetic algorithms, let's make clear why we really *need* to use a directed search procedure on solution spaces of bitstrings. Why is it that we can't just look at *all* the possible bitstrings in some kind of alphabetical order, evaluate each of the strings with the fitness function, and then choose the highest-scoring string as the answer?

The problem with such a *brute force search* is that there will normally be too many strings. Suppose, for instance, that I'm interested in some computer a-life creatures each of whom has a genome of exactly one hundred bits. There are two-to-the-hundredth possible such genomes in the search problem's solution space, which is a number in excess of ten-to-the-thirtieth, or 100, 000, 000, 000, 000, 000, 000, 000, also known as one hundred octillion.

Because brute force searches are impossibly time consuming for most problems, we really do need some method for conducting a directed search. And, unlike classical hill climbing, our method has to work even for unsmooth and discrete spaces. The method we need is genetic algorithms.

THE STANDARD GENETIC ALGORITHM

Insofar as the computer always represents things by strings of bits, we may as well suppose from now on that we are going to be looking at a search problem whose solution spaces consist of strings of zeroes and ones.

To ground the discussion, you might best think of a bitstring as encoding the description of some a-life creature like a turmite that is trying to get a good score, or fitness, in an a-life world. But the genetic algorithm is also useful for practical problems where the bitstrings might code up, for example, different proposed production schedules for a factory. In the case where bitstrings code up factory production schedules, their fitnesses might correspond to the profitability of running the factory according to them.

The earliest work on genetic algorithms was done by John Holland in the 1960s. In this section we'll describe one of Holland's standard approaches. The idea is that you work with a fixed-size population of candidate gene strings. Your starting population is normally created at random. Repeatedly you (1) *evaluate the fitness* of every genome in the population and (2) *create a new population* consisting of copies of some of the old population's genomes. Then you (3) perform a *crossover* operation on some pairs of the new population's genomes and (4) *mutate* some of the new population's genomes as well. And then you go back to step (1).

Let's look at the four steps, and then we'll talk about why the process is supposed to work.

(1) *Evaluate the fitness.* Evaluating the fitness of the various genomes is usually the most time-consuming part of the process. In an artificial life search problem, each genome will need to be translated into the parameters of a creature, and then you will need to let each creature run around for a while so you can see how it does.

(2) *Create a new population.* The guiding principle here is that the fitter a genome of the old population is, the more representatives it should receive in the new population. This is known as *fitness-proportional reproduction.*

When carrying out fitness-proportional reproduction, you need to use a certain amount of subtlety to avoid prematurely wiping out genetic diversity. This can happen quite easily if you are working on a small-sized population.

This pitfall is known as *premature convergence.* It's like suddenly everyone looks like a platypus—not because platypus genes are so great but only because they were so lucky. Premature convergence is an unproductive condition to be in—it's as if a group of hill-climbing surveyors were to cluster on the side of one particular hill before having really looked around the landscape.

Here's an example of a *crude approach* to fitness-proportional reproduction that is quite likely to produce premature convergence: Divide the population into two halves according to score, give each of the high-scoring genomes two representatives, and give each low-scoring genome no representatives, as illustrated in Figure 3-5.

The crude approach gives you a new population the same size as the old one, as it should, but each application of the crude approach *halves* the number of different kinds of genomes. In a population of 16, the crude approach can lead to complete genetic homogeneity in four steps, as shown in Figure 3-5. The crude

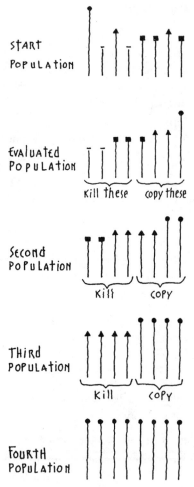

Figure 3-5 Crude fitness-proportional reproduction

approach can homogenize a population of 64 in five steps, and can homogenize a population of one thousand in ten steps.

The problem with the crude approach is that it insists that each old genome gets either *two* representatives or *no* representatives in the new generation. The subtle approach that Holland invented instead allows the process of fitness-proportional reproduction to say that some old genomes may get 0.7 representative, others may get 1.1, others 1.3, and so on. The idea is to cluster the numbers near 1.0, rather than pushing them out to the 0.0 and 2.0 extremes of the crude approach.

But how do you give someone 1.2 representatives in the next generation? The idea is that a number like 1.2 is taken like a *probability*. That is, if a genome were to get 1.2 representatives ten times in a row, this would average out to 12 representatives. The preferred fitness-proportional representation algorithm implements this by imitating the behavior of a fortune wheel with different size slices, as drawn in Figure 3-6. For each genome in the new population, you spin the fortune wheel once to decide which old genome the new genome should be a copy of.

The fortune wheels in Figure 3-6 are drawn for a population of only six genomes. For each fortune wheel, the respective sizes of the pie slices represent respective fitnesses of the genomes. To pick a new population of six genomes, we spin the chosen fortune wheel six times and create copies of the six genomes whose numbers come up.

The idea is that to prevent premature convergence, we do not let the pie slices get too excessively small or large. For the details of how this is implemented for the *Boppers* program, see the discussion of the Death Level parameter in the Colonies Dialog section of Chapter 6, *Boppers User's Guide.*

(3) *Crossover.* We talked a little about crossover and mutation in Chapter 1, *Life and A-Life,* but let's go over them again.

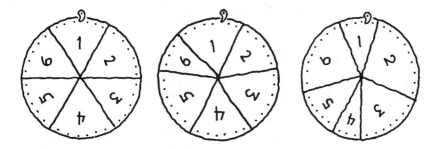

Figure 3-6 Some six-number fortune wheels

Like the fitness-proportional reproduction process, the crossover process can be thought of as something that replaces an existing population of genomes by a new population. This is sometimes emphasized by referring to fitness-proportional reproduction and to crossover as *genetic operators*. A genetic operator transforms a given population of genomes into different populations of the same size.

Crossover works by using a randomizer to split the population into distinct randomly selected pairs of genomes, as shown in Figure 3-7. Each pair of the old population produces a pair in the new population.

Depending on the rate at which you wish sex to happen, some or all of the new pairs are obtained from the old pairs by the process of crossover, as illustrated in Figure 3-8.

(4) *Mutation*. The final step in the standard genetic algorithm cycle is to mutate the bits of the new genomes with some probability per bit of being mutated. Thus you might set the mutation probability at .01, meaning that each bit has a one in one hundred chance of being changed. Like fitness-proportional reproduction and crossover, mutation is an operator that transforms a population of genomes. A picture of a bitstring mutation was shown in Figure 1-9.

When you are comparing bitstrings, you can speak of the *Hamming distance* between two bitstrings as being the number of positions at which the strings differ. When you mutate a genome, you are moving to a genome that is "near" in the sense of having a relatively low Hamming distance from the original

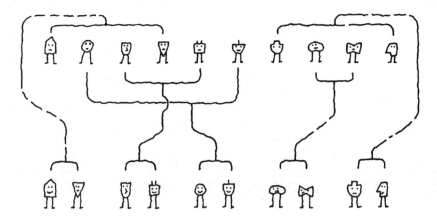

Figure 3-7 Crossover groups population into random pairs

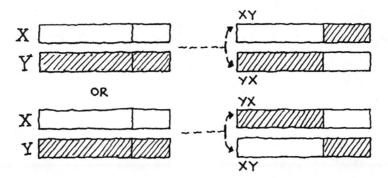

Figure 3-8 Crossover replaces an old pair by a new pair

genome. In this way, mutation is quite similar to the hill-climbing notion of exploring nearby points.

Summing up, we can say that the standard genetic algorithm consists of repeatedly measuring a population's fitness and using this information to apply genetic operators to the population. The standard genetic algorithm uses these three genetic operators: the fitness-proportional reproduction operator, the crossover operator, and the mutation operator.

Note that the information about fitness is only used by the fitness-proportional reproduction operator. The crossover operator and the mutation operators don't pay any attention to the genomes' fitnesses.

It is pretty clear that the role of fitness-proportional reproduction is to reduce the number of different kinds of genomes in the population. The role of mutation, on the other hand, is to increase the diversity of the genomes.

But what about crossover? What is crossover actually doing for us? At one level, crossover simply acts as a kind of super mutation that changes a population's diversity. If you have two identical genomes and one of them happens to get crossed over with a different genome, then the original genomes will no longer be identical.

A deeper effect of crossover is that it sets off a hidden game in which small stretches of the genomes compete with each other to reproduce and to form useful alliances.

In Holland's terminology, a consecutive stretch of a genome's bits is a *schema* (plural form is *schemata*). Some of a bitstring's schemata are shown in Figure 3-9. During crossover, some schemata are cut in half, but others get the opportunity to join up with schemata from a different genome.

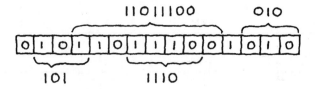

Figure 3-9 Schemata are pieces of bitstrings

If it turns out that one schema is particularly valuable in a certain location, then fitness-proportional reproduction will ensure that more and more of the population's genomes have this schema at the right location. And crossover will keep letting this winning schema try to ally itself with other winning schemata.

Holland and his students have produced a number of formal proofs that the standard genetic algorithm does a good job of selectively breeding the *schemata* as well as the *genomes*. The standard genetic algorithm keeps working on the detailed makeup of the genomes for as long as you let it run.

GENETIC ALGORITHMS AND ARTIFICIAL LIFE

The field of genetic algorithms might be thought of as a part of artificial life—insofar as artificial life is about getting man-made systems to behave like living things. Historically, however, genetic algorithms became a recognized field of study some ten to 15 years earlier than a-life. Much of the work in genetic algorithms is focused on getting specific solutions to real problems; while the ultimate goal of a-life is the more cosmic question of imbuing our programs, processes, and machines with lifelike behavior.

In any case, genetic algorithms seem to be very well suited for evolving interesting forms of a-life. In a typical situation, you have some a-life creatures that move about according to algorithms that use a list of parameters. Deciding what values to use for the parameters is often an impractically difficult problem. It's like your new a-life creature is this little virtual robot that you've created, and you don't fully understand the implications of what all your new machine's switches do, nor do you have any more than the foggiest grasp of how the different switch settings will interact. So, you try and let some good settings evolve.

The idea is to pick some fitness function that makes sense for your a-life creatures, and then to use a genetic algorithm that tries to solve the search problem for that particular fitness function over the solution space of all the possible parameter settings for your a-life creatures.

In order to use a genetic algorithm on a-life creatures, it is customary to represent the creatures' genomes as bitstrings of a certain length. An important consideration here is that *every possible bitstring* of the correct length has to be usable as a genome. This is because crossover and mutation switch the bits of the genomes around in arbitrary ways, and the genetic algorithm would grind to a halt if some bitstrings turned out to be unacceptable.

Yet the parameters that determine the motions of a turmite or a boid are usually limited to certain ranges. How can we use arbitrary bitstrings as genomes, yet be sure that these bitstrings encode usable values of turmite and boid parameters?

The trick is to give each bopper two kinds of genetic material, which I call DNA and RNA. The DNA Parameters are the arbitrary bitstrings that the genetic algorithm can work on. The RNA Variables are the tweaked values that can be used as turmite and boid parameters. The *Boppers* program uses a function, called *DNAToRNA*, which turns a bopper's DNA bitstring into a suitable set of values for the bopper's RNA Variables.

The *Boppers* program groups its creatures into three colonies: green, red, and blue. Each colony uses a genetic algorithm on the genomes of its member boppers. The boppers have fitness functions which are primarily based on the colors of pixels they encounter. You can use the Controls menu's Colonies dialog to control the genetic algorithm that each colony uses, choosing the intensity of each of five genetic operators: Death (fitness-proportional reproduction), Sex (crossover), Mutation, Zapping, and Transposing. The Cycles Between Breeding parameter controls how many simulation steps the boppers perform to compute their fitnesses.

More information on the *Boppers* breeding methods can be found in the "Colonies and Genes" section of Chapter 4, *Installation and Quick Start,* in the "Colonies" section of Chapter 5, *The Boppers and Their World,* and in the "Colonies Dialog" section of Chapter 6, *Boppers User's Guide.*

The boppers' scores tend to improve up to a certain point, and then do not get much better. This may mean that the boppers are fairly quick in getting to a maximum fitness—or it may mean that they are very slow in getting past a mediocre fitness.

One problem, of course, is that the *Boppers* populations are of rather small size: the most boppers you can have at once is 27. Also the solution spaces which the boppers search can be exceedingly large—we allow boppers with DNA strings that contain over nineteen thousand bits. But judicious use of genetic algorithms seems to give some good results. As long as you are careful to avoid premature convergence of the genomes, the genetic information can be processed and reprocessed very many times. An advantage of *Boppers* is that it runs fast enough to make it possible to evolve populations through many thousands of generations. The ultimate answer as to how effective the genetic algorithms are for evolving boppers is something that you may experimentally decide to your own satisfaction.

One special feature of the *Boppers* world fitness functions is that the fitness value of each creature is affected by what the other creatures are doing. The result is that a process of *co-evolution* is possible, under which each colony's evolution is influenced by the evolution of the other colonies. Co-evolution is of course the order of the day for natural biological systems—prey species continually evolve new ways of escaping their predators, while at the same time the predators evolve new ways of pursuing their prey.

Chapter 1, *Life and A-Life,* stated that true a-life should always be *gnarly*. Are the boppers that evolve under our fitness functions gnarly? That is, do they tend to have measures of disorder up near the edge of total randomness? This is a hard thing to answer definitively, but it often does seem that as a *Boppers* world evolves it becomes more beautiful and, yes, more gnarly.

The question of whether scoring well on some particular fitness function *requires* gnarliness is an interesting issue that is currently being debated by a-life researchers. There is a feeling that gnarly behaviors are computationally richer— and hence more likely to perform well on fitness functions.

In human terms, we know that very rigid and inflexible people—with behavior that might be called highly ordered—do not do well in changing situations. At the other extreme, very distracted and erratic people tend not to do well either. So we are predisposed to suppose that behaviors that lie somewhere in between are most likely to succeed. One of the things that makes a-life exciting is that it is possible to conduct experiments that can empirically test these kinds of beliefs in a scientific way.

NOTES AND REFERENCES

- The first book on genetic algorithms was John Holland's *Adaptation in Natural and Artificial Systems*, University of Michigan Press, 1975. I have drawn most of my information about the field from David Goldberg's *Genetic Algorithms in Search, Optimization and Machine Learning*, Addison-Wesley, 1989.

- Jorge Luis Borges' famous story about a library with all possible books is called "The Library of Babel," and appears in his collection *Labyrinths*, New Directions, 1962. If you've never seen this collection, make a point of getting it the next time you're in a library; it's incomparably great. I have my own raps about the "Library of Babel" in my nonfiction book *Infinity and the Mind*, Birkhauser, 1982 and in my novel *White Light*, Ace, 1980.

If you wanted to list all possible strings of zeroes and ones, you might go about it by (1) using an "alphabetical" order in which 0 comes before 1, and by (2) first listing all strings of length 1, then all strings of length 2, then all strings of length 3, and so on. The list this process leads to would start out like this: 0, 1, 00, 01, 10, 11, 000, 001, 010, 011, 100, 101, 110, 111, 0000, 0001, ...

- Biologist Richard Dawkins created a program called *The Blind Watchmaker* in which the fitness function is simply the user's aesthetic preference. The program presents the user with an array of nine variegated shapes of a vaguely zoological appearance. Each of these static shapes is generated by algorithms based on the idea of a branching binary tree. The "genes" specify the angles at the branchings, also the genes specify whether or not to mimic animal segmentation by printing several copies of the image in a row. The user points and clicks to select the shape he or she likes, and then nine variations on this shape appear. In time, the user can guide the evolution toward a desired form.

- Karl Sims has carried out some *Blind Watchmaker* type experiments in which the genomes of the images consist of LISP functions that describe how to compute a pixel's color from its position. Sims' end images are yummy and eldritch. Writing a Sims-style image evolver for the PC is a stiff programming challenge, as LISP programs tend to run quite slowly. Sims himself does his work on a Connection Machine!

The idea of using genomes that are LISP programs rather than bitstrings was pioneered by John Koza, author of *Genetic Programming*, MIT Press, 1992. Koza argues that it is better to be able to evolve actual computer *programs* instead of evolving *bitstrings* that still must be interpreted by computer programs. LISP is so suitable for program evolution because you can do crossover on LISP expressions by writing them as "parse trees," and swapping a branch of one tree with a branch of another tree. Nobody seems to be able to think of a way to do this for programs in ordinary C—simply cutting two C programs in half and sewing the different halves together won't produce working programs.

- As an example of a-life co-evolution, see D. Hillis' article "Co-Evolving Parasites Improve Simulated Evolution as an Optimization Procedure," in the *Artificial Life II* anthology. This paper describes an experiment in which a genetic algorithm was used to discover an optimally fast algorithm for sorting lists of numbers. Hillis avoids getting stuck at the tops of small hills by simultaneously evolving the test cases that are best at demonstrating the nonfitness of proposed algorithms.

- The theme of whether the fittest a-life creatures are likely to be complex and gnarly is discussed in Christopher Langton's paper "Life At The Edge of Chaos" in the *Artificial Life II* anthology, as well as in, "Revisiting the Edge of Chaos: Evolving Cellular Automata to Perform Computations," by M. Mitchell, P. Hraber, and J. Crutchfield which is to appear in the journal *Complex Systems* in 1994.

- Running a genetic algorithm involves using a lot of *randomization*—as when one decides which members of the population to pair up for sex. The only source of *true* randomness is the physical world. But as nobody is producing a physical randomizer chip, computers make do with so-called *pseudorandom* algorithms for things like the genetic algorithm.

Boppers uses a pseudorandomizing algorithm based on a certain one-dimensional cellular automaton known as Rule Thirty, which was first studied by Stephen Wolfram, and is extensively described in Wolfram's anthology, *Theory and Applications of Cellular Automata*, World Scientific, 1986.

Each time Boppers is started up, the Rule Thirty randomizer is seeded with a bitstring representing the number of seconds that have elapsed since 1970. This ensures that the randomizer will give different numbers during different *Boppers* sessions. Loading a *Boppers* experiment file (as described in Chapter 6, *Boppers User's Guide*) will, however, set the randomizer's seed to whatever value got stored in the experimental file.

Note that in *Boppers* the motions of the turmites, boids, and turboids contain no randomness at all. Randomization is used only during the breeding process.

PART TWO: THE BOPPERS PROGRAM

4

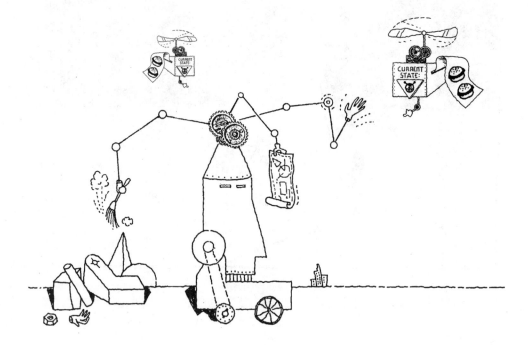

Installation and Quick Start

This chapter describes how to install and run the Boppers *program. It also includes a tutorial-style quick start section that walks you through a demonstration of some of the program's features.*

REQUIREMENTS AND INSTALLATION

In order to run *Boppers*, your computer must have Windows 3.1 installed. You should also have a VGA or SuperVGA color monitor, a mouse, and four megabytes of RAM. The creatures of *Boppers* can be of various types: turmites, boids, wolves, beavers, or dogs. Worlds that include any type of creature other than turmites will run noticeably faster if your computer has a math coprocessor.

To install and run *Boppers* on your hard disk, you will need about 1.5 megabytes of free space. Create a new directory called BOPPERS on your hard disk, and copy all the files on the *Boppers* distribution disk to this directory.

You can create the directory and copy the files by using the Windows File Manager. Alternatively, you can switch from Windows to DOS (either by exiting Windows or by selecting the DOS prompt icon within Windows) and use the following series of DOS commands (replace the "A" and "C" with other letters if you want to use other drives). Press (ENTER) after each command is typed.

```
C:
CD \
MKDIR BOPPERS
COPY A:*.* BOPPERS
```

Your next task is to alert Windows that the *Boppers* program is present. If you are not in Windows, start up Windows by entering:

```
WIN
```

Or, if you are running DOS from within Windows, return to Windows by entering:

```
EXIT
```

Click on the group where you'd like the *Boppers* program to have its icon—either Applications or Games would be appropriate.

Now choose the New option from the Program Manager's File menu. Choose Program Item from the New Program Object dialog. This brings up the Program Item Properties dialog.

You can now use the Browse option to find the BOPPERS.EXE program, or you can simply click on the Command Line field and directly type:

```
C:\BOPPERS\BOPPERS.EXE
```

Now click on the Working Directory field and type:

```
C:\BOPPERS
```

If you chose to copy the *Boppers* distribution disk to a different drive or directory, you should adjust the Command Line and Working Directory fields of the Program Item Properties dialog to match the correct location of the *Boppers* files.

There is no need to enter anything in the Description or Shortcut Key fields, although if you would like your icon to show a name other than "BOPPERS," you can type this name into the Description field.

Now choose OK and *Boppers* should be fully installed in Windows. The icon for *Boppers* will be found inside the currently highlighted group inside Program Manager.

Windows frequently puts a new file icon off in an invisible corner of the highlighted group. Click the upward-pointing arrow in the upper right-hand corner of the highlighted group to maximize it, and use your mouse to drag the *Boppers* icon into a position where it will be visible when you return the group to its normal size. Return the group to normal size by clicking the double arrow found just below the upper right-hand corner.

If you change your mind about what group to keep *Boppers* in, you can always drag the icon to a different group.

RUNNING BOPPERS

In Windows, you start up *Boppers* by double-clicking its icon, or by highlighting its icon and pressing (ENTER). In DOS you can normally start *Boppers* by moving to the BOPPERS directory and entering:

`WIN BOPPERS`

You can resize the *Boppers* window by dragging its lower right-hand corner. You can maximize the *Boppers* window by clicking the upward-pointing arrow in the upper right-hand corner of the window. After the *Boppers* window is maximized, clicking the double arrow in the upper right-hand corner of the window returns the window to its prior size. The downward-pointing arrow near the upper right-hand corner of the window minimizes *Boppers* to an icon.

Note that *Boppers* continues to run even if it is hidden or minimized. If you notice that another application is running slowly, or is unable to run, find and close the *Boppers* program.

If you have a lot of windows open and lose track of where *Boppers* is, you can find it by clicking the System Menu box in the upper left-hand corner of a window and by then choosing the Switch To selection. This opens the Task List dialog. Here you choose the line that says BOPPERS.

Once you get *Boppers* running, you can try a quick tour of its features by following the instructions found in the following Quick Start section.

To close the *Boppers* program, choose the *Boppers* File menu and then choose Exit. Alternatively, you may double-click the System Menu box in the upper left-hand corner of the *Boppers* window.

When you exit *Boppers*, the Ready To Exit Boppers dialog asks, "Save Current Parameters And Genes?" Either "Yes" or "No" is a good answer—see the Exit subsection of the File Menu section in Chapter 6, *Boppers User's Guide,* for details.

While *Boppers* is running, you can use the scroll bars to change your view of the *Boppers* world. Clicking the scroll arrows moves the view a little, and clicking in the scroll bars moves the view a lot. You can also drag the scroll-bar markers, which are commonly known as *thumbs*. The *Boppers* world is *toroidal*, meaning that what scrolls off the right side scrolls back onto the left side, what scrolls off the bottom scrolls back on from the top, and vice versa and vice versa.

The absolute size of the *Boppers* world is adjusted to match the Windows display mode you have chosen—in general the *Boppers* world has just about as many pixels as the current Windows display size.

What display resolution is best for running *Boppers*? *Boppers* runs at the same speed at every resolution, so speed is not an issue. Many of the *Boppers* patterns include pixel-sized details, so a very high resolution may make these details hard to see. On the other hand, if you use a higher resolution you will have room to increase the lengths of the worm-like trails that the boppers leave.

When running *Boppers*, you have the choice of a black or a white background for the screen. You can select between the two by using the Tools menu's Background Color.

QUICK START

So, okay, you've got *Boppers* up and running. Now it's time to get your hands on some artificial life.

One of the first things you can try is to repeatedly press the (CONTROL)-(V) combination and look at the patterns you see. Try this several times. (CONTROL)-(V) is a control key shortcut for the File menu Randomize popup's Everything selection. The effect of this selection is to randomly change all of the settings in all of *Boppers'* dialog boxes.

Next, try to load some of the parameter files included on the *Boppers* disk. These files all have the extension *.BL. Brief descriptions of these files can be found in Chapter 7, *Examples*.

To load a parameter file, click on the File menu's Open selection, and then click on Open Params. The Open dialog box appears.

If the directory listed under Directories in the Open dialog box is not your *Boppers* home directory (which is likely to be "C:\BOPPERS"), then you have to use the dialog box's Drives and Directories controls to get into the BOPPERS directory. Once you are in this directory, you should see a list of file names of the form "*.BL" on the left of the dialog box.

You can try loading files and looking up the comments on them in Chapter 7, *Examples*. When you are ready to read through the next subsection, load the START.BL file.

To load a *.BL file, type the name of one of the displayed file names in the File Name field, or scroll the list of *.BL files until you see a file name you want, and then click on it. Next, press (ENTER) or click the dialog box's OK button. An alternative way to select a file name is to double-click on it. After a slight pause, the *Boppers* window should erase itself, and the right part of the *Boppers* window's title bar should read something like "Last File: C:\BOPPERS\START.BL."

Boppers and Their Trails

If the right-hand part of the *Boppers* title bar does not end with "START.BL," load the START.BL parameter file by the process just described. You may not even need to bother loading START.BL, because the START.BL parameters are hard-coded into BOPPERS.EXE, and will automatically be in effect the first time you start BOPPERS.

Yeah! There they are, little red, green, and blue clumps of pixels on a black background, each clump with a racing white dot. The white dots are the heads of the individual boppers, and the colored pixel clumps are the trails the bopper heads leave. With each step, each bopper adds a pixel to its trail. Once the trail reaches a certain length, an old pixel is erased for each pixel added.

Note that one of the boppers has a pattern like a Maltese cross for its head. This bopper is called the *edit bopper*. By moving the cursor and left-clicking near other boppers, you can change the identity of the edit bopper and the position of the Maltese cross.

According to the color of the pixels they leave, boppers are called green, red, or blue. We think of the boppers as belonging to one of three *colonies*: the green colony, the red colony, and the blue colony. In the START.BL world, each colony has six members and the colony members breed and compete only with fellow members of their own colony. The number of members in each colony stays fixed, but the genetically determined behaviors of the boppers change.

All the boppers in START.BL are of the kind known as turmites. As labelled in Figure 4-1, the ones that race along in straight lines are called rail turmites, the ones that move in regularly toothed circles are cog turmites, and the ones who make messy patches are sand turmites. The kind of pattern a turmite makes depends on its genes. More information about turmites is in the "Turmites" section of Chapter 2, *Computer A-Life,* and in the "Turmite Motion" section in Chapter 5, *The Boppers and Their World.*

You can change the genes of all the boppers at once by clicking the File Randomize Bopper Genes selection, or by using the control key shortcut (CONTROL)-(G). As the genes change, you will notice that the patterns of the boppers' trails change as well.

If you look closely at the boppers, you may be able to see that there are two shades of each of the three colors. (If you can't see this, adjusting the contrast or brightness of your computer screen may help.) I call the two color shades *faint* and *strong*. If you look *very* closely, you may even notice that when two different-colored trails cross each other, the pixels where the trail cross are given a combination of the two trail colors.

As an aid to looking closely at the boppers' trails, you can turn the cursor into a lens. Do this by selecting the Tools menu Cursors popup and clicking Lens. The cursor will

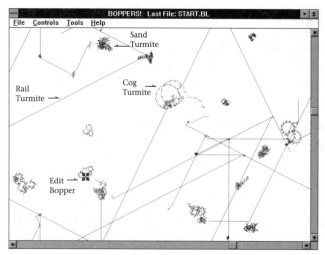

Figure 4-1 The START.BL world showing rail, cog, and sand turmites

now have the form of a magnifying glass. If you left-click the mouse, a magnified patch appears at the cursor location, as shown in Figure 4-2. Right-clicking the mouse turns off the magnified patch. You can get rid of the lens cursor by using the Tools menu Cursors popup to choose Pick.

As mentioned before, a bopper is a moving trail like a worm that grows at one end while shrinking at the other end. The little white pixels show the current head positions of the boppers, and the places where pixels are disappearing are the current tail positions of the boppers. A bopper is a moving filigreed pattern that stretches from its head to its tail. As its head moves along, its tail follows.

You can experiment with different lengths of trails by using the Controls menu's World Dialog. The – and + buttons in the Average Pixels Per Bopper Trail box allow you to adjust the sizes of the green, red, and blue bopper trails. Try clicking the – buttons until the three displayed values are all less than 500, and then click the DO IT! button. The screen will clear itself, and the boppers will start up again, only with shorter trails.

Watch this for a while, and then use the Controls menu's World dialog to make the trails longer again. Click the + buttons in the Average Pixels Per Bopper Trail box until the numbers are bigger than 3,000. Note, by the way, that if you click a + button enough times, the trail length changes from a number to the phrase "Permanent Trail." This means that the boppers in the colony in question never have their trail cells erased. Pressing the corresponding – button turns the trail length back into a number which is the maximum length of an erasable trail for that colony.

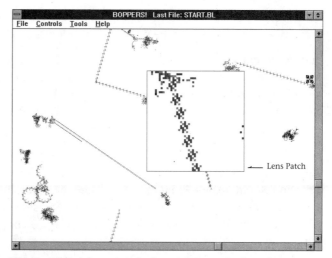

Figure 4-2 A lens patch showing two shades of trail color

Now practice keeping all of a given bopper's trail in the middle of the screen by using the *Boppers* scroll bars to move the world right and left or up and down. Note that when something scrolls off one side of the *Boppers* world it comes back from the other side.

When the boppers have long trails, it can be difficult to see where each bopper's head is. You can replace the small head dot by a graphic icon as follows. Open the Controls menu's Individuals dialog. Click the All Boppers radio button at the upper left of the dialog. Then click on the combo box next to the Body Icon radio button and click the Single Body selection. Accept this change by clicking the DO IT! button, and close the Individuals dialog by clicking the EXIT button.

How Boppers Score

Now open the Controls menu's World dialog again and turn on the checkboxes marked "Food Patch" and "Poison Patch." Accept these choices and close the World dialog by using the DO IT! button. You should see something like Figure 4-3.

The screen shows a gold rectangle and a mauve rectangle which are being eaten away by the boppers who happen to run into them. A red bopper that wanders into the gold rectangle, for instance, draws a bunch of faint-colored and strong-colored red pixels over the gold. When its tail end erases the older red pixels, the black background pixels appear instead of the gold pixels. It's as if the red bopper ate some of the gold.

The gold rectangle is "food," while the mauve rectangle is "poison." The poison does not actually *kill* any of the boppers, it just lowers their scores.

In order to monitor a bopper's score, open the Tools menu's Scorebox dialog. The Scorebox shows four picture icons and some numbers. Focus on the right-most picture and the number under it. The picture represents the current edit bopper, and the number is that bopper's current score. Try moving the cursor and left-clicking near different boppers to see how their scores are doing.

Isolated boppers who stay in one spot tend to have a score of zero, boppers near the food have positive scores, and boppers near the poison have negative scores. You can get a more detailed idea of how the scores work by grabbing hold of a bopper and moving it about. To do this, use the Tools menu Cursors popup and select Drag. Note that you do *not* have to close the Scorebox dialog before doing this.

Once you select the Drag cursor, the cursor should look like a pointing hand. If you left-click the mouse, the closest bopper is attached to the cursor and can be dragged about. Drag a bopper across the food and watch how its score increases. Drag it across the poison and watch the score decrease. Right-click the mouse to release the bopper.

The exact values of the scores for various colors can be seen by opening the Controls menu's Ecology dialog. The three rows of numbers in the upper part of the Ecology dialog box specify the score values that the green, red, and blue

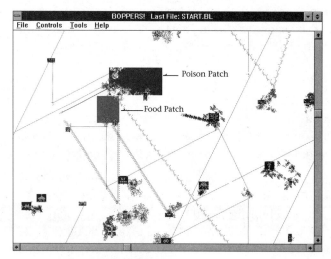

Figure 4-3 Turmites with single body icons in a world with food and poison patches

boppers get by eating different kinds of pixels. Note that in the START.BL ecology, boppers get positive points for encountering trails of differently colored boppers. Also note that the mauve poison pixels are worth minus two each, while the gold food pixels count for three points.

Now change the ecology by clicking the Food Loop radio button. Note that this changes the values of eating green, red, and blue cells. The effect is as if the green boppers like blue pixels and dislike red pixels, the red boppers like green pixels and dislike blue pixels, and the blue boppers like red pixels and dislike green pixels. Accept this by clicking the DO IT! button, and then close the Ecology dialog by clicking the EXIT button.

Left-click the Drag cursor near a red bopper and note how the red bopper's score is increased by crossing green bopper trails and is decreased by crossing blue bopper trails. Right-click to release the bopper and use the Tools menu's Cursors popup to select the Pick cursor again. Close the Scorebox Dialog by double-clicking on the gray button in its upper left-hand corner.

If you have a Sound Blaster card attached to your computer, this is a good time to use the Tools menu's Sound dialog to turn on the Eating Sounds checkbox. This causes the *Boppers* program to make a sound whenever the edit bopper encounters a different colored pixel. Close the Sound dialog with the DONE! button. When you get tired of the sounds, you can turn them off by reopening the Tools menu's Sound dialog, selecting No Sounds, and clicking the DONE! button.

Fancier Trails

Now open the Controls menu's Individuals dialog. Make sure the All Boppers radio button is selected. Now click the + button next to the Speed radio button, changing the displayed Speed from 1 to 2. Click the DO IT! button and notice that the boppers are moving in bigger steps. You can leave the Individuals dialog open for now, clicking and dragging its title bar if you want to move it out of the way or drag it back to center screen.

Now click the combo box next to the Trail Lines radio button. Click the Thin Lines selection and then click the DO IT! button. The boppers' trails now look like scribbled lines. Clear the old bopper trails off the screen by using the File menu's Clear Screen selection. You should see something like Figure 4-4.

Now go back to the Controls menu's Individuals dialog and click repeatedly on the – button next to the IQ radio button until the IQ value is 1. Click the DO IT! button and notice how the boppers now tend to move in simple straight lines. This is easier to see if you clear the old bopper trails off the screen by using the File menu's Clear Screen

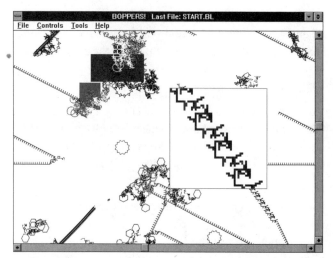

Figure 4-4 Speed two turmites with thin line trails and lens patch

selection. Now use the + button next to the IQ radio button to increase the IQ to 32 and press the DO IT! button.

Still using the Individuals dialog, click on the combo box next to the Turmite Windrose radio button and select 24. Click the DO IT! button. The boppers will now move in larger steps, and in a greater variety of directions.

Now click the second radio button in the Individuals dialog's Scope of Changes box. Keep clicking this button until its caption says "Green Colony." Now open the combo box next to the Trail Nodes selection and select Small Squares. Click DO IT! and then click EXIT.

At this point, the green boppers should have small squares at each "node" where successive sections of the boppers' trails connect. You might want to let this configuration run for a while, and use the Lens cursor to look at some of the details. It is striking how precisely designed the turmite trails can be.

Next use the Controls menu's World dialog to set the trail lengths to less than 1,000. As long as you have the World dialog open, turn off the Food Patch and Poison Patch checkboxes, and choose the Walled World radio button. When you use the DO IT! button to accept the changes and close the World dialog, a gray rectangular wall appears in the *Boppers* world. If the wall is not located at the edge of the screen, as in Figure 4-5, you can bring the wall to the edge of the

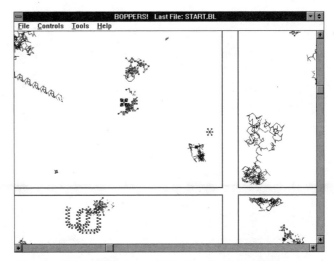

Figure 4-5 A walled world that is scrolled off center

screen by dragging the horizontal scroll bar's slider to the left of its range and dragging the vertical scroll bar's slider to the top of its range.

Boids and the Third Dimension

Now open the Controls menu's Individuals dialog again. In the Scope of Changes box on the left, select the second radio button from the top, clicking it until it says Blue Colony. Now open the combo box next to the Bopper Type radio button on the right and select Boid. Click the DO IT! button and then click the EXIT button. The blue boppers should now be flying around in a smooth fashion, more or less as shown in Figure 4-6.

Information about how boids move can be found in the "Boids" section of Chapter 2, *Computer A-Life,* and in the "Boid Motion" section in Chapter 5, *The Boppers and Their World.*

To make the motions of the blue boppers easier to follow, use the Controls menu's World dialog to make the blue trail length be about 100 and click DO IT! You should see something like Figure 4-6.

Watch this for a while, then open the Controls menu's World dialog and click the Wrapped World radio button and the DO IT! button. Note how the blue boid boppers fly off the edges of the screen and return from the opposite sides.

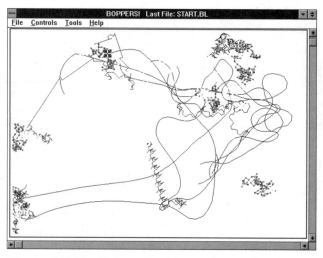

Figure 4-6 A walled world with turmites and boids

Next use the Controls menu's World dialog to select the radio button marked 3 Dimensional. Note that this changes all of the trail lengths to the same value. Click the DO IT! button. The bopper icons are all now green figures of various sizes; the sizes correspond with how far away the bopper is supposed to be in the third dimension, which is perpendicular to your computer screen.

In the Wrapped World mode, a bopper can move out through the back of the three-dimensional boppers world and return from the front, or vice versa. Visually, this has the effect of an icon that gets smaller and suddenly gets big, or that gets big and then suddenly turns small.

To enhance the effect of three-dimensionality, open the Controls menu's Individuals dialog, check the All Boppers radio button, and open the combo box next to the Trail Lines radio button. Choose the Thick Lines selection and click DO IT! Because the green colony's nodes won't show anyway with a thick line, you might as well turn them off. With the All Boppers radio button still checked, open the combo box next to the Trail Nodes radio button and choose the Dots selection. Click DO IT! to make this change take effect as well. (Because only the green colony has Trail Nodes that are not Dots, you would get the same effect by making this last selection with the Green Colony radio button checked in the Scope of Changes box.)

Clear the screen with the File menu's Clear Screen selection. Notice now that the trails are thick lines which are drawn under and over each other according to their distance. That is, a trail is drawn on top of an existing trail only if the new trail is closer than the old trail. Otherwise, the new trail is drawn with a gap in it, to show that it passes behind the old trail. In this mode, the program runs fast at first, and then slows down a bit when each of the boppers' trails reaches its maximum length and the work of erasing old trail cells has to start being done.

With the All Boppers radio button still active in the Individuals dialog, open the combo box next to the Bopper Type radio button and select Boid. Click DO IT! to change all the boppers to boids and then click EXIT to close the Individuals dialog. The screen should look something like Figure 4-7.

At this point, the program may be running slower than you like. You can speed it up by opening the Controls menu's World dialog and clicking the – buttons in the Population Per Colony box. Change each of the colony populations to three and click DO IT! Notice how the boppers twine their trails around each other.

Next open the Controls menu's World dialog again and select the Walled World radio button. Also click on any of the - buttons in the Average Pixels Per Bopper Trail to reduce the trail lengths to around 500. Press DO IT! If the gray wall is not at the edges of the screen, drag the horizontal scroll bar sliders to the left end, and drag the vertical scroll bar slider to the top. Open the Controls menu's Ecology dialog and make sure that the Food Loop radio button is checked. Press DO IT! and then EXIT to close the Ecology dialog.

You may notice now that the green boppers chase the blue boppers and avoid the reds, the red boppers chase the greens and avoid the blues, and the blues chase the reds and

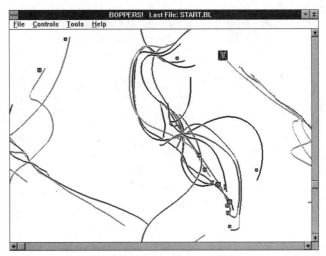

Figure 4-7 A three-dimensional world with boids. Trails are rendered in back to front order

avoid the greens. Also, each color of bopper tries to group itself with other boppers of the same color.

This behavior is visible in Figure 4-8, where you can see that the three flocks of boids are effectively chasing each other around and around in a circle. One of the green boids has just escaped from a gang attack by three reds.

Use the Tools menu's Cursors popup to select the Drag cursor and then left-click near a red bopper. As you drag the red bopper around, you will notice that the greens move away from it, particularly if they are at the same depth—as indicated by the sizes of their icons.

To speed up the program, go back to a two-dimensional world by using the Controls menu's World dialog to select the 2 Dimensional radio button. Change the trail lengths for the three colonies to around 200 each, and then click DO IT! You should see nine boppers swarming around inside a walled two-dimensional world. The green boppers should still have the square nodes. Try dragging some of the boppers around and watch how the others react. Then use the Tools menu's Cursors popup to select the Pick cursor again.

Next open the Controls menu's Individuals dialog and click the All Boppers radio button. Click on the combo box next to the Bopper Type radio button and select Owl. Click DO IT! and EXIT. The motions of the boppers should be smoother than before.

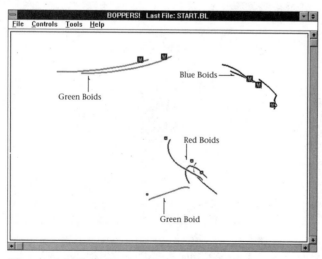

Figure 4-8 Three boid colonies chasing each other

Now randomly change all of the parameters that you can set with the Individuals dialog. You can do this by clicking on the File menu's Randomize popup's Individuals' Params selection. Pick out a bopper whose behavior interests you and left-click on it with the Pick cursor to make it be the Edit Bopper. Now open the Controls menu's Individuals dialog, and you can read off the properties of the edit bopper. Note that you can left-click on another bopper to change the edit bopper even while the Individuals dialog is open. Close the Individuals Dialog with the EXIT button.

Next try randomly changing all the parameters that you can set with the World dialog. You can do this by clicking on the File menu's Randomize popup's World Params selection. Do this a few times, looking at the variety of worlds you get. When you find an interesting world, open the Controls menu's World dialog to read off the properties of this world. Close the World dialog with the EXIT button.

Colonies and Genes

In this section, we'll look at how the boppers' scores are used as fitness functions to evolve their genes. Reload the START.BL parameter file by using the File menu's Open popup's Open Parameters selection, as described at the beginning of the Quick Start section.

Use the Controls menu's World dialog to make the trail lengths longer than 4,000. To do this, click the + buttons in the Average Pixels Per Bopper Trail and then click the World dialog's DO IT! button.

Open the Controls menu's Colonies dialog. Click the – button in the Cycles Between Breeding box to change the displayed number to 400. Open the combo box next to the Sex label in the Breeding Methods box and select None. You will have to use the up arrow key to scroll the None selection into visibility. Now click the Colonies dialog's DO IT TO ALL! button, and close the Colonies dialog with the EXIT button.

Open the Tools menu's Scorebox dialog and focus your attention on the left side of the Scorebox. There are two rows of three numbers each; the rows are labelled Curr and Last. Note that every so often the Curr numbers all change to 0. At the same time the Last numbers are changed. Each time this happens, the three colonies are undergoing a breeding process. Because you just used the Colonies dialog to change the breeding times for all three colonies to 400, the breeding process is taking place after every 400 updates of the boppers' positions.

To get a cumulative view of the scores, open the Tools menu's Graph dialog. You will see green, red, and blue dots corresponding to score values. Move the slider in the vertical scroll bar upward to increase the vertical separation between the score dots. You can move the slider by clicking on the scroll bar's arrows, by clicking in the blank part of the scroll bar, or by clicking and dragging the scroll bar's slider. Note that as you change the slider's position, the caption in the Graph dialog's title bar changes to reflect the visible vertical range of the graph.

If you have been running *Boppers* for some time, it may be that the graph dots run completely across the horizontal axis of the graph. You can scroll out to the active end of the graph by using the Graph dialog's horizontal scroll bar. If you watch the active end of the graph, you should be able to see fresh green, red, and blue data points being drawn every so often. These points are drawn at the same time the Scorebox is updated.

If you have a Sound Blaster card, open the Tools menu's Sound dialog, click a checkmark into the Breeding Sounds box and click DONE! Each time the edit bopper's colony undergoes breeding, the edit bopper will send out a sound which differs depending on whether that bopper's genes are saved or are overwritten by some other bopper's genes.

Close the Scorebox dialog and the Graph dialog by right-clicking inside each of these dialog boxes. Now open the Tools menu's Gene Viewer dialog box.

The top of this dialog shows three horizontal bars with fine vertical stripes. The bars represent the bitstring genes of three boppers. The top bar corresponds to the bopper in the Mother Bopper box, the middle bar corresponds to the Father Bopper box, and the bottom bar corresponds to the Child Bopper. Try clicking on the Colony and Rank buttons in the three boxes to change the boppers, and watch how the different boppers have different genes. Note also that boppers in the same colony often have similar or identical genes.

Click on the Breeding Method radio button labelled Zap Child Bopper and then repeatedly click the Gene Viewer dialog's DO IT! button. Note that each time you do this, there is a big change in the bar representing the Child Bopper's gene.

Now click on the Colony and Rank buttons until the top two gene bars are quite different from each other. Also make sure that the Child bopper is not the same as the Mother or Father. Now click on the radio button labelled Crossover Mother and Father to Child. Click the Gene Viewer dialog's DO IT! button, and note that the third, or Child bopper, gene pattern resembles one parent on its left side and resembles the other parent on its right side. Click the DO IT! button several more times to look at different ways a crossover can be performed.

Now, without closing the Gene Viewer dialog, open the Controls menu's Individuals dialog. Click the Individuals dialog's All Bopper radio button, and then go down and click on the – button next to the Individuals dialog's IQ radio button until the IQ is 16. Now click the Individuals dialog's DO IT! button.

The gene patterns in the Gene Viewer dialog should now be coarser. Reducing the IQs of the boppers shortens the bitstrings that control their behavior. Press the Gene Viewer's DO IT! button again to see how zapping and crossover look with the reduced IQ. Crossover should look something like Figure 4-9, where the crossover point is below the "r" in "Viewer."

Now close the Gene Viewer dialog with a right-click or the EXIT button, close the Individuals dialog with a right-click or the EXIT button, and open up the Tools menu's Graph dialog again to take another look at how the evolution is progressing. As before, use the Graph dialog's scroll bars to adjust the view, and close the Graph dialog with a right-click.

Cursor Tools

Find a bopper you like and copy its genes onto its fellow colony members. An interesting choice might be to load the ALGAE.BL parameter file and then copy one of the green boppers to the others.

You copy a bopper's genes and parameters by using the Tools menu's Cursors popup and selecting Copy. The cursor then takes on the appearance of two smiley faces with an arrow between them. Left-click this Copy cursor on the head of a bopper whose pattern you like, and all the boppers in its colony will start to act the same way. You can see this especially clearly if you use the File menu's Clear Screen selection to clear the screen. Now right-click the Copy cursor on a bopper you like and *all* the boppers in *all* the colonies act like the bopper that you click. Note that this makes everyone act

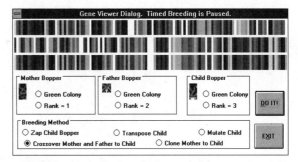

Figure 4-9 The top two gene patterns are crossed over to make the bottom gene pattern

the same, as shown in Figure 4-10. But if Zapping or Mutating or Transposing are set to levels higher than None, the next occurrence of Timed Breeding may change some of the boppers.

When you get tired of seeing everyone being the same, use the Tools menu's Cursors popup to select the Zap cursor, which is shaped like a lightning bolt. Left-clicking the bottom tip of the bolt near the head of a boppers randomizes that bopper's genes. Repeated clicks cause repeated randomizations.

Once you see a bopper you like, use the Tools menu's Cursors popup to select Isolate. The cursor takes on the appearance of three concentric squares. If you left-click on a bopper, the other boppers disappear, and you can see the activity of the edit bopper on its own. Boids tend to fly only in straight lines when on their own, but turmites are more interesting. Try and find a turmite that avoids getting stuck or falling into a periodic behavior when isolated. Right-clicking the mouse with the Isolate cursor brings back the other boppers.

Cellular Automata

Open the Controls menu CAs popup and click the CA On selection. A patch of changing color will appear on the screen. This is a cellular automaton patch. Use the *Boppers* scroll bars to move the CA patch to the center of the screen.

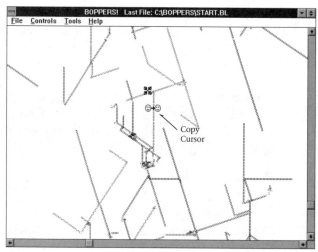

Figure 4-10 A right click of the copy cursor makes everyone the same

The CA patch will run the Rug rule, which shows a pattern a bit like the grain of wood. Every time a bopper moves across the CA patch, the activity gets stirred up again, as shown in Figure 4-11.

Use the Controls menu's CAs popup's More Cells selection to make the CA patch bigger. If you like, you can choose this selection twice to make the CA patch even bigger, although the bigger the CA patch gets, the slower it runs. Now use the Controls menu's CAs popup's Select Rule popup to try some different CA rules; try Life, then Zhabotinsky, and then Faders. Try reseeding these rules with the Controls menu's CAs popup's Seed CA selection.

Now try to tailor the shape of the CA patch. First make sure the *Boppers* window is not maximum size by clicking the window button that has an up-pointing and a down-pointing arrow in it. This button is near the upper right-hand corner of the *Boppers* window. Now click and drag the lower right-hand corner of the *Boppers* window until the window is the shape of a small rectangle. Now click the Controls menu's CAs popup's Resize CA To Window selection, and the CA will resize itself. Click the up-pointing arrow near the upper right-hand corner of the *Boppers* window to make the window big again.

Now magnify the cells of the CA. Choose the Controls menu's CAs popup's Stretchable CA selection. Resize the *Boppers* window, and observe how the CA resizes its stretching factor as well. Turn off the magnification by choosing the Controls menu's CAs popup's Stretchable CA selection again.

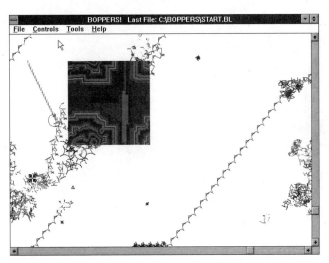

Figure 4-11 The Rug rule being stirred up by turmites

Finally, try looking at a series of random CAs of the Lambda rule type. The easiest way to do this is to use the control key shortcut (CONTROL)-(D). Use this combination a number of times. Note that some CAs die out, others seethe wildly, and certain rare ones generate localized crawling patterns similar to the patterns seen in Faders and in Brain.

NOTES AND REFERENCES

- Note that although all 486 chips originally came with a math coprocessor on board, there are now some that do not. If you're buying a computer, the first 486 the salesman offers you will normally *not* have a math coprocessor. It's a point worth bringing up. Some "non-math" 486 chips can be upgraded with inexpensive 387 math coprocessors rather than with the much higher priced 487 and other 486-specific upgrades. To shop for a math coprocessor, find whatever manual or documentation you got with your computer, and talk to as technical a person as you can find in the biggest computer store that you can drive to or phone up. With luck you should be able to upgrade for about a hundred dollars, although some may find that a high price to pay for faster turboids and boids.

5

The Boppers and Their World

Boppers *is a computer a-life world in which* phenomes *depend on* genomes. *That is, the* appearance *and* motion *of the boppers are a direct reflection of the* bitstrings *that code their parameters.*

The boppers move about in a world that can be either two-dimensional or three-dimensional. This world is divided into cells. Each bopper is represented as a moving head the size of one cell.

If the world is 2D, each cell corresponds to a single pixel on the screen. If the world is 3D, the nearest cells still match the pixels on the screen, but there are additional layers of cells "behind" the screen up to a depth equal to the screen's height. That is, the 3D version of the *Boppers* world is shaped like a fish tank with squares at the ends of the long axis, as shown in Figure 5-1.

As a bopper's head moves, it lays down a colored trail, which can be thought of as that bopper's *body*. Each bopper's body has a length, which is controlled by the Controls menu's World dialog's Average Pixel Per Bopper Trail box.

If you look closely (or use the Lens cursor), you can see that each bopper has two different shades of trail color that it can leave.

The boppers can use one of six different kinds of algorithms for moving: they can be turmites, boids, wolves, beavers, dogs, or owls.

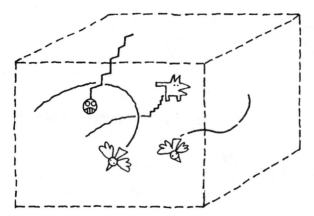

Figure 5-1 The shape of the 3D boppers world

The boppers notice when they run across other boppers trails, and they can also notice the positions of the other boppers' heads. They continually adjust their behavior according to the things they notice in the world.

Each bopper has a running score which tracks how well it is doing. As discussed in the following text, these scores are used to compute the boppers' fitness levels for use in a genetic algorithm whose goal is to breed higher-scoring boppers.

Each bopper's running score is primarily based on the colors of the cells the bopper encounters. The numerical score values of the different colors are something that can be adjusted by using the Controls menu's Ecology dialog.

In a sense, the boppers generate the problem they are trying to solve, because they generate the pattern of trails they are trying to feed on in a high-scoring way.

Note that the boppers' scores are normally changed not by actually touching the *heads* of other boppers, but merely by running across the colored pixels of the other boppers' *trails*. Moving toward another bopper's head is, however, a likely method for encountering cells of that bopper's trail. By the same token, moving away from another bopper's head is a good way to avoid its trail cells.

Although the boppers often chase and flee each other, they do not normally destroy each other, and the relative populations of the boppers stay the same. If you *do* want to see boppers destroying each other, put a check in the Recruit Prey checkbox of the Colonies dialog.

The boppers are grouped into three colonies according to their trail colors: green, red, and blue. At periodic intervals, each colony applies a variant of the standard genetic algorithm to the genomes of the boppers in the colony. Each colony uses its own version of the genetic algorithm.

So that the genetic algorithm can be meaningfully applied to the boppers in a single colony, all the boppers in a given colony use the same fitness function. The three fitness functions are specified in terms of the score values for encountering different colored pixels, and in terms of minimum motion and entropy.

This chapter gives a detailed description of the boppers and how they move, followed by a description of the colonies and how they breed.

BOPPERS

A bopper is a collection of data which is updated according to certain rules. In this section, we first describe the way in which a bopper's data is structured, then we look at the boppers' update cycle, and then we look at the details of how the boppers move.

The Bopper Data Structure

A bopper is an example of what computer scientists call a *data structure*. A data structure is an arrangement of slots that can be filled with information. We call the slots *parameters* or *variables*, usually using "parameter" to mean a data value that you can change from the outside, and using "variable" to mean a data value that is automatically determined by the parameters and by workings of the program. In the case of a bopper, its position is an example of a variable, while its minimum speed is an example of a parameter. Table 5-1 lists the names of the different bopper parameters and variables along with a short comment on each of them.

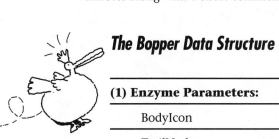

The Bopper Data Structure

(1) Enzyme Parameters:

BodyIcon	// Body Icon off, on, or continuous.
TrailNodes	// Trail Nodes: dot or square.
TrailLines	// Trail Lines off, on, or thick.
BaseSpeed	// Speed multiplied times steps.
BopperType	// Type of Move function being used.
TurmiteWindrose	// Which windrose the bopper uses.
IQ	// IQ, or the number of states used.

continued on next page

continued from previous page

(2) DNA Parameters:

DNA[ ]	// An array of *DNA_length* bytes.

(3) RNA Variables:

DNALength	// Depends on *BopperType* and *IQ*.

Turmite RNA Variables:

WriteColorTable[ ][ ]	// Double array size *IQ* by *two*.
TurnTable[ ][ ]	// Double array size *IQ* by *eight*.
NewStateTable[ ][ ]	// Double array size *IQ* by *eight*.
WindroseDirections	// How many directions in the windrose.
WindroseX[ ],	
WindroseY[ ],	// Three single arrays of length.
WindroseZ[ ]	// *WindroseDirections*. Set by *TurmiteWindrose*.

Boid RNA Variables:

WatchTwoFlag	// Watch one or two closest boppers.
NearWallDistance	// When wall is too close.
CruiseDistance	// Desired distance from flockmates.
VisionAngle	// Field of vision.
CopyWeight	// Fly parallel to nearest boid.
CenterWeight	// Fly to center of flock.
AttackWeight	// Fly towards prey boppers.
FleeWeight	// Fly away from predator boppers.
VeerWeight	// Fly away from wall.
MaxSpeed	// Fastest allowable speed.
Acceleration	// Rate at which speed changes.

Turboid RNA Variables:

NearPrey[ ]	// Both arrays of length *IQ*.
NearPredator[ ]	// Beaver uses these.

DogBrain[ ]	// Array length *IQ*, used by dog turboids.
Move Procedure:	
Move	// Can be turmite, boid, wolf, beaver,
	// dog, owl, or dragged by cursor.

(4) Situation Variables:

Score	// Score from eating.
x, y, z	// Location.
State	// Used by turmites and by all turboids.
TurboidState	// Used by beaver and by dog turboids.
ReadColorCode	// Color code of the cell being eaten.
WriteColor	// Trail color to leave behind.
Turmite Situation Variable:	
Direction	// Turmite windrose index.
Boid Situation Variables:	
RealSpeed	// Current speed.
Tangent	// Current unit direction vector.
Metric Situation Variables:	
To[ ]	// Array of unit vectors to other boppers.
NearestBopper	// ID of the nearest visible bopper.
SecondNearestBopper	// ID of second nearest visible bopper.
NearestDistance	// Distance to the nearest bopper.
NearColonyCode	// Same, predator, prey, or neutral.
ToCentroid	// Unit vector to center of flock.

(5) Memory Variables:

ID Variables:	
BopperID, ColonyID	// Personal ID and the number of colony.
Old Situation Variables:	

continued on next page

continued from previous page

oldx, oldy, oldz	// Last position. Used to draw lines.
oldoldx, oldoldy, oldoldz	// Position before last. Used for squares.
OldWriteColor	// Last WriteColor. Used for squares.
OldScore	// Last Score. Used by wolf.
OldTangent	// Last Tangent. Used by boid and turboid.
Low Motion Variables:	
startx, starty, startz	// Position at time of last breed.
LowMotionFlag	// Stays on until bopper moves far enough.
Entropy Tracking Variables:	
TurnFrequency[ ]	// Array of length *WindroseDirections*.
Entropy	// Based on numbers of different turns.

Table 5-1 The bopper data structure

Note that the data structure breaks into five main parts:

1. *Enzyme Parameters*

2. *DNA Parameters*

3. *RNA Variables*

4. *Situation Variables*

5. *Memory Variables*

You control the (1) Enzyme Parameters and the (2) DNA Parameters , but they can also be changed by the breeding process. The parameters in these two groups make up the genome of a bopper.

The *Boppers* program computes the (3) RNA Variables from the values of the Enzyme Parameters and the DNA Parameters. The close relationship between the first three groups of parameters and variables is explored in the next section.

The (4) Situation Variables keep track of where a bopper currently is and what it is doing. The Situation Variables normally change values during each bopper update. The (5) Memory Variables keep track of the bopper's identity, where the bopper has been, and what it has done.

Before going into details about the meanings of the parameters and variables, we should first be clear about the *types* of the variables. Most of the parameters and variables in Table 5-1 stand for whole numbers, or *integers*, but the following stand for other types of data.

RealSpeed, CopyWeight, CenterWeight, AttackWeight, FleeWeight, VeerWeight, and Acceleration are *real numbers*, meaning numbers with decimal points, like 0.9735 or 1.12.

Tangent, ToCentroid, and OldTangent are *vectors*, where a vector is a triple of three real numbers, one number for each of the possible coordinate directions *x*, *y*, and *z*.

Move is a variable that stands for the name of the procedure used to update the bopper's position. Different types of boppers use different kinds of Move procedures.

DNA, NearPrey, NearPredator, DogBrain, and TurnFrequency are *arrays* of integers; To is an array of vectors.

An *array* is an indexed list of a certain length. The DNA array, for instance, has length DNALength, and each member of the array is supposed to be an eight-bit integer, also known as a *byte*. Thus, DNA[1], DNA[2], DNA[3], and so on up through DNA[DNALength] are all bytes. The value of DNALength is computed from the BopperType and the IQ parameters, by the way, as will be discussed in the next section.

Saying that To is an array of vectors means that To[1], To[2], and so on are all vectors. To has one entry for each active bopper.

WriteColorTable, TurnTable, and NewStateTable are *double arrays* of integers.

The TurnTable Array

TurnTable[1][1]	TurnTable[1][2] ...	TurnTable[1][8]
TurnTable[2][2]	TurnTable[2][2] ...	TurnTable[2][2]
TurnTable[3][1]	TurnTable[3][2] ...	TurnTable[3][8]
TurnTable[4][1]	TurnTable[4][2] ...	TurnTable[4][8]

Table 5-2 A four by eight double array

A *double array* like TurnTable[ ][ ] can be thought of as a two-dimensional table, as shown in Table 5-2. When TurnTable is used, the first index number is supposed to be a State value, like 3, and the second is supposed to be the code number of a color that the bopper has encountered, like 2. The corresponding value in the TurnTable table is called something like TurnTable[3][2]. The picture of TurnTable in Table 5-2 is for a bopper that has an IQ of four, and that distinguishes eight different colors. (Why there are exactly eight colors that a bopper distinguishes is something we will discuss in the next section.)

In looking at Table 5-2, you can think of the first line as specifying how the bopper turns when it is in state 1, the second line as specifying how the bopper turns when it is in state 2, and so on.

Enzymes, DNA, and RNA

As was already mentioned, there is a close relationship among a bopper's Enzyme Parameters, DNA Parameters, and RNA Variables. The idea is that the Enzyme Parameters control the *type* of motion algorithm the bopper uses, the DNA Parameters are the source of the variable settings that the motion algorithm uses, and the RNA Variables store these DNA-determined settings in an easily usable form.

The names *Enzyme*, *DNA,* and *RNA*, are used in analogy to living cells. A cell uses its DNA to make RNA, and it is the RNA which is actually used to construct the proteins that control cell functions. Certain enzymes that are present in the cell are instrumental in converting DNA into RNA, and in converting RNA into proteins. The mental image is of the enzymes using the DNA instructions to build the RNA-described proteins, as suggested by Figure 5-2.

You can directly change the Enzyme Parameters from the Individuals dialog box or by using the Randomize Individuals' Params selection. During the breeding process, the enzymes may also be changed, as will be discussed in this chapter's section on Breeding. Table 5-3 shows the correspondence between Enzyme Parameter names and the names on the Individuals dialog. (The Individuals dialog can be seen in Figure 6-7 in the following chapter.)

Bopper Data Structure Name	Individuals Dialog Name
BodyIcon	Body Icon
TrailNodes	Trail Nodes
TrailLines	Trail Lines
BaseSpeed	Speed
BopperType	Bopper Type
TurmiteWindrose	Turmite Windrose
IQ	IQ

Table 5-3 Bopper enzyme parameter names and Individuals dialog names

The DNA Parameters consist of the DNA array of bytes that you can change by choosing the File Randomize Genes selection, or by using the Gene Viewer dialog box. The DNA Parameters are altered whenever the breeding process takes place.

The Enzyme Parameters and DNA Parameters can also be changed by using the File Open selection to load files. Loading a parameters file (with extension *.BL) changes the Enzyme Parameters of all the boppers, but it does not change their DNA Parameters. Loading an experiment file (with extension *.BEX) changes the Enzyme Parameters and the DNA Parameters of all the boppers. Loading a bopper file (with

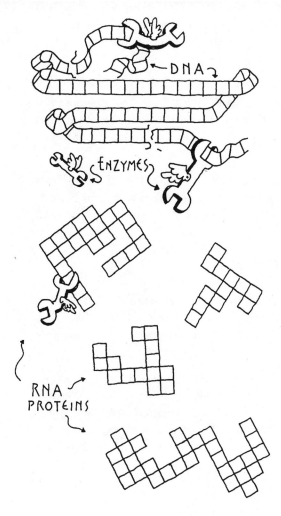

Figure 5-2 Enzymes turn DNA into RNA proteins

extension *.BOP) changes the Enzyme Parameters and the DNA Parameters of the edit bopper. For more information on loading files, see Chapter 6, *Boppers User's Guide*.

One final way in which you can directly affect the boppers' Enzyme Parameters and DNA Parameters is by using the Copy cursor, which copies the selected bopper's Enzyme Parameters and DNA Parameters to other boppers.

The DNA Parameters contain information about how the bopper moves, but this information is not in readily usable form. The RNA Variables are the settings the bopper uses when the Move procedure updates its position. These variables are not directly set by you. The Boppers program includes a procedure called DNAToRNA, which fills up a bopper's RNA Variables on the basis of, first, the contents of the boppers DNA array and, second, the values of the bopper's Enzyme Parameters.

As already mentioned, the DNA array is a list of bytes, and the parameter DNALength keeps track of how many bytes are active in the DNA. A bopper will allow any possible byte-string of length DNALength as its DNA. This means that you can freely mutate and crossover boppers' DNA arrays without worrying that you might get an unusable bitstring.

The value of the DNALength variable depends both on the size of the bopper's IQ variable and on what BopperType the bopper has. Let's talk about the size of DNALength for each of three possibilities for BopperType: **turmite**, **boid**, and **turboid**.

Turmite DNA

For a turmite, DNALength is equal to the number of entries that will be used in the three double arrays WriteColorTable, TurnTable, and NewStateTable. The DNAToRNA procedure uses one byte of DNA to compute each entry in these three double arrays.

In these double arrays, the first index number corresponds to a State the bopper might be in, while the second index number corresponds to the ReadColorCode of the pixel the bopper has examined. A bopper uses eight different values for ReadColorCode: BLANK, SELF, JABBER, WOCKY, FOOD, POISON, WALL, and OTHER. The meaning of these is fairly evident except for, sigh, "JABBER and WOCKY."

ReadColorCode

		JABBER	SELF	WOCKY
	GREEN	Blue	Green	Red
Colony Color	**RED**	Green	Red	Blue
	BLUE	Red	Blue	Green

Table 5-4 Colony-specific ReadColorCode values

The idea is that each bopper has a color associated with it depending on what colony it belongs to: green, red, or blue. If a bopper is red, then it views red pixels as having ReadColorCode SELF, for instance. Now think of green, red, and blue as being arranged in a cycle that goes around and around like: green, red, blue, green, red, blue, ... JABBER stands for the colony that can be found immediately to the left of your colony name, while WOCKY stands for the colony found immediately to the right of your colony name, as spelled out in Table 5-4.

Why bother to use the confusing JABBER, SELF, and WOCKY ReadColorCodes? Why not just say GREEN, RED, and BLUE? Well, the idea is that a bopper's motion code should be independent of what color it actually is. By doing the ReadColorCodes in this jabberwocky way, *Boppers* fixes it so that if you copy a red bopper's Enzyme Parameters and DNA Parameters to a blue bopper, the blue bopper will act just like the red one did. As for the choice of the words "jabber" and "wocky," well—what programmer *isn't* a Lewis Carroll fan? And doesn't Figure 5-3 look like the caucus race in *Alice in Wonderland*?

Anyway, before we went off into jabberwocky here, we were saying that a bopper uses eight different ReadColorCodes, and we were leading up to a calculation of how big DNALength is for a turmite. Recall that we had gotten to the point of saying that for a turmite DNALength is equal to the number of entries in the three Turmite RNA tables: WriteColorTable, TurnTable, and NewStateTable. Let's start by looking at the size of the NewStateTable.

A turmite computes its new State by using an instruction of the form:

```
State = NewStateTable[State][ReadColorCode];
```

This means that NewStateTable needs to have an entry for each combination of State and ReadColorCode that the bopper might come up with. The IQ parameter specifies

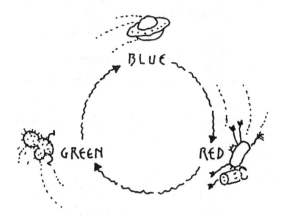

Figure 5-3 Chasing the Jabber and fleeing the Wocky

how many states are allowable, and we know there are eight possible ReadColorCode values, so we conclude that NewStateTable has (8 * IQ) entries. It turns out that each of these entries is computed from a single byte of DNA array. The length of DNA in bytes is DNALength, so this means that NewStateTable adds (8 * IQ) to DNALength.

Also note in NewStateTable that each of its entries must be a number between 1 and IQ. This is because NewStateTable is used to compute a turmite bopper's next State, and the next State must stay in the range allowed by the IQ setting. This limitation on the range of numbers allowed as entries in NewStateTable is an example of why we must use the DNA and RNA distinction. Any byte can be used in the DNA array, but only values that fall in the accepted range of State values can be used in the NewStateTable.

TurnTable and WriteColorTable are both the same size as NewStateTable. For each combination of State and ReadColorCode, a turmite uses the value of TurnTable[State][ReadColorCode] to see how much to turn. The turmite uses the value of WriteColorTable[State][ReadColorCode] to decide whether to leave a faint or a strong trail marking.

As with NewStateTable, there is a limitation on the allowable values in these tables. In TurnTable, the listed values must range from 1 to WindroseDirections, where WindroseDirections itself is determined by the TurmiteWindrose. In WriteColorTable, the values must correspond to the faint and the strong trail colors the bopper can leave. More details on how the turmites move are to be found in the "Turmite Motion" section that follows.

Adding up the sizes of WriteColorTable, TurnTable, and NewStateTable, we get (8 * IQ) + (8 * IQ) + (8 * IQ), which is 24 * IQ. When a turmite has the maximum allowable IQ of 100, this makes for a DNALength of 2,400 bytes, or 19,200 bits.

It is worth noting that when we use the DNA array to calculate the values for the three tables, we walk out through the DNA, peeling off 24 bytes for each of the bopper's possible states, as depicted in Figure 5-4. That is, the lower end of the DNA array affects a turmite bopper's behavior for low State values, and the higher end of the DNA array affects a turmite bopper's behavior for high State values.

Boid DNA

A boid does not use the turmite RNA Variables at all; instead it organizes its motion solely according to the eleven Boid RNA Variables. Four of these are coded by byte-sized integers: WatchTwoFlag, MaxSpeed, CruiseDistance, and NearWallDistance. Seven of these are real numbers that are coded by two bytes each: RealSpeed, CopyWeight, CenterWeight, AttackWeight, FleeWeight, VeerWeight, and Acceleration. This makes a total of 18 bytes of DNALength needed to fill the Boid RNA Variables.

The bytes for the Boid RNA parameters are taken from the very beginning of the DNA array, as shown in Figure 5-4.

Turboid DNA

All of the turboids, except the owl, can act like a turmite sometimes, so all of them need at least as much DNALength as a turmite: 24 * IQ.

Each of the turboids also uses Boid RNA parameters; as with a regular boid, these are set from the first 18 bytes of the DNA array. Note that this means that the first 18 bytes of the DNA array are used both for specifying the turmite behavior in State 0 and for specifying the Boid RNA parameters. This means that the same stretch of DNA is expressed in two different ways by a turboid.

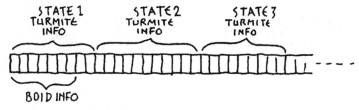

Figure 5-4 Bopper DNA showing turmite and boid info

In addition, the Beaver turboid uses the NearPrey and NearPredator arrays, and the Dog turboid uses the DogBrain and the NearPredator arrays. These are single arrays of length IQ. The NearPrey or DogBrain arrays are computed by skipping past the first 18 bytes of the DNA array (which were already used for the Boid RNA Variables) and looking at the next IQ bytes, as shown in Figure 5-5. The NearPredator array uses the next IQ bytes after that, for a total of 18 + (2 * IQ) bytes. This number is always less than the 24 * IQ bytes used for the turmite RNA Variables.

Although the owl turboid never acts like a turmite, it uses 18 * IQ bytes of DNA. The reason is that, according to which State it is in, the owl picks out a different 18 bytes of DNA to turn into boid RNA Variables. State one uses the first 18 bytes, State two uses the second 18 bytes, and so on, as shown in Figure 5-5.

Unlike the other types of boppers, the owls keep doing the DNAToRNA conversion on the fly to keep so much memory from being tied up for Owl RNA.

One last thing to point out about DNA and RNA is that the DNAToRNA conversion is performed because it is faster for the boppers to simply consult the precomputed RNA Variables than it would be for them to look up and convert the relevant bytes of DNA each time. The DNAToRNA procedure is called whenever a bopper's Enzyme Parameters or DNA Parameters have been changed.

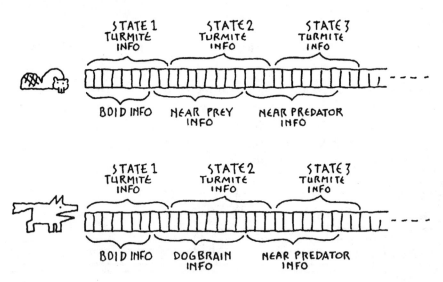

Figure 5-5 DNA of turboid boppers

At this point, we've explained what kinds of data are in a bopper data structure, and we've talked about the relationships between some of these pieces of data. Now let's look at how the boppers get updated.

The Boppers Update Cycle

During each full *Boppers* update, the boppers go through the following steps:

1. *Store positions*

2. *Update the metric*

3. Compute the *move* to the next position

4. *Read and eat* what's at the new position

5. *Draw the trail shapes*

6. *Draw the heads*

7. *Update the body icon*

All the boppers do step 1, then all do step 2, then all do step 3, and so on. Organized in this way, the process behaves almost as if it were *parallel*, meaning that there are almost no effects due to the order in which the individual boppers are processed within each of the seven steps. The one slip in perfect parallelism comes in step 5 when the trails are drawn, as will be discussed.

We'll spend the rest of this subsection talking about the seven steps.

Store Positions

In this step, each bopper sets the Old Situation Variables to match the current values of the Situation Variables. That is, each bopper sets: oldoldx equal to oldx, oldx equal to x, oldoldy equal to oldy, oldy equal to y, oldoldz equal to oldz, oldz equal to z, OldTangent equal to Tangent, OldScore equal to Score, and OldWriteColor equal to WriteColor.

There are diverse reasons for doing this. Each bopper needs to know its old positions, its "oldold" positions and its old WriteColor so that it can maintain its trail markings. The bopper's OldTangent is used during boid updates to ensure parallelism. And the OldScore is used so a turboid wolf bopper can subtract OldScore from Score to see how it fared during the latest update.

Update the Metric

In this step, for each bopper that is not a turmite, we set the values of the bopper's Metric Situation Variables: its To array, its NearestBopper and SecondNearestBopper indexes, its NearestDistance variable, its NearColonyCode variable, and its ToCentroid vector. If a particular bopper is a turmite, then it won't need this information, so we don't compute the information for that bopper.

Let's look at how a bopper that is not a turmite gets its Metric Situation variables updated during the *update the metric* step.

The To array of vectors consists of vectors that each have length one. Each of these unit vector points *from* the bopper that owns the To array *to* one of the other boppers. That is, To[1] will point to the bopper with BopperID 1, To[2] points to the bopper with BopperID 2, and so on, as indicated in Figure 5-6. In the process of computing the To vectors, we also compute the actual distances from our bopper to each of the other boppers.

By using the To vectors, the bopper can now decide which of the other boppers are visible to it. This is done by calculating the angle between the bopper's Tangent vector and each of the To vectors. Mathematically, it is very easy to calculate the angle between two unit-length vectors, which is one reason why we compute the To vectors in unit length form.

So now, by using the To vectors as well as the tabulated distances to the other boppers, our bopper can figure out the identity of the NearestBopper and the

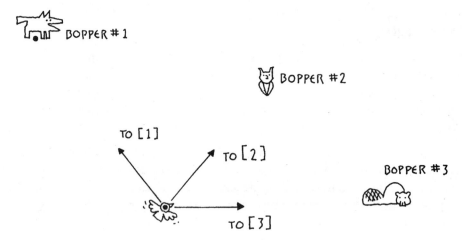

Figure 5-6 The To vectors

SecondNearestBopper. These are the closest and second closest boppers that are *visible*. If there don't happen to be any boppers that lie within the bopper's cone of vision, it sets the NearestBopper and SecondNearestBopper to be itself.

The NearColonyCode depends on which colony the nearest bopper belongs to. It can be SAME, PREY, PREDATOR, or NEUTRAL.

Here is how the NearColonyCode gets set. Suppose that Andrea and Bartholomew are two boppers. Andrea is a boid that is being updated, and Bartholomew is the closest visible bopper to Andrea. If Bartholomew is in the same colony as Andrea, then Andrea's NearColonyCode is set to SAME. Otherwise, Bartholomew is in a different colony from Andrea. Looking at the Ecology dialog, you can see three possible cases according to the Eat Value for Andrea-colored boppers eating Bartholomew-colored trail cells: the Eat Value is positive, the Eat Value is negative, or the Eat Value is zero. According to which case arises, we set Andrea's NearColonyCode to PREY, PREDATOR, or NEUTRAL.

Next the bopper's ToCentroid vector is updated. ToCentroid is a unit length vector that points toward a weighted average position based on the positions of the other boppers in the same colony. The simplest way to get a centroid is simply to average the other boppers' *x* positions, average their *y* positions, and average their *z* positions, as suggested in the top of Figure 5-7.

In nature, a bird in a large flock is not really aware of the positions of all the birds in the flock. A real bird heads toward the centroid not of the whole flock, but of the nearest group of birds. We imitate this in the boids algorithm by using a *weighted centroid*, which has a boid average the weighted positions of the other boids, with the nearest boids' positions being given a higher weight, as suggested in the bottom of Figure 5-7.

Move

In this key step, each bopper uses its Move function to compute its new position. The *x*, *y*, and *z* variables are updated to match the bopper's new position. No marks are made in the bopper world yet. Details on how the boppers move can be found in the "Bopper Motions" section.

Eat and Read

Here, each bopper looks at the color of the pixel at its new location. The bopper *eats* the pixel by adding an increment or decrement to its Score according to the eat value for that color which is set in the Ecology menu. The bopper *reads* the color value by storing it in its ReadColorCode variable. Note that here "eat" is not used in the sense of "erase," but in the sense of "add this cell's value to your Score." That is, the *eat and read* step changes the boppers' Score and the ReadColorCode variables, but this step does not change anything that you see on the *Boppers* screen.

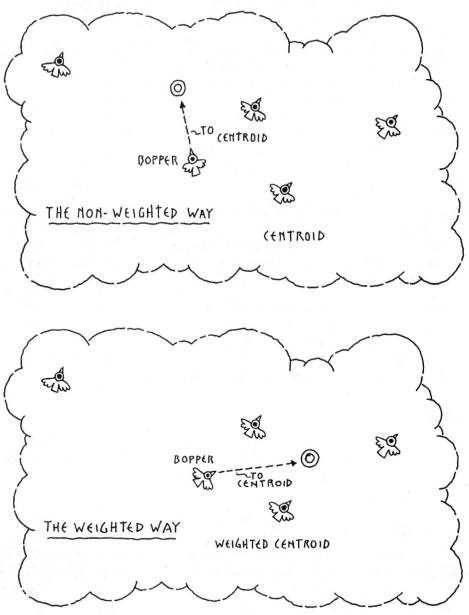

Figure 5-7 Weighted centroid pays more attention to nearby boids

If the bopper is drawing lines between its nodes or drawing squares around the nodes, then it will eat and read some more during the next step, otherwise it is now done eating and reading.

Details on the eating and reading that takes place during the drawing of trails is found in the "More About Eating and Reading" subsection.

Draw Trail Shapes

Every bopper leaves a trail of dots, but some draw lines between the dots and/or draw squares around the dots.

According to which colony a bopper is in, it leaves trails that are green, red, or blue. Each of these colors comes in two shades, which I call *faint* and *strong*. While in boid mode, a bopper always uses the strong trail color, but when in turmite mode, a bopper may use either the faint or the strong trail color.

How do we deal with a situation where two trails intersect? One way is to *combine* the colors by a logical OR operation. That is, a red pixel on top of a green pixel gives a yellow pixel, a blue pixel on top of a red pixel gives a purple pixel, and so on. Because there are really six trail colors—the faint and the strong versions of green, red, and blue—quite a variety of overlapped colors can arise. The more colors your display supports, the more distinctions you will be able to see. The boppers view all of these overlapped colors as corresponding to the ReadColorCode OTHER, except in the rare situation where a combination of colors may happen to match one of the FOOD, POISON, or WALL colors.

Whenever a bopper colors a pixel, it adds the position of this pixel to a memory buffer that belongs to the bopper's colony. If the buffer of trail cells is already full, then before adding the new pixel position to the trail buffer, the bopper erases the pixel corresponding to the oldest pixel position in the buffer.

The further details of the *draw trail shapes* step are best explained by breaking it into three substeps: *draw square*, *draw line*, and *draw dot*. It is useful to look at Figures 5-8, 5-9 while reading about these three substeps.

Draw Square. This applies if the Controls menu's Individuals dialog's Trail Nodes setting is Small Squares, Medium Squares, or Large Squares for the bopper in question. When a bopper is using squares nodes, the bopper begins the draw trail shape process by drawing an OldWriteColor square around the oldoldx, oldoldy, oldoldz position. The bopper looks at the color of each pixel it overwrites. It *eats* these color values, but it *does not read* them. That is, when the square is drawn, the value of each pixel that is overwritten is added to the bopper's Score, so the bopper *eats*; but the bopper's

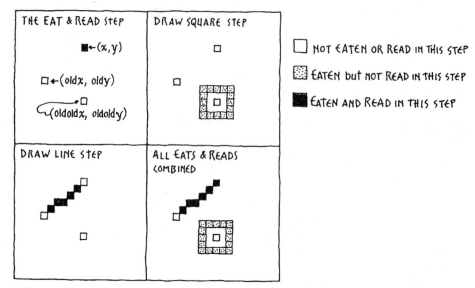

Figure 5-8 What gets eaten and read during a bopper update

ReadColorCode variable is *not* changed by anything the bopper encounters while drawing a square around an oldold position, so the bopper *does not read*.

Draw Line. Next, if the bopper is drawing lines between successive nodes, it draws a WriteColor line from oldx, oldy, oldz to x, y, z. The line does not include its end points. While drawing the line, the bopper *eats and reads*. That is, the bopper changes its Eat Values according to any colors it writes over, *and* it changes its ReadColorCode variable to match the last non-blank pixel (if any) that it encounters while drawing the line.

Note that the last paragraph says "last *non-blank* pixel." The boppers read along its trail lines, rather than only letting them read at their new head positions, to prevent a bopper from crossing someone's trail without noticing it. In general, the BLANK ReadColorCode is the one the bopper is going to be working with the most often, and we want to try and decrease the frequency with which this ReadColorCode occurs. So if a bopper's ReadColorCode is already different from BLANK, we don't want the bopper's action of reading along its trail line to be able to set the ReadColorCode back to BLANK. Therefore, as a bopper reads along its trail line, it *will* change the ReadColorCode with each non-blank pixel it encounters, meaning that, once again, it changes its ReadColorCode variable to match the last non-blank pixel. If all the pixels along the line are blank, then the ReadColorCode remains at the value that was set when the bopper read the color at its new position in during step 4.

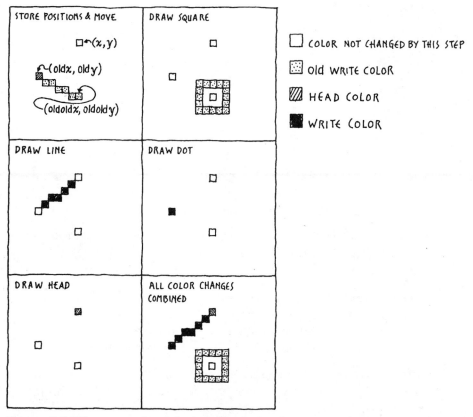

Figure 5-9 What gets colored during a bopper update

Draw Dot. For the final substep of drawing the trail, the bopper replaces the head-colored pixel at oldx, oldy, oldz by a pixel with WriteColor. No change to Score or to ReadColorCode is effected by this step. When the bopper does not draw squares around its nodes and does not draw lines between its nodes, this substep is the entirety of the *draw trail shapes* step.

As previously mentioned, parallelism can fail while drawing the trails. One way this can happen is that drawing, say, a red line crossing a blue line will have a different effect on the boppers' Scores depending on whether the blue line or the red line is drawn first. There are two excuses for this lack of full parallelism. First of all, if you run boppers that only leave trails made of single dots, then the update *is* perfectly parallel. Second of all, the update order of the boppers is expressly randomized every time that breeding is performed, so that no bopper gets a lasting order-position advantage. Visually, the program *appears* perfectly parallel because when trail colors overlap, the overlapped region is drawn as a mixture of the colors.

Draw Heads

Here each bopper draws a head-colored pixel at its current head position. This is the final step of a bopper's drawing anything on the screen during its update step. See Figure 5-9 for a summary of what a bopper *does* draw on the screen.

Update Body Icons

When a bopper has a single icon on to mark its position, the icon at the old position is erased and a new one is drawn. The icons are a purely visual effect, and are not visible to the boppers in their world.

More About Eating and Reading

The eating steps that take place during a bopper's update cycle affect the bopper's Score variable, while the reading steps serve to set the values of the ReadColorCode variables.

During an update, The Score is changed by adding in the values of all the pixels the bopper eats. In order, the bopper eats the pixel at the new position of its head, possibly eats a square of pixels around the bopper's oldold position, and possibly eats a line from the bopper's old position to its new position.

All boppers in a colony use the same Eat Values. These values are displayed by the Ecology dialog, which shows values for Green, Red, Blue, Food, Poison, Wall, Prey Head, and Other.

Green, Red, and Blue all can come in either faint or strong shades, but both shades are regarded as identical for the purposes of adding in Eat Values.

Food is usually given a negative Eat Value, and Poison a positive Eat Value. Wall cells are often given a negative Eat Value.

If a bopper that is moving as a boid comes within NearWallDistance of a wall, the bopper's Score will have the Wall value added to it. A bopper moving as a turmite, on the other hand, must actually try to move into a space occupied by a wall cell before the Wall Eat Value is added to its Score.

The Prey Head case can occur if a bopper eats a cell which is the color of the head color which the boppers use. In the case where the screen background color is black, the head color is white; and when the screen background color is white, the head color is black.

It is possible that the presence of a cellular automaton patch, or the accumulation of several colors on top of each other might produce a pixel that is read as head-colored, even though no bopper's head is really there. Once a bopper detects that it has eaten a head-colored cell, it checks the positions of the other boppers to find out which (if any) bopper has its heads at that position. If the other bopper's colony color is given a positive weight by the bopper's colony, then the bopper is thought of as a prey species, and the Prey Head Eat Value is added to the original bopper's score.

One other way in which a bopper may receive the Prey Head Eat Value is if the bopper happens to be moving as a boid during an update. A boid need not land directly on another bopper's head for the encounter to be thought of as a direct hit. Instead, a boid bopper need only come within Boid Hit Radius pixels of another bopper's head in order to be thought of as hitting the other bopper's head. If the other bopper is a prey species relative to the original bopper, then the Prey Head score is added to the original bopper's score. Boid Hit Radius, by the way, is set from the Colonies dialog.

For a pixel that is not classified in one of the other color categories, the Other Eat Value is added to the bopper's score.

As mentioned in the "Enzymes, DNA, and RNA" section, the ReadColorCode can be BLANK, SELF, JABBER, WOCKY, FOOD, POISON, WALL, or OTHER. Recall that a bopper refers to its own colony color with the ReadColorCode SELF; and that, relative to the cycle *green, red, blue, green, red, blue,...*, a bopper refers to the colony one lower as JABBER, and to the colony one higher as WOCKY.

During an update, the ReadColorCode is changed by looking at the values of all the pixels the bopper reads. In order, the bopper first reads the pixel at the new position of its head, and then reads the pixels along a line from the bopper's old position to its new position. As mentioned before, the bopper takes the last non-blank ReadColorCode it encounters as its final value.

Because we do not use a special HEAD ReadColorCode, when a bopper encounters the head of another bopper it sets the ReadColorCode to OTHER. Note, however, that the bopper *does* change its Eat Value in a unique way if a head pixel from a prey colony is encountered—as described previously.

Another difference between reading and eating is that a bopper will *read* its own faint-colored trail cells as being BLANK. The reason for this is that a turmite bopper is thought of as a Turing machine that is marking space with ones and zeroes. Its faint-colored trail cells are like its zeroes, and its strong-colored trail cells are like its ones.

You might wonder why the *Boppers* program doesn't just have a bopper use *one* color of trail cell, and let the bopper set its faint-colored trail cells to the same as the background color. There are two reasons. First, it is more interesting to watch *Boppers* if the trail of where a turmite has been is always visible. Second, since the boppers get much of their Eat Values from eating other boppers' trails, it is a good thing to leave as many trails around as possible.

Because boids do not use the ReadColorCode in their update, they do not need to make the distinction of leaving two shades of trail color, so while in boid mode, each bopper uses only its strong trail color.

Instead of using the ReadColorCode, the boids use the NearColonyCode, which was previously discussed in the "Update the Metric" subsection.

Bopper Motion

The Move function uses the bopper's State, ReadColorCode, and NearColonyCode to update the bopper's direction of motion, position, and State. This section will give full details about the six kinds of possible motion: *turmite*, *boid*, *wolf*, *beaver*, *dog*, and *owl*.

In order to precisely describe these algorithms, a *pseudocode* version of each motion algorithm, along with a brief explanation will be provided.

"Pseudocode" is a computer science word that means "a way of expressing yourself that is almost like computer code, but is easier to read." Every writer gets to invent his or her own pseudocode conventions and standards. The pseudocode used here is a hybrid between Pascal and C that is supposed to be easy to read. Here are some of the conventions used:

`expression1 = expression2;` means that *expression1*'s value is to be set equal to the value of *expession2*.

```
IF [situation]
  THEN [action]
```

means that if the [situation] is true, then the [action] is to be taken.

```
IF [situation]
  THEN [action]
  ELSE [other action]
```

means that if the [situation] is true, then the [action] is to be taken, and if the [situation] is not true than the [other action] is taken.

An action can either be a single command, such as `expression1 = expression2;`, or an action can be a compound list of commands. BEGIN and END are used to mark the start and end of compound lists of actions.

Within the pseudocode, the lines that are merely *comments* to increase comprehensibility are set off by a "//" at their start. For each of the six kinds of motion, a pseudocode version along with an explanation and some comments is listed.

Turmite Motion

This motion uses the bopper's State and ReadColorCode as indices into three tables: the WriteColorTable, the TurnTable, and the NewStateTable. The tables are used, respectively, to change the bopper's WriteColor, Direction, and State, as shown in the pseudocode displayed in Listing 5-1.

Listing 5-1 The Turmite Motion algorithm

```
BEGIN
// Compute WriteColor
        WriteColor = WriteColorTable[State][ReadColorCode];
// Compute new Direction.
        Direction = Direction + TurnTable[State][ReadColorCode];
        IF (Direction > WindroseDirections)
            THEN Direction = Direction - WindroseDirections;
// Compute new State
        State = NewStateTable[State][ReadColorCode];
// Compute new position
        x = oldx + BaseSpeed   WindroseX[Direction];
        y = oldy + BaseSpeed   WindroseY[Direction];
        z = oldz + BaseSpeed   WindroseZ[Direction];
END
```

Although we do not explicitly mention the *bopper* itself in this listing of the Turmite Motion algorithm, the understanding is that all the variable names refer to information in the data structure of the bopper being updated.

According to what the bopper's WindroseType is, its WindroseDirections will be some fixed number. In addition, the bopper's WindroseType will have been used to fill three arrays of length WindroseDirections: WindroseX, WindroseY, and WindroseZ.

The bopper's new Direction is computed by looking up a turn value from the TurnTable, and by adding this turn value to the current Direction, as shown in Figure 5-10.

A turmite bopper's new *x, y,* and *z* position values are computed by looking up the corresponding displacements in the WindroseX, WindroseY, and WindroseZ arrays. A picture of the different windroses used by *Boppers* appears in Figure 6-10 in the next chapter.

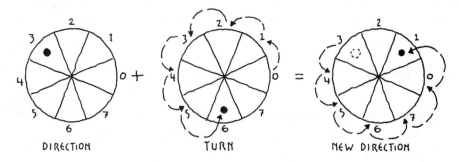

Figure 5-10 On an eight-direction windrose, three plus six is one!

Note that before adding in the windrose displacements, these values are multiplied by a bopper's BaseSpeed. It is sometimes interesting to give the boppers a BaseSpeed greater than one so that they move around faster. In this situation, it is usually a good idea to have the boppers leave trails that are lines—otherwise they are not likely to encounter each other's trails as they take their big steps.

One consideration to keep in mind when adjusting turmites' speeds is that the windroses with more directions tend to have larger sized steps in their Windrose arrays. This is for the simple reason that there are a limited number of small, discrete steps you can take! In practice, lower speeds with the higher windroses seem to work well.

Something the pseudocode does not explicitly state is that once the new values of *x, y,* and *z* are computed, the values that lie outside the confines of the boppers' world need to be clipped or wrapped. If the world is in wrapped mode, then values that run off one side of the world are wrapped around to the other side. If the world is in walled mode, then a value that would extend out past a wall is clipped back to a value that does not go beyond the wall.

Boid Motion

The Boid Motion algorithm uses a secondary algorithm called Flock Motion, which is shown in Listing 5-2. The Flock Motion algorithm changes a bopper's Tangent vector and RealSpeed variables; that is, Flock Motion changes the direction and the speed of a bopper's motion.

Note that the Flock Motion algorithm refers to a bopper called "nearbopper." The idea is that Flock Motion is an algorithm that a bopper applies to itself relative to some nearbopper. We assume that when the Flock Motion algorithm is used, the NearColonyCode has been set to reflect the relationship between the bopper and the nearbopper. Any variable name that is not explicitly tied to nearbopper (like "near-bopper's OldTangent") is assumed to belong to the bopper being updated.

Listing 5-2 The Flock Motion algorithm

```
BEGIN
// Apply one of the following four methods, according to NearColonyCode.
// Flock with own SAME colony boppers.
   IF (NearColonyCode is SAME)
   THEN
          BEGIN
                 // Fly parallel.
                 Tangent = Tangent + CopyWeight  (nearbopper's OldTangent);
                 // Maintain CruiseDistance.
                 IF (nearbopper is ahead, closer than CruiseDistance)
                      THEN RealSpeed = RealSpeed/Acceleration; // Back off.
                 IF (nearbopper is ahead, further than CruiseDistance)
                      THEN RealSpeed = RealSpeed  Acceleration; // Catch up.
                 IF (nearbopper is behind, closer than CruiseDistance)
                      THEN RealSpeed = RealSpeed  Acceleration; // Rush away.
                 IF (nearbopper is behind, further than CruiseDistance)
                      THEN RealSpeed = RealSpeed / Acceleration; // Wait up.
          END
// Or pursue PREY boppers.
   IF (NearColonyCode is PREY)
   THEN
          BEGIN
                 // Chase prey in the direction of the To vector.
                 Tangent = Tangent + AttackWeight  To[nearbopper];
                 // Rush headlong.
                 RealSpeed = RealSpeed  Acceleration;
          END
// Or flee PREDATOR boppers.
   IF (NearColonyCode is PREDATOR)
   THEN
          BEGIN
                 // Flee along the negative of the To vector.
                 Tangent = Tangent - FleeWeight  To[nearbopper];
                 // Slow for sharp turn.
                 RealSpeed = RealSpeed / Acceleration;
          END
// Or slow down near NEUTRAL boppers.
   IF (NearColonyCode is NEUTRAL)
          THEN RealSpeed = RealSpeed / Acceleration;
END
```

As far as direction goes, Flock Motion says to fly parallel to nearbopper if nearbopper is in your own colony, to fly toward a prey nearbopper, and to fly away from a predator nearbopper. The strengths of these influences are adjusted by CopyWeight,

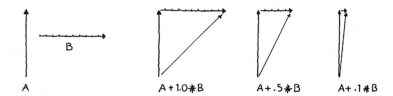

Figure 5-11 Weighted vector addition

AttackWeight, and FleeWeight, which range from 0.0 to 1.0. At the beginning of the algorithm, Tangent, nearbopper's OldTangent, and the To vectors all have the same length of one, so the effect of changing the weights is as drawn in Figure 5-11.

Note that when NearColonyCode is SAME, the bopper adds in a multiple of nearbopper's *OldTangent* vector, rather than a multiple of nearbopper's *Tangent* vector. The reason for this is so the update will work in a *parallel* fashion, meaning, once again, that it shouldn't matter what order the boppers are updated in. All of the OldTangent values were set at the beginning of the full bopper update cycle during the store positions step.

As far as speed goes, the Flock Motion algorithm tries to keep the bopper at a constant distance from its nearest visible flock mates in the SAME case. In the PREY case, the bopper speeds up, and in the PREDATOR case it slows down, as if for a sharp turn. In the NEUTRAL case, the bopper slows down as well.

The bopper's Acceleration variable determines how rapidly it slows down or speeds up. *Boppers* allows acceleration to range from 1.01 to 1.3. These values may look small, but keep in mind that each boid is updating its velocity repeatedly, and repeated multiplications or divisions by even small numbers do make an impact.

Flock Motion is *part* of the Boid Motion algorithm, but it is not *all* of it. Note, for instance, that Flock Motion does not actually change the bopper's *position*; it only adjusts the bopper's speed and direction of motion. In addition to actually executing the motion, the Boid Motion algorithm also includes these three additional behaviors: veer away from nearby walls, chase prey boppers, and flee from predator boppers.

There are two small things that need to be mentioned before discussing the Boid Motion algorithm as shown in Listing 5-3. First of all, a flag variable such as WatchTwoFlag can have one of two values: OFF and ON. (Like the other boid variables, WatchTwoFlag cannot be set directly by the user.) Second of all, a vector V is formally defined as an *array of length three*. The *x, y,* and *z* components of V are V[1], V[2], and V[3].

Listing 5-3 The Boid Motion algorithm

```
BEGIN
// Avoid the walls
            IF (The world is in walled mode and x, y, or z is within
                NearWallDistance pixels of a wall)
                THEN (Add to Tangent components of size VeerWeight pointing away
                      from the walls that are too near);
// Flock with neighbors.
            Do Flock Motion with NearestBopper;
            IF (the WatchTwoFlag is ON)
                THEN do Flock Motion with SecondNearestBopper;
// Head towards centroid.
            Tangent = Tangent + CenterWeight  ToCentroid;
// Clamp speed and get the unit tangent.
            Make RealSpeed be between (3  BaseSpeed) and (MaxSpeed  BaseSpeed);
            Make Tangent be a unit vector;
// Compute new position.
            x = oldx + RealSpeed  Tangent[1];
            y = oldy + RealSpeed  Tangent[2];
            z = oldz + RealSpeed  Tangent[3];
END
```

Boid Motion consists of five steps:

1. Avoid the walls

2. Flock with neighbors

3. Head toward centroid

4. Clamp and normalize

5. Compute new position

(1) *Avoid the walls.* If the *Boppers* world is in walled mode, then the boids need to avoid the walls. Each boid bases its wall-avoiding behavior on two of its Boid RNA Parameters: NearWallDistance and VeerWeight. NearWallDistance ranges from 30 to 60 pixels, while VeerWeight ranges from 0.4 to 0.8. Figure 5-12 shows how a weighted "Bounce" vector pointing away from a wall gets added to a bopper's Tangent vector.

Each time a boid executes a veering motion to avoid a wall at the edge of its world, *Boppers* adds the Eat Value corresponding to WALL to the boid's Score. According to whether you set the WALL Eat Value to negative, zero, or positive, the boids will evolve to avoid, be indifferent to, or seek out the walls.

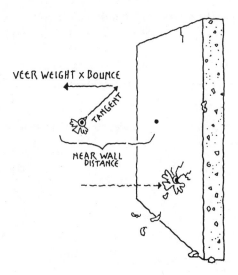

VEER WEIGHT x BOUNCE

TANGENT

NEAR WALL DISTANCE

Figure 5-12 A boid avoids a wall

Boids do *not* react to walls that are part of a maze other than by plowing through maze walls and adding the WALL Eat Value to their scores for each wall pixel they eat.

(2) *Flock with neighbors.* According to the setting of its Boid RNA parameter WatchTwoFlag, each bopper has the option of flocking with one or two of its nearest neighbors. Note that if the Flock Motion function is called for the SecondNearestBopper as well, then the value of the NearColonyCode is adjusted to reflect the colony of the SecondNearestBopper before Flock Motion gets called a second time. Note also that since Flock Motion does not change the bopper's position, the order in which you flock with the NearestBopper and SecondNearestBopper doesn't matter.

If, by the way, you do Flock Motion with a nearbopper in your colony who is a turmite, what happens? At start-up, each bopper's Tangent and OldTangent vectors get set to some random unit vector value. Turmite motion does not change the values of these vectors. So each time you do Flock Motion with a turmite, you'll be adding in a direction parallel to the unchanging OldTangent value that happens to be in the turmite bopper's memory.

(3) *Head toward centroid.* This is a straightforward step. CenterWeight is between 0.0 and 1.0. As mentioned, the centroid of a flock is computed in a weighted form, that is, a boid pays more attention to flockmates that are closer to it. This

is a necessary step for if all boids headed toward the same centroid point, they'd probably end up stuck in a glob at one spot.

(4) *Clamp and normalize.* In this step, we make sure the speed adjustments from the Flock Motion calls have not pushed the bopper's RealSpeed out of range. We also "normalize" the bopper's Tangent vector (that is, we make the Tangent vector be of unit length).

Each bopper has a Boid RNA integer parameter, MaxSpeed, that can range between 3 and 8. These speeds are in terms of pixels per step. No bopper is allowed to have its RealSpeed fall below 3 * BaseSpeed and no bopper is allowed to go faster than its MaxSpeed * BaseSpeed. The bottom-level speed of 3 given to the boid motions keeps the boids moving at a nice, lively pace, a pace comparable to the 25-direction turmite windrose.

The Tangent vector has to be normalized because in the process of adding all those other vectors to it during the Boid Motion algorithm, you have probably changed its length.

(5) *Compute new position.* If we were to think of OldPosition and Position as vectors, the three equations of this step could be expressed as the vector equation, Position = OldPosition + RealSpeed * Tangent. Because the Tangent has length one, the length of RealSpeed * Tangent is RealSpeed. So in this step, there is a move of length RealSpeed from the old position to the new position. The relative sizes of Tangent's components determine how the motion is shared out among the axes. In the two-dimensional case, by the way, we make sure that Tangent has a 0.0 Z component.

As in the turmite case, we have to wrap around the edges of the world if a point falls off one side or the other. Another thing to mention about wrapping is that the boids can see past the edge of their world. That is, if a boid is closely following a second boid, it will continue to do so even while the boids wrap around from one side of the screen to the other.

Wolf Motion

A bopper of the wolf turboid BopperType decides between acting like a turmite or a boid depending on the change in the bopper's score during the last update. The change in score is computed by subtracting the OldScore variable from the Score variable; if this quantity is negative, the last update reduced the bopper's score. If, on the other hand, Score minus OldScore is positive, the bopper's score increased over the last update.

As you can see from the profile in Listing 5-4, the wolf's strategy is to act like a turmite when the change in Score is favorable, and act like a boid when the most recent change in Score is neutral or unfavorable.

Lising 5-4 The Wolf Motion algorithm

```
BEGIN
   IF (Score minus OldScore is negative or zero)
         THEN do Boid Motion;
   IF (Score minus OldScore is positive)
         THEN do Turmite Motion;
END
```

The wolf is supposed to be a turboid that gets high scores. The idea is to take advantage of the fact that turmites tend to move across the screen more slowly than boids. So acting like a turmite is one way to try and stay in a region where the Score changes are favorable, and acting like a boid is a way to try and leave regions where the Score changes are negative or zero.

If you turn a food patch on, and set one of the turmite colonies to act like wolves, you will notice how they like to swoop down on the food, and how they really rip into it.

Boids and turboids don't see the food from afar; they only see other boppers at a distance. But they do notice when they run over food because this increases their scores. When a wolf runs across the food, it starts acting like a turmite and bounces around inside the food patch for as long as it can. But since it stays inside the food patch and the other wolves tend to flock with it when in boid mode, the other wolves will tend to end up near the food as well. So ultimately, thanks to wolf teamwork, it is almost as if the wolves *can* see the food!

The wolves are equally likely, by the way, to congregate on any clusters of prey colony boppers they find. The wolves are particularly apt to cluster on a prey colony whose member boppers are in turmite mode. For a wolf, turmites are sitting ducks!

Beaver Motion

A beaver turboid generally acts like a turmite, although sometimes it will act like a boid. The beaver's method of deciding whether to act like a turmite or a boid involves the use of the variable we call TurboidState.

TurboidState is very similar to the State variable; in fact, the State variable could have been used in place of TurboidState. But it seems better to let State just control the turmite activities of the beavers, and to use a different variable called *TurboidState* to control the beaver's turmite-or-boid decision-making.

Listing 5-5 The Beaver Motion algorithm

```
BEGIN
// Decide between Turmite and Boid motion.
   IF (NearColonyCode is SAME or NEUTRAL)
         THEN do Turmite Motion;
   IF (NearColonyCode is PREY)
   THEN
         BEGIN
               IF ( NearestDistance <= NearPrey[TurboidState])
                     THEN do Turmite Motion;
               IF ( NearestDistance > NearPrey[TurboidState])
                     THEN do Boid Motion;
         END
   IF (NearColonyCode is PREDATOR)
   THEN
         BEGIN
               IF ( NearestDistance >= NearPredator[TurboidState])
                     THEN do Turmite Motion;
               IF ( NearestDistance < NearPredator[TurboidState])
                     THEN do Boid Motion;
         END
// Update the TurboidState.
   TurboidState = NewStateTable[TurboidState][NearColonyCode];
END
```

In the pseudocode shown in Listing 5-5, we see that the beaver uses the NearPredator and the NearPrey arrays, which are Turboid RNA Variables of the bopper. The exact values of NearPrey and NearPredator for different TurboidStates are determined by the bopper's DNA during the DNAToRNA conversion process. But *Boppers* does ensure that all the NearPrey values lie between zero and 255, while the NearPredator values lie between 256 and 511, as is suggested by the relative sizes of the two circles in Figure 5-13.

Whether a beaver turboid is currently acting like a boid or like a turmite, it always updates its Boid Situation Variables, so it always knows who is the NearestBopper. Recall that the direction of NearestBopper lies within VisionAngle degrees of the beaver's Tangent direction. Although regular turmites do not waste time updating their Tangent vectors, a turboid (such as a wolf, dog, or beaver) always updates its Tangent vector even when it is temporarily acting like a turmite. The Tangent vector of a turboid always points in the direction in which it most recently moved.

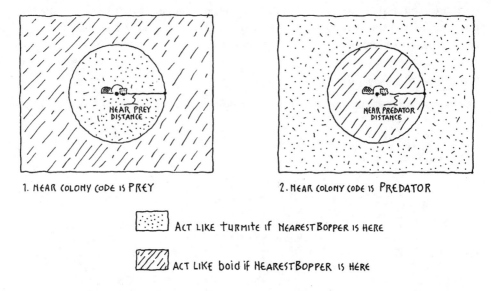

1. NEAR COLONY CODE IS PREY

2. NEAR COLONY CODE IS PREDATOR

[illustration box with dots] ACT LIKE tuRMite if NEAREST BOPPER IS HERE

[illustration box with diagonal lines] ACT LIKE boid if NEAREST BOPPER IS HERE

Figure 5-13 How a beaver turboid decides between acting like a turmite and a boid

As well as knowing who is the NearestBopper, a beaver also is aware of the NearestDistance, which is the distance to NearestBopper, and aware of NearColonyCode, which expresses whether the NearestBopper belongs to a colony that is SAME, PREY, PREDATOR, or NEUTRAL—relative to the bopper's own colony.

If NearColonyCode is SAME or NEUTRAL, the beaver acts like a turmite. If NearColonyCode is PREY or PREDATOR, the beaver uses the NearestDistance variable to decide whether to act like a turmite or a boid, as shown in Figure 5-13.

Depending on what TurboidState the beaver is in, it will have different values for its NearPrey distance lookup value and its NearPredator distance value, although NearPredator will always be larger than NearPrey.

Basically, the beaver wants to act like a turmite. But if the NearestBopper is PREY and is farther away than NearPrey, then the beaver will act like a boid, as if to fly closer to the prey. And if the NearestBopper is PREDATOR and is closer than NearPredator, the beaver will act like a boid as if to fly away from the predator. But otherwise the beaver acts like a turmite.

NearColonyCode	ReadColorCode	Code Number
<Not Used>	BLANK	0
SAME	SELF	1
PREY	JABBER	2
PREDATOR	WOCKY	3
<Not Used>	FOOD	4
<Not Used>	POISON	5
<Not Used>	WALL	6
NEUTRAL	OTHER	7

Table 5-5 The NearColonyCodes and ReadColorCodes. Some stand for the same code numbers

When the beaver updates the TurboidState, it uses the NewStateTable. Instead of using ReadColorCode as the second parameter, it uses NearColonyCode. The ReadColorCodes and NearColonyCodes both stand for small integer Code Numbers that are used in the *Boppers* program, as is spelled out in Table 5-5. Also keep in mind that TurboidState is a variable that ranges over the same values as State. So the expression "NewStateTable[TurboidState][NearColonyCode]" in the Beaver Motion algorithm makes as much sense as the expression "NewStateTable[State][ReadColorCode]" in the Turmite Motion algorithm.

Dog Motion

A dog is about equally likely to act like a boid or a turboid. The dog maintains a TurboidState like the beaver turboids, and it uses this TurboidState to decide whether to act like a turmite or a boid. A dog decides by looking into the DogBrain array and determining if the entry at the position corresponding to TurboidState is odd or even, as you can see in Listing 5-6.

Listing 5-6 The Dog Motion algorithm

```
BEGIN
// Decide between turmite and boid.
        IF ( DogBrain[TurboidState] ) is odd )
            THEN do Boid Motion;
```

continued on next page

continued from previous page

```
        IF ( DogBrain[TurboidState]) is even )
              THEN do Turmite Motion;
// Update the TurboidState.
        // Use the first of the following three methods which applies.
        IF (ReadColorCode is FOOD or POISON)
              THEN TurboidState = NewStateTable[TurboidState][ReadColorCode];
        //Otherwise.
        ELSE IF NearestDistance > NearPredator[TurboidState] )
              THEN TurboidState = NewStateTable[TurboidState][BLANK];
        // Otherwise.
        ELSE TurboidState = NewStateTable[TurboidState][NearColonyCode];
END
```

The DNAToRNA function uses the bopper's DNA to fill up the DogBrain array with bytes that are the same as the bytes used for the NearPrey array, as discussed in the "Enzymes, DNA, and RNA" section. Initially, these bytes are equally likely to be odd or even, but depending on whether the boid or the turmite behavior produces better results, the dog turboid may evolve to lean toward one or the other kind of action.

Most commonly, though, the dog turboids tend to vacillate quite regularly between turmite and boid motions, meaning that their trails have a brambly look to them, much like the path of an old male dog like my dog Arf, who stops to sniff and urinate as often as possible.

Like the beaver, the dog reserves its State for the turmite calculations, and uses its TurboidState for deciding between turmite and boid motion. The dog updates its TurboidState by using the NewStateTable according to one of three methods.

- If the ReadColorCode is FOOD or POISON, then TurboidState is set to NewStateTable[TurboidState][ReadColorCode].

- Otherwise, if the NearestBopper is at a distance greater than NearPredator[TurboidState], then the lonely dog sets TurboidState to NewStateTable[TurboidState][BLANK]. As we mentioned in the discussion of Beaver Motion, the NearPredator values range between about 250 and 500.

- *Otherwise*—that is, if the ReadColorCode isn't FOOD or POISON, and the NearestBopper is closer than NearPredator[TurboidState]—the dog uses the NearColonyCode as the second lookup index into the NewStateTable and sets TurboidState to NewStateTable[TurboidState][NearColonyCode]. Recall that the correspondences between ReadColorCodes and NearColonyCodes are given in Table 5-5.

Owl Motion

The owl turboids always act like boids. But, unlike boids, they update the State variable, and they adopt different values of the Boid RNA Parameters depending on what the value of their State is. The Owl pseudocode appears in Listing 5-7.

Listing 5-7 The Owl Motion algorithm

```
BEGIN
// Update the Boid RNA Variables.
        Set the Boid RNA Variables based on the eighteen bytes found
        in the bopper's DNA array at the location 18  State;
// Fly.
        Do Boid Motion;
// Update the State.
        State = NewStateTable[State][NearColonyCode];
END
```

Instead of using the State as an index for looking up pre-stored RNA parameters, the owl turboids use the State to look up a swatch of DNA which they convert into RNA parameters on the spot. Because the owls don't need two different kinds of state variables, they don't bother with the TurboidState. Note that the turmites and all the turboids use the State variable, and the TurboidState is used only by the beaver and the dog turboids.

Math Alert

As mentioned in the "Enzymes, DNA, and RNA" section, the reason for this programming strategy is that it would increase the size of the bopper data structure to include up to a hundred (the largest possible range of States) different versions of Boid RNA. Boid RNA Variables are so bulky because many of them stand for real number variables, which use up a minimum of four bytes of memory apiece. According to one way of calculating it, the Boid RNA Variables use a net amount of 34 bytes, so a hundred sets of these values would use 3,400 bytes. This is larger than the 2,400 bytes it takes to store the three Turmite RNA lookup tables for a hundred states and eight ReadColorCodes.

Even though they have to convert 18 DNA bytes into Boid RNA parameters with each update, the owl turboids seem to move around at a respectable speed. The calculations involved in updating the Boid Situation Variables are in fact much more taxing.

Like the beavers, the owls update their state on the basis of the NearColonyCode.

As a practical matter, the owl turboids use more computation than any of the other boppers, and this is visible in the subtlety and complexity of their flocking behavior. The owls' gnarl is *elegant*.

COLONIES

The boppers are grouped into colonies of three colors: the greens, the reds, and the blues. One reason for having the boppers in colonies is to make it easier to invent stories about what they are doing.

The greens can be thought of as the most likely to be prey. The reds are the guys in the middle, and blues are the ones on top. The Food Chain button in the Controls popup's Ecology dialog reflects this ordering, with green fearing red, red fearing blue and liking green, and blue liking red.

You might go a step further, and think of the greens as plants, the reds as cows, and the blues as cattle-mutilating UFOs. The UFOlogy button in the Controls popup's Ecology dialog reflects this notion. In the UFOlogy ecology, the blue saucers like the red cows, the red cows fear the UFOs and like the green grass, and the grass likes both the cows and the UFOs. To make this scenario rigorously logical, the grass likes the cows because of the cowpies they leave, and the grass likes the UFOs because the saucers' powerful antigravity drives fix vast amounts of nitrogen in the soil! Making up little stories about the food values settings helps you interpret the boppers' actions more easily.

Dividing the boppers into colonies helps us to make up stories about them, but more importantly, we can let the different colonies use *different fitness functions* and *different breeding methods*.

As regards the fitness functions, the boppers in each colony are working on a search problem as described in Chapter 3, *Genetic Algorithms*: they are trying to find genomes that will optimize their scores according to their colony's fitness function. Each colony's fitness function is primarily set by assigning Eat Values to the different colors of pixels the bopper's move across. It is also possible to make some additional adjustments to a colony's fitness function; the additional adjustments involve the magnitude and the disorderliness of the boppers' motion.

As regards the breeding methods, the boppers within each colony evolve according to a genetic algorithm whose parameters are set at the colony level. Five genetic operators are allowed, each with an adjustable weight. In addition, a colony can also evolve using a completely different breeding method, known as Hit Breeding, under which boppers have sex with other boppers only when their heads touch or come very close to touching.

The ability to independently adjust both the question (the fitness function) and the method of solution (the genetic algorithm) for each colony makes a wide range of experiments possible. One might, for instance, give two colonies the same fitness functions and different genetic algorithms to see which genetic algorithm works better.

Another effect of the division into colonies is that the fitness functions the boppers work on may become more difficult as time goes by. For if the reds get points by coming close to the greens, but the greens lose points by being near the reds, then the better the reds get, the harder the greens have to work, and vice versa.

Table 5-6 lists the colony data structure. The structure breaks into three parts as labelled: (1) Population Information, (2) Score Parameters, and (3) Breeding Parameters.

The Colony Data Structure

(1) **Population Information:**	
Population Parameter:	
PopulationSize	// The colony's population count.
Population Variable:	
Member[MAXBOPPERS]	// Lists index numbers of the members.
(2) Score Parameters:	
Ecology Parameters:	
GreenValue	// Score per green cell eaten.
RedValue	// Score per red cell eaten.
BlueValue	// Score per blue cell eaten.
FoodValue	// Score per food cell eaten.
PoisonValue	// Score per poison cell eaten.
WallValue	// Score per wall cell touched.
PreyHeadValue	// Score per prey head hit.
OtherValue	// Score per other color cell eaten.
Low Motion Fitness Parameters:	
MinTotalMotion	// Minimum pixels to move, or
LowMotionValue	// this is added to your Score.
Entropy Fitness Parameters:	

continued on next page

continued from previous page

TargetEntropy	// The closer you get to this Entropy, the
GoodEntropyValue	// more of this is added to your Score.

(3) Breeding Parameters:

Timed Breeding:	
BreedTime	// Steps between timed breeding cycles.
DeathLevel	// Maximum number of copies per bopper.
SexLevel	// Percent of pairs which do crossover.
MutationLevel	// Probability per bit of getting flipped.
ZapLevel	// Number of boppers to zap.
TranspositionLevel	// Number of bopper genomes to transpose.
ZapCode	// Things to zap.
Hit Breeding:	
BoidHitRadius	// Boid within this distance scores a hit.
ExogamyFlag	// Hit crossover with other colonies.
EndogamyFlag	// Hit crossover with own colony.
RecruitPreyFlag	// Enlist prey colony hits.

Table 5-6 The colony data structure

With the exception of the Member array in the Population Information group, all of the colony's data consists of parameters which are controlled by the user, as described in Chapter 6, *Boppers User's Guide*.

All of the colony data entries are integers; except for DeathLevel, SexLevel, MutationLevel, ZapLevel, and TranspositionLevel, which are decimal real numbers; and except for Member, which is a single array of bopper IDs.

Population Information

PopulationSize is controlled from the Controls popup's World dialog.

The Member array has a length the same as the colony's PopulationSize. The Member array is the only *variable* data in the colony data structure; all the other colony data fields are *parameters* which are set by the user.

The Member array is organized by the program itself, simply to keep a list of which boppers are currently being used by a given colony. When the size of a colony's population is increased, the handiest unaffiliated bopper is added to that colony's Member array.

Score Parameters

The Score Parameters include Ecology Parameters, Low Motion Fitness Parameters, and Entropy Fitness Parameters.

The Ecology Parameters are controlled from the Controls popup's Ecology dialog, while the Low Motion Fitness and Entropy Fitness Parameters are controlled from the Controls popup's Colonies dialog.

During each timed breeding cycle, a colony's boppers continuously accumulate scores by eating pixels and by (occasionally) coming near prey boppers' heads. After BreedTime updates of the colony's boppers, the timed breeding process takes place. Just before timed breeding, the colony's boppers add corrections to their scores based on the Low Motion Fitness Parameters and the Entropy Fitness Parameters.

Ecology Parameters

Earlier in this chapter, the "Eating and Reading" section talked about what happens when boppers eat pixels of various colors. The GreenValue, RedValue, BlueValue, FoodValue, PoisonValue, WallValue, PreyHeadValue, and OtherValue specify the sizes of the Eat Values that are added to the colony's boppers as they eat, or try to eat, pixels of various colors.

In the case of a turmite encountering a wall pixel, the turmite will not eat the wall pixel, although it will add WallValue to its score. This behavior breaks down for some combinations of turmite speed and windrose.

A boid will add WallValue to its score if it comes within NearWallDistance of a wall bounding the edge of the world, even if it does not touch the wall. This is so boids can be bred to avoid or to seek out walls. If a boid runs over a wall, such as a maze wall, the boid adds an increment of WallValue to its score for each wall pixel eaten.

Recall that a bopper views another bopper as prey if the bopper's Eat Value for the other bopper's trail color is positive. The PreyHeadValue is added to a bopper's score when it hits the head of a prey bopper. A turmite bopper needs to have its head land directly on the other bopper for a hit to occur, but a boid need only be within BoidHitRadius of the other bopper, as you'll see in the "Hit Breeding" section.

Low Motion Fitness Parameters

If a bopper's total motion over all the updates in the last breeding cycle is less than MinTotalMotion, then the bopper gets a penalty equal to LowMotionValue added to its score. LowMotionValue is always zero or negative, so it truly is a penalty.

The calculation works like this. After each timed breeding, the bopper's current position is recorded as startx, starty, and startz, and the bopper's LowMotionFlag is set to ON. During each succeeding update, the bopper compares its *x, y, z* position to the position stored as startx, starty, startz. We compute a kind of "taxicab distance" here by summing the *x, y,* and *z* displacements, viewed as positive numbers. If this distance becomes greater than MinTotalMotion, then the bopper sets its LowMotionFlag to OFF until the end of the current breeding cycle. When breeding takes place, each bopper that still has its LowMotionFlag set to ON gets LowMotionValue added to its score. By the way, taxicab distance is used instead of standard Pythagorean distance just to make the program run a touch faster.

The point of this is to try and eliminate those boppers who just stay jittering in one boring spot for update after update. The idea is to pick the MinTotalMotion value so that any reasonably lively bopper will have time to move that far before BreedTime runs out; leaving the slow and lazy boppers to get penalized with the LowMotionValue.

Entropy Fitness Parameters

The Entropy Fitness Parameters dovetail with some of the theoretical work on a-life. Each bopper calculates an Entropy that reflects how disorderly its turmite motion, if any, is. Based on how closely a bopper's Entropy matches its colony's TargetEntropy, the bopper will be given a reward that ranges from zero up to the size of its colony's GoodEntropyValue.

The Entropy and TargetEntropy values are normalized to range between zero and one hundred; they might be thought of as percentages, with zero being the least possible Entropy, and one hundred being the most possible Entropy.

The GoodEntropyValue can be set to any positive value. The reward given the bopper is computed by a tent-shaped graph that peaks at TargetEntropy, as shown in Figure 5-14. The further a bopper's entropy is from the TargetEntropy, the lower is its reward. But no bopper gets a negative reward; so the use of a GoodEntropyValue will tend to make all of the colony's boppers' scores a bit higher. The goal, of course, is for genomes that cause a motion closest to TargetEntropy to have a bigger influence on the colony.

As already mentioned, the bopper Entropy is a quantity that measures the disorderliness of the turmite motions the bopper performs. Thus, Entropy is only meaningful for boppers who are turmites or who are turboids of the type wolf, beaver, or dog—who vary between acting like boids and acting like turmites.

A bopper's Entropy is computed at the end of BreedTime updates by using the information in the bopper's TurnFrequency array. This array keeps count of how many times the bopper does a turmite-style turn of each possible size.

The TurnFrequency array has the same length as the value specified by the bopper's WindroseDirections variable. At the beginning of each breeding cycle, all of the TurnFrequency entries are set to zero. During the succeeding updates, every time the bopper does a turmite turn of size 0, the TurnFrequency[0] number is increased by one; every time the bopper does a turmite turn of size 1, the TurnFrequency[1] number is increased by one, and so on.

The bopper's Entropy measures how evenly distributed the bopper's turns are, statistically speaking. If a turmite chooses equally often among all the possible amounts to turn, then it has an Entropy of one hundred—the maximum entropy. If, on the other hand, a turmite always turns by the same amount, over and over, then it has an

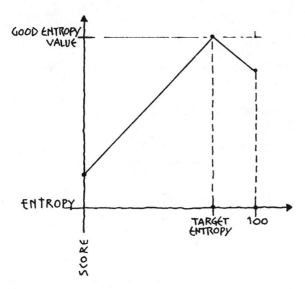

Figure 5-14 Computing a bopper's entropy fitness reward

Entropy of zero—the minimum entropy. Further details on how Entropy is calculated appear in this chapter's "Notes and References" section.

In the terminology of the "Turmites" section of Chapter 2, *Computer A-Life,* sand turmites tend to have high Entropy, while polygon turmites have low Entropy. A rail turmite is likely to have a low Entropy as well, but a lace turmite's Entropy should be higher.

If we believe that the fittest a-life forms lie at the interface between order and disorder, then we might suppose that boppers with some medium Entropy level might be the most successful.

If you want to get an idea of what some bopper's Entropy actually is, you can set the TargetEntropy to 100 and the GoodEntropyValue to 100, in which case the Entropy reward given each bopper during Timed Breeding will be precisely equal to each bopper's Entropy. Conversely, you can set the TargetEntropy to zero and the GoodEntropyValue to 100, in which case each bopper's Entropy rewards will be 100 minus its Entropy.

Breeding Parameters

The breeding parameters are controlled from the Controls menu's Colonies dialog. There are two distinct types of breeding that can be used: Timed Breeding and Hit Breeding.

Timed Breeding

Timed Breeding is a variation on the standard genetic algorithm that was discussed in Chapter 3, *Genetic Algorithms.*

The BreedTime parameter specifies how many updates the boppers in the colony go through before undergoing the breeding process. As soon as BreedTime updates elapse, the bopper's Scores are adjusted according to the Low Motion Fitness Parameters and the Entropy Fitness Parameters as described in the last section.

At this point, the genetic algorithm is applied in five steps: fitness-proportional reproduction, also known as *death*; crossover, also known as *sex*; and then *mutation*; *zapping*; and *transposing*.

Death

Based on its score relative to the other boppers in the colony, each bopper has a certain probability of being able to pass one or several copies of itself for the next generation. The higher a bopper's score is, the more representatives it is likely to get. The DeathLevel parameter specifies how many representatives the highest-scoring bopper is likely to get. The higher the DeathLevel is, the more low-scoring boppers will have to die in the sense of having their genomes overwritten by other boppers.

As discussed in the section on "The Standard Genetic Algorithm" in Chapter 3, *Genetic Algorithms,* and in the section on the "Colonies Dialog" in Chapter 6, *Boppers User's Guide,* the process needs to be delicately adjusted to prevent the colony's genomes from prematurely converging to all look the same. More information about the implementation of this process can be found in the section on the Controls popup's Colonies dialog in Chapter 6.

Sex

Once you have decided which new bopper representatives go into the next generation, you choose a percentage of pairs from the new group and mate them together using crossover. SexLevel is the percentage of pairs chosen for sex.

In order that wolf, beaver, and dog turboids can have rapidly evolving boid parameters, we actually do *two* crossovers on the genomes of these turboids. One crossover is picked from the whole length of the DNA, while the other is picked to be inside the boid and turboid genes the bopper uses. We don't need to bother with this trick with boids and owls; their DNA is all devoted to boid activities anyway.

Note that in Timed Breeding, the sex partners are chosen completely randomly, with no regard to screen position or to relative scores. Hit Breeding, which we describe in the next section, is a different approach under which boppers only have sex when they are very close to each other.

Mutating

The colony MutationLevel specifies the probability per bit of being flipped. Mutation is like a hard rain of radiation that changes everyone. See the section on the "Colonies Dialog" in Chapter 6, *Boppers User's Guide,* for details.

Zapping

Zapping is a process whereby one or two individual boppers can be completely randomized. This often seems to work better than simply mutating all of the boppers. We pick the two lowest scoring boppers in a colony as the ones to possibly Zap. The ZapLevel specifies the probability with which these two boppers get Zapped.

By using the Things To Zap group in the Controls popup's Colonies dialog, you can specify which of a bopper's parameters gets Zapped. Normally, the DNA is zapped, but you can also request that some of the bopper's Enzyme Parameters be randomized as well.

Very rapid evolution effects can be seen when the Enzyme Parameters are zapped—for instance if a colony's Eat Values are all set to positive numbers, then it will be to the advantage of that colony's boppers to eat as much as possible. A good way to eat more is to draw trail lines and squares around your trail nodes, so if you allow these Enzyme Parameters to be zapped, the colony will quickly evolve to have lines and squares for most of its boppers.

Transposing

Transposing is another very strong way of changing the boppers' genomes. Here bits of the genetic bitstring are swapped, as discussed in Chapter 1, *Life and A-Life*. Transposing is applied to the colony's *best-scoring* bopper, and the TranspositionLevel specifies the probability of doing this.

Transposition is good at preventing some single genome from taking over a colony, but if used too much it can churn the colony's genomes more rapidly than Death can make them converge, leading to a nearly random pool of genomes.

Hit Breeding

Hit Breeding can occur when two boppers' heads are near each other. In order to discuss these controls, it will be useful to have names for the two boppers involved. Let's call the bopper whose colony parameters we are setting Andrea, and let's call the bopper that Andrea hits Bartholomew.

In the case where Andrea is a turmite, we say Andrea hits Bartholomew only when Andrea's head is in the same position as Bartholomew's. If Andrea is a boid, we say that Andrea hits Bartholomew so long as the distance between Andrea and Bartholomew is *less than* Boid Hit Radius.

The distance, by the way, is computed using the usual Pythagorean distance formula, and the units of distance are pixels. Thus, if Andrea has a Boid Hit Radius of two, and Bartholomew's head is located on a pixel right next to Andrea's head, then Andrea says that she hits Bartholomew. Some pixel distances are illustrated in Figure 5-15. When looking at this figure, keep in mind that the pixel to pixel distance must be less than the radius in order for the pixel to be in the Hit neighborhood. Thus, for instance, the only pixel whose distance from the center pixel is *less than* one is the center pixel itself.

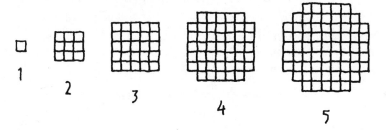

Figure 5-15 Pixel neighborhoods for different values of Boid Hit Radius

Note that if Andrea and Bartholomew are both turmites and Andrea hits Bartholomew, it is also true that Bartholomew hits Andrea—for when turmites hit, their heads are in the same position. It can happen however, that a boid hits a turmite, say, without the turmite hitting the boid, as shown in Figure 5-16.

Given that Andrea hits Bartholomew, what happens next? This depends on which colony Bartholomew belongs to, and on the settings of (1) EndogamyFlag, (2) ExogamyFlag, and (3) RecruitPreyFlag for Andrea's colony.

(1) If *EndogamyFlag* is ON, *and* if Bartholomew is in the *same* colony as Andrea, then Andrea and Bartholomew have sex, with each replacing his or her genes by a joint crossover of their genetic bitstrings.

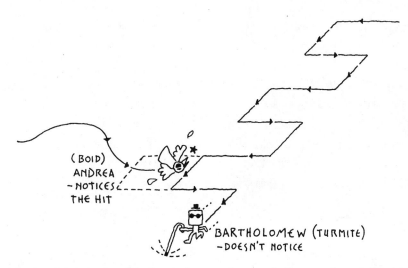

Figure 5-16: Andrea hits Bartholomew, but Bartholomew doesn't hit Andrea

(2) If *ExogamyFlag* is ON, *and* if Bartholomew is in a *different* colony from Andrea, then Andrea replaces her genes by a crossover of her and Bartholomew's genes. She has sex onto herself. If at the same time Bartholomew is hitting Andrea and if Bartholomew's colony has ExogamyFlag ON, then Bartholomew is also replaced by a crossover of Andrea and Bartholomew.

(3) If *RecruitPreyFlag* is ON, *and* if Bartholomew is in a different colony from Andrea, *and* if Andrea's colony views Bartholomew's colony as a *prey* colony; then Andrea will copy her parameters onto Bartholomew, and add Bartholomew to her colony by altering the colonies' PopulationSize parameters and Member arrays, and by changing the color of trails that Bartholomew leaves. Bartholomew's genomes are left intact, however, as a way of bringing new information into the colony.

Using Hit Breeding in place of, or in addition to, Timed Breeding opens up a lot of possibilities for experimentation. One might try, for instance, turning off each colony's Timed Breeding by increasing the BreedTimes until they all read "No Breeding." Next one could turn on all the Exogamy Flags. Finally, one might set the Ecology to Dog Eat Dog so that all the boppers view the other colonies as prey. While this simulation runs, the only boppers that breed will be the ones that come near the heads of boppers in other colonies. Will this lead to a world of boppers who are more likely to hit each other?

NOTES AND REFERENCES

Math Alert

The Entropy we use in the Controls Colonies Additional Fitness Measures Turmite Entropy Bonus group is more correctly known as *normalized entropy*.

The definition of normalized entropy goes like this. Suppose that you keep track of some variable V over a period of time, and suppose that V can take on values that range from 1 to N. (In the case of our Turmite Entropy Group, V is the amount that the turmite changes direction at each step.) You can use your tracking information about V to compute a Probability array so that for each *i* between 1 and N, *Probability[i]* is the percent of times that V took on the value *i*. The *entropy* of V's distribution is obtained by letting *i* run from 1 to N and summing up all the values:

Probability[i]   (-log (Probability[i]))

Here "log" means "logarithm base two." If the distribution of V's values happens to be uniform, then a maximal entropy of log(N) is attained. The *normalized entropy* is obtained by dividing the entropy by the maximal entropy value log(N).

- The low end of a Turmite's DNA array specifies its behavior in state 1, the next swatch of DNA specifies its behavior in state 2, and so on. An alternative approach would be to let the low end of the DNA to specify a turmite's behavior for ReadColorCode BLANK, let the next stretch of DNA specify the behavior for ReadColorCode SELF and so on down the list of possibilities in Table 5-5. The alternate representation would make different kinds of schemata likely to be preserved by the crossover operator. This kind of issue is discussed in a fascinating book by Yuval Davidor: *Genetic Algorithms and Robotics,* World Scientific, 1991.

6

Boppers User's Guide

In this chapter, we describe how to use the Boppers *menus, and what to try if problems arise. A version of this chapter can be found in the Help menu under the Help on Boppers selection.*

The first three chapters talked about the theory and history of a-life techniques, the fourth chapter got you running, and Chapter 5, *The Boppers and Their World,* gave a detailed description of how the *Boppers* program is supposed to work. This chapter lets you take control of the boppers and start your own experiments with artificial life.

BOPPERS MENUS AND DIALOGS

There are four main menus you can open from the *Boppers* menu bar: the File menu, the Controls menu, the Tools menu, and the Help menu.

The File, Controls, and Tools menus allow you to do all sorts of things with the *Boppers* program. You can open these menus by clicking on them or by pressing (ALT) and one of the letter keys underlined on the menu bar as shown in Figure 6-1. Thus (ALT)-(F) opens the File menu.

Once a menu is open, you can choose one of its selections by clicking a selection, or by pressing the appropriate underlined letter key (no (ALT) key is needed on open menus). You can also choose a highlighted menu entry by pressing (ENTER), and you can mouselessly move the highlight by pressing arrow keys.

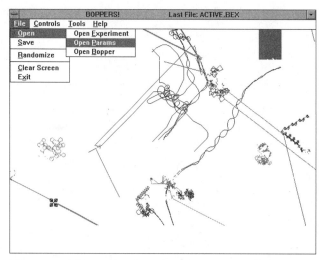

Figure 6-1 The menu bar, the File menu, and the Open popup

Suppose that you open the File menu and then choose the Open selection. The Open selection leads to a submenu known as a *popup*. You choose a selection from a popup just as you choose a selection from a menu. That is, you click your selection, press (ENTER) while your selection is highlighted, or press the underlined code key for the selection.

The menu selections which lead to popup menus have a "▶" symbol (right-pointing arrowhead) next to them. You can move up out of a cascade of popup menus one menu at a time by using the (ESC) key, or you can just bag the lot of them by clicking the mouse down in the uncovered region where the boppers live.

Some other menu selections lead to *dialog boxes*. A dialog box is a *child window* with interactive controls such as *pushbuttons*, *checkboxes*, *radio buttons*, and *combo boxes*.

Choosing a pushbutton changes the value of something or performs an action. Choosing a checkbox toggles it between the checked and the unchecked state. Choosing a radio button highlights one out of a range of possible selections. Clicking a combo box displays a list of selections you can choose from. You can use the arrow keys to scroll up and down to all the entries of a combo box—this is important in the event one of the combo box entries is not visible. Once the desired combo box selection is highlighted, you can choose this selection by clicking it or by pressing (TAB).

The menu selections that lead to dialog boxes have a "..." symbol (ellipsis) next to them. Position and click the mouse to make the desired selections in a dialog box.

To close a dialog box, you may choose the dialog's Exit button, double-click on the System Menu box in the dialog's upper left-hand corner, or right-click your mouse in a blank region of the dialog box. A final method of closing a dialog box is to rechoose the menu selection that opened the dialog in the first place.

You can reposition a dialog box by using the mouse to drag the dialog box's title bar. The dialog boxes are designed to reopen in the same location they were in the last time you closed them.

It is possible to mouselessly navigate a *Boppers* dialog box by using the (TAB) key to move among the dialog box's subgroupings, using the arrow keys to move about within a subgrouping, and using (SPACE) to press a selection. You can choose a dialog box action by pressing (ALT) and the underlined letter key (such as (ALT)-(D) for "DO IT!" or (ALT)-(X) for "EXIT").

Using Real-Time Dialog Boxes

Almost all of the *Boppers* program's dialog boxes control the program in *real time*. This means that the active boppers keep moving while these dialogs are open. You can have a lot of the real-time dialogs open at once, with large parts of the dialog boxes shoved offscreen so you can see the boppers. Do note, however, that *Boppers* runs slightly slower when many real-time dialogs are open.

The only two *non* real-time dialogs are the Controls menu's *World* dialog and the Help menu's *About* dialog. When either of these dialogs is open, the boppers stop moving, and no additional dialogs can be opened. Generally, you should close the World and About dialogs as soon as you are done using them so the program can continue running. Sometimes, however, it may be convenient to leave one of these dialogs open in order to effectively suspend the *Boppers* program while you are using another application.

The changes you make in a real-time dialog box take effect as soon as you press the DO IT! button. Note that pressing the DO IT! button does not close a real-time dialog box. Pressing the DO IT! button transfers the changes from the Dialog box to the boppers, who are actively running in the background.

As you have not pressed the DO IT! button in a real-time dialog box, the newest changes are *not* in effect. If you decide not to use the changes you've made in a real-time dialog box, you may close the dialog by pressing the EXIT button. If you want to use the changes *and* close the dialog box, you should first press DO IT! and then press EXIT. If you close the dialog by pressing EXIT without first pressing DO IT!, then the proposed changes will not be made.

There is no need to close any of the dialog boxes before exiting *Boppers*.

FILE MENU

The File menu allows you to *open*, or load, files from your disk that encode various gene and parameter settings for *Boppers*. You can also use the File menu to save and to randomize these settings. Finally, the File menu can be used to clear the screen and to exit *Boppers*. You can look ahead to Figure 6-3 for a picture of the File menu (with some additional popups hanging off it).

Open Popup and Open Common Dialog

The quickest way to get an idea of what the *Boppers* program can do is to use the Open Experiment and Open Parameters options to open some files and see what happens.

If you choose Open from the File menu, you see a popup menu that offers you three selections: Open Experiment, Open Parameters, and Open Bopper.

Each of these selections leads to an instance of the Open common dialog box. The Open common dialog enables you to choose the desired file with the appropriate file extension, as shown in Figure 6-2. Experiment files have the extension .BEX (for "bopper experiment"), parameter files have the extension .BL (for "bopper land"), and individual files have the extension .BOP (for "bopper").

Boppers installs as a flat directory with no subdirectories, so all the distribution experiment, parameter, and individual files that we give you will be in the BOPPERS directory after installation. You will find more parameter files available

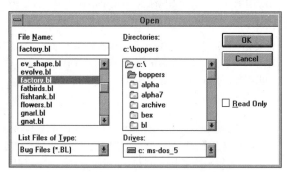

Figure 6-2 Windows common dialog for opening a parameter file

than anything else. Chapter 7, *Examples,* has details on the .BL parameter files provided with this release of BOPPERS.

To choose a file, make sure the common dialog box directory is set to C:\BOPPERS, or to whatever directory you have the files in. Then choose a file by highlighting a selection and pressing OK, or simply by double-clicking a selection.

An *experiment file* includes all the parameters that you can change from the menus and dialogs, along with the genes of the active boppers.

A *parameter file* includes the parameters that can be changed from the menus and dialogs. Each active bopper's parameters are saved in a *Boppers* parameter file, but the individual bopper's genes are not saved.

An *individual file* consists of an individual bopper's genes plus all the parameter settings for the bopper that might be changed with the Individuals dialog. This information is written onto the *edit bopper.*

The *edit bopper* is the one whose icon is a cross in a circle. If you cannot see the edit bopper icon, maximize the *Boppers* window, or use the scroll bars to look for it.

When you open a parameter or experiment file, the screen is cleared and the file's name appears on the *Boppers* title bar. When you open a individual file, the behavior of the edit bopper will normally change in a noticeable way.

Save Popup and Save Common Dialog

When you find an interesting *Boppers* world, you may want to save the whole world's parameters and genes as an experiment file, save the world and the individuals' parameters as a parameter file, or save some individual bopper's parameters and genes as an individual file.

Keep in mind that the suffixes used for experiment, parameter, and individual files are .BEX, .BL, and .BOP, respectively.

Due to the amount of information involved, a .BEX experiment file ranges from 10K to 200K in size, while a .BL parameter file is well under a K, and a .BOP file is between 1K to 8K. (Recall that a K is about a thousand bytes.) The sizes range because various worlds have differing numbers of boppers, and different boppers may have greater or lesser numbers of genes.

Given the finiteness of disk space, one normally prefers to save interesting *Boppers* configurations as the small parameter files instead of as the large experiment files. But if you have been evolving some boppers' genes for a long time, then you need to save the world as an experiment file. Saving an individual file is a good idea whenever you notice a bopper that is doing something really cute or weird.

The Save Experiment, Save Params, and Save Bopper menu selections all lead to a Windows common dialog box. Before saving a file, make sure the correct directory is selected—ordinarily you might as well save all your files in the BOPPERS directory, although if you do extensive experimentation, you may want to keep some of the files in special subdirectories.

Be warned that if you do use separate directories, the last directory you used for a common dialog box will always be the active directory the next time you open a common dialog box. This is not a problem when you Open a file, because if you're in the wrong directory, there are no files there to open. But when you Save a file, it is very easy to put it in the wrong directory.

Note also that the first time you use a common dialog, you may well find that you are in the drive and directory where Windows lives. The moral is to try and remember to check the active directory in the common dialog whenever you save a file. You can actually change the directory and then cancel out of a Save (or out of an Open for that matter), and the directory change will stay in effect.

Randomize Menu

The File *Randomize* selection shows a popup with seven kinds of randomization, plus a lower-level popup that allows you to exclude some parameters from being randomized. See Figure 6-3 for a picture of the popups. A rapid randomizer is used to accomplish each of these changes quickly. Not all random possibilities are equally weighted; in most cases the "randomization" is constrained to set values within some not too unreasonable ranges.

Repeatedly using the File Randomize selections, especially the File Randomize *Everything* selection, is a good way to get an idea of some of the various kinds of *Boppers* worlds you might encounter. The seven kinds of randomization are

1. World Params

2. Bopper Params

3. Bopper Genes

4. Ecology Params

5. Colony Params

6. Positions

7. Everything

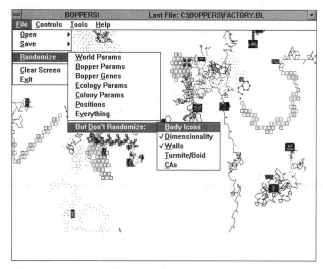

Figure 6-3 The File popup with the Randomize popup, and the But Don't Randomize popup

Note that as soon as you request one of these randomizations, the change is made right away, without any more prompts. Sometimes, a too-hasty Randomization choice may cause you to lose a world you've been working on.

(1) *World Params* changes all the parameters that are affected by the Controls World dialog. These include the numbers of boppers of each color, the lengths of the boppers' trails, the dimensionality of the *Boppers* world, whether or not the world wraps around or has walls, whether food or poison patches are present, and whether or not a cellular automaton patch is displayed. Randomize World Params is useful if you have a nicely evolved bunch of boppers you'd like to try in a different environment.

(2) *Bopper Params* changes the parameters that are affected by the Controls Individuals dialog. These include whether the boppers show body icons, whether they draw squares along their trails, whether their trails are dots or lines, how far they move with each step, whether they act like turmites or like boids, how many directions a turmite can move in, whether a turmite treats its own faint color differently from a blank color, and how many internal states a turmite has. Randomize Bopper Params is useful if you are letting the boppers' parameters evolve, and would like to jolt or restart the evolution.

(3) *Bopper Genes* changes the genetic bitstrings, or genomes, used to compute each bopper's turmite lookup tables and boid parameters. These bitstrings can be viewed and manipulated with the Tools Gene Viewer dialog. Randomize Bopper Genes is

appropriate for restarting a run of genetic evolution, or for trying to prospect for some interesting new boppers of a particular parameter type.

(4) *Ecology Params* changes the food value weights found on the Controls Ecology dialog. This option can be used to show how dependent bopper evolution is on the particular fitness function created by the food values, although normally one would be more likely to change the settings by hand.

(5) *Colony Params* changes the parameters that are found in the Controls Colonies dialog. These include the Timed Breeding parameters, the Hit Breeding settings, and the Additional Fitness Measures. In general, all of these parameters affect the way in which the individual same-colored bopper colonies breed and evolve. Normally, it's better to change these settings by hand rather than randomizing them, but there is always the possibility that randomizing can produce some interesting and unexpected phenomena.

(6) *Positions* clears the screen and moves each bopper to a new random position. This is an interesting thing to do if you have a *Boppers* world that has converged on a stable population that arranges itself in a characteristic pattern of groupings or knots. Using Randomize Positions enables you to see if the world's pattern reemerges. This control is also useful if many boppers seem to be stuck against a wall.

(7) *Everything* is a good shotgun method for finding new bopper ecosystems. It has the effect of doing all of the prior six randomizations at once.

But Don't Randomize Popup

When using the Randomize controls, there may be certain parameter settings you especially want to avoid changing. This is what the *But Don't Randomize* popup is for. The idea is that you get *Boppers* into a configuration you like and then use the But Don't Randomize popup to specify the things you don't want to change from the present setting.

The things you can exclude from randomization are *Body Icons*, *Dimensionality*, *Walls*, *Bopper Type*, and *CAs*. The things currently excluded are indicated by checkmarks in the But Don't Randomize popup, as shown in Figure 6-3.

The But Don't Randomize exclusions apply to all seven different kinds of randomization. If, for instance, the Dimensionality entry is checked on the But Don't Randomize popup, then none of the seven possible randomizations can change your present world from two dimensional to three dimensional—or from three dimensional to two dimensional, as the case may be.

Note that the But Don't Randomize exclusions do *not* prevent parameters from being changed as a result of using the File menu to open experiment, parameter, or individual files.

You can toggle a checkmark on or off by selecting that entry from the But Don't Randomize popup. Each time you do this, the triple cascade of menus closes and you need to open them all again if you want to change something else—which is mildly tedious. The good news is that your But Don't Randomize selections are permanently saved on disk, so that the next time you run the *Boppers* program your preferred But Don't Randomize selections will still be in effect.

The reasons for wanting to exclude some properties from randomization have to do with both aesthetics and speed.

Body Icons. If you are interested in running *Boppers* as rapidly as possible, you might use the Tools popup's Controls Individuals dialog to turn all the boppers' body icons off. Showing the icons takes up a little extra time. If you then want to try randomizing things without having to worry about the icons getting turned back on, you can use the But Don't Randomize popup to make sure that Body Icons is checked. Alternatively, you might be interested in the visual effects created by having all of, or some of, the boppers' Body Icon parameters set to Body Trail. In this case, you would still want the But Don't Randomize Body Icons entry checked, but you'd make sure to use the Controls *Boppers* menu to set most of the Body Icons parameters to Body Trail.

Dimensionality. You can check this entry if you want to look at a variety of worlds of one particular dimensionality. If, again, you are interested in speed, you should use the Controls World dialog to set the dimensionality to two. But another time you might want to look at a series of three-dimensional worlds, and this could be done by setting dimensionality to three on the Controls World menu, checking the But Don't Randomize Dimensionality entry, and repeatedly randomizing World or Everything.

Walls. *Boppers* runs at about the same speed with or without walls around the edge of the arena. Generally, walled worlds don't look as nice when you scroll them. But here again, you have the option of picking walls or no walls from the Controls World menu, checking the But Don't Randomize Walls entry, and then using the Randomize selections to look at a slew of this kind of world.

Bopper Type. If your machine does not have a math coprocessor, the turmites will run noticeably faster than the other types. In this case, you may well want to use the Controls Individuals dialog to set all boppers' Bopper Type parameters to Turmite. Then make sure that the But Don't Randomize Bopper Type entry is checked before randomizing.

CAs. The CAs, or cellular automata, take up many extra computation cycles, so if you are interested in maximum speed while Randomizing things, you will want to check But Don't Randomize CAs and then turn CAs off by using the Controls World dialog or Controls CAs popup.

Clear Screen and Exit

The *Clear Screen* selection is self-explanatory: it erases everything on the screen and starts all the boppers on a fresh trail. If food or poison patches are present, these patches are restored to solidity. Note that the Clear Screen selection does *not* erase the contents of the CA patch, if such a cellular automaton patch is active.

The Exit selection closes down the *Boppers* program, including any *Boppers* dialogs that might be open. After you make the Exit selection, the *Ready To Exit Boppers* dialog appears with the question, "Save Current Parameters And Genes?" If you answer "Yes," a Save Experiment command is carried out, saving the current parameters and genes to a file called ACTIVE.BEX.

ACTIVE.BEX will be placed in whichever directory is currently active in the File Open and File Save common dialog boxes. Generally, this will in fact be the home BOPPERS directory, but sometimes it will end up being another directory.

If you answer "No," no attempt to write an ACTIVE.BEX file is made, and the next time you open *Boppers* the same old ACTIVE.BEX (if there is such a file on your disk) will be used again.

When *Boppers* is started, the program looks for an ACTIVE.BEX file and does an Open Experiment on it, loading the parameters and genes so that your program starts right where you left off.

Boppers first looks for ACTIVE.BEX in the BOPPERS directory, then in the WINDOWS directory, and then in whatever directories are in the standard search path. Confusion can arise if you have ACTIVE.BEX files in several different directories. It's a good practice to search out and destroy any stray ACTIVE.BEX files every now and then.

If *Boppers* does not find an ACTIVE.BEX, it starts with randomized genes and some hardcoded parameters that are identical to the parameters in START.BL. This will work even if no START.BL is present—so that a naked BOPPER.EXE file can still run. If there is in fact no START.BL, *Boppers* creates one after starting up from its hardcoded parameters.

CONTROLS MENU

The Controls menu allows you to open dialog boxes that control the parameter settings of the World, the Ecology, the Colonies, and the individual boppers. The Controls menu also includes a popup menu that controls the CAs, or cellular automata. If you look ahead, you can see a picture of the Controls menu in Figure 6-11, with some secondary popups hanging off it.

When using the dialog boxes from the Controls menu, keep in mind that, with the exception of the World dialog, the boppers will keep moving and evolving even while these dialogs are open. It is sometimes convenient to leave a frequently used dialog open, perhaps dragging it by the title bar to one corner of the screen. The program will, however, suspend updating the boppers for as long as the World dialog is open.

World Dialog

The World dialog allows you to change various global features of the *Boppers* world, including: the number of boppers in each color-coded colony, the lengths of the trail the boppers in each colony leave, whether the world wraps around or has walls at its edges, whether the world is two or three dimensional, whether the world has patches of food or poison, whether the world includes a maze of walls, and whether the world includes a CA patch that runs a cellular automaton rule. A picture of the World dialog is shown in Figure 6-4.

The boppers suspend their motion for as long as the World dialog is open. The changes you make on the World dialog do not take effect until you press the DO IT! button. The DO IT! button closes the World dialog, makes the requested changes, and

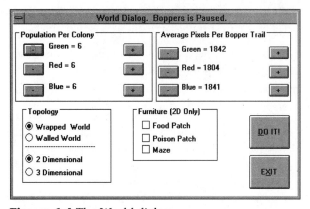

Figure 6-4 The World dialog

sets the boppers back into motion. If after making some changes you decide not to implement them, use the EXIT button to close the World dialog and to set the program back into motion where you left off.

The World dialog behaves slightly differently in the two- and three-dimensional cases. Let us first discuss how it behaves in the two-dimensional case and then discuss the differences in the three-dimensional case.

Population Per Colony Group

You can use the – and + buttons in the Population Per Colony group to adjust the number of boppers in each colony. The largest total number of boppers allowed is 27, and the smallest total number allowed is one. Sometimes you may need to reduce the size of one of the other colonies in order to be able to increase the size of a particular chosen colony. When you add boppers to a colony, the new boppers have their parameters adjusted to match the parameters of the highest scoring member of that colony, but their genes are left unchanged.

Average Pixels Per Bopper Trail Group

You will notice that as the boppers move along, they usually erase their oldest trail cells. In order to keep track of which cells still need to be erased, each colony has access to some fixed amount of memory—enough for 42,666 trail cells per colony in the two-dimensional case.

The – and + buttons of the Average Pixels Per Bopper Trail allow you to adjust the lengths of the trails of the boppers in each of the three colonies. If a colony has a low population, its members can have an accordingly longer maximum trail length, up to the maximum of 4,266 cells if the colony has only one member. The shortest trail length allowed is two pixels.

Whenever possible, a colony's average trail length value is kept the same when you adjust the population of the colony. But if adding additional colony members would force the total trail length to an unacceptably high value, the average trail length is adjusted downward.

The average trail length per colony member is just that: an *average*. A bopper that leaves larger trail markings (by having a nonzero radius or by drawing lines between its nodes) will get to use more of its colony's trail record resource than boppers that leave a simple trail of dots.

If you keep pressing the + button for a trail length, the trail length eventually changes from a number to the phrase "Permanent Trail." This means that the old trail cells of this colony will not be erased (unless the screen is cleared). This option sometimes produces interesting visual effects.

While on the subject of visual effects, note that fairly short trail lengths give the most dynamic looking effects of motion. Longer trail lengths, on the other hand, build up complex and intricate structures that might be thought of as bopper nests.

One further consideration in changing trail lengths is that these parameters affect the ecology in which the boppers live—if trail lengths are short, then boppers will run into other bopper trails less frequently. Over time, this has an effect on the boppers' evolution.

Topology Group

This group has two pairs of radio buttons: Wrapped World and Walled World, and 2 Dimensional and 3 Dimensional. In a wrapped world, any bopper that runs off one edge of the screen comes back on the opposite edge. In a walled world, a gray wall line is drawn around the edges of the bopper world. When a turmite's motion would make it run into a wall, the turmite normally stops short of hitting the wall but assigns itself a *wall value* change in its Score, where *wall value* can be adjusted in the Controls Ecology dialog. The boids look ahead and turn to avoid hitting the walls.

When you scroll a screen with walls on it, the walls scroll along with the world.

Details on the difference between the two-dimensional and three-dimensional worlds are in the "Three-Dimensional Case" subsection.

Furniture Group

The Furniture group checkboxes can be used to specify that the *Boppers* world includes a gold patch of food, a mauve patch of poison, and/or a gray maze of walls.

The boppers' Scores are adjusted when they encounter these furnishings by the amounts of the *food value*, *poison value*, and *wall value* that are set in the Controls Ecology dialog. The turmites use a different part of their lookup tables when they encounter food, poison, or a wall, and tend to move differently in these regions. Although the boids' Scores are changed by crossing the food or poison patches or the maze walls, they do not sense these objects from afar; a boid only sees the other boids and possibly the walls at the edge of the world.

The *Boppers* program keeps track of how many food cells and poison cells are present at any given time. If the food patch or poison patch is on, and the count of that type of cell falls below the hardcoded minimum value of 350, then a fresh food or poison patch is drawn at some random location in the world.

Each time you turn the Maze option on, the program draws a new spiral maze with a random position and a randomly determined number of turns. A food patch is placed at the center of the maze.

If you don't like the first maze you get, you can change it by the following slightly tedious procedure: open the World dialog, turn the maze checkbox off, press the DO IT! button, reopen the Word dialog, turn the maze checkbox on, and press the DO IT! button again.

The maze is intended to act as an impermeable group of walls that boppers try to find their way to the center of. This works correctly for a bopper with a low speed such as one, and with a low windrose number such as eight. (You can alter the boppers' speeds and windroses by using the Individuals dialog under the Controls popup.)

A picture of a *Boppers* world with a maze appears in Figure 7-19 in the next chapter.

The boids generally plow right through maze walls, and many turmites do not work well with the maze either. Turmites that draw lines for their trail tend to pock the maze's walls, and turmites that use a high speed or a high windrose number may sometimes step right over one of the maze's walls. The moral is that you need to adjust the types of boppers present in order to have the maze behave in the expected way.

Whenever you make the File Clear Screen selection, the poison patch, food patch, and maze will be redrawn in their most recent position, if present.

Three-Dimensional Case

If you choose the 3 Dimensional radio button in the Topology group of the Controls World dialog, the world of the boppers becomes three dimensional.

In the two-dimensional case, the world of the boppers is an array of cells of about the same size as the array of pixels on your screen. In the three-dimensional case, the world of the boppers acquires depth; you can think of it as extending in past the screen. The exact depth of a three-dimensional boppers world is set to be the same as the world's height.

There are two ways to notice when the world of the boppers is three dimensional. First of all, a different set of body icons is used in the three-dimensional case. Each bopper receives an icon which is drawn smaller as the bopper moves farther away and larger as the bopper moves closer. Secondly, the trails of the boppers are overlapped in the correct way, so that if one trail passes behind another, it does not break the line of the closer trail. This is particularly striking if the boppers are using the Thick Lines selection in the Parameter To Change group of the Controls Individuals dialog. Figures 7-2 and 7-3 in the next chapter show two views of three-dimensional worlds.

Due to memory considerations, you are not allowed to have poison, food, a maze, or a CA patch in a three-dimensional world, so the World dialog does not allow you to make these combinations of choices. That is, once you choose the 3 Dimensional button, the Food Patch, Poison Patch, Maze, Boppers and CA, and CA Only checkboxes and radio buttons cannot be turned on.

Another feature of the World dialog in the three-dimensional case is that all three colonies are required to have the same trail length. Pressing any of the – or + buttons in the Average Pixels Per Bopper Trail group will change the trail length values of all three colonies at the same time. The reason for this limitation has to do with the algorithm used to correctly order or *zbuffer* the trails according to their distance behind the screen.

If the Walled World button is chosen, the three-dimensional world acts like a fish-tank, with top, bottom, sides, front, and back. If the Wrapped World button is chosen, the three-dimensional world wraps front/back as well as left/right and up/down.

The front/back wrap means that if a bopper moves out through the front of the screen, it reappears back at the deepest part of the world, and if it goes out the back, it reappears at the front. In terms of the icon sizes in a wrapped three-dimensional world, the first case corresponds to an icon that gets larger and then suddenly gets small; the second case corresponds to an icon that gets smaller and smaller and then suddenly gets big.

Most first-time viewers of the wrapped three-dimensional mode have to make a little effort to wrap their minds around what's happening, but it's really no more unnatural than things flying off the left of the screen and coming back on the right.

Ecology Dialog

The Ecology dialog, which is shown in Figure 6-5, enables you to adjust the Eat Values of the *Boppers* colors. Each bopper keeps a running Score based on the total Eat Values of the cells it crosses. The higher a bopper's Score is, the more likely it is that the bopper will continue behaving in the same way.

You can set the entries in the Eat Values group individually, or you can choose patterns of Eat Values by pushing one of the radio buttons in the Preset Eat Values group.

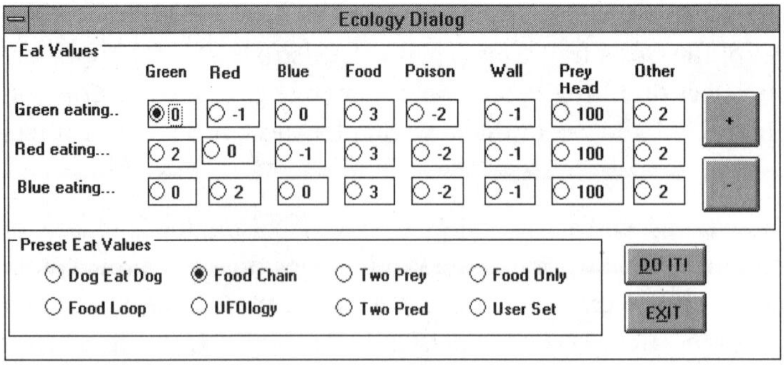

Ecology Dialog

Eat Values

	Green	Red	Blue	Food	Poison	Wall	Prey Head	Other
Green eating..	0	-1	0	3	-2	-1	100	2
Red eating...	2	0	-1	3	-2	-1	100	2
Blue eating...	0	2	0	3	-2	-1	100	2

Preset Eat Values

- ○ Dog Eat Dog ● Food Chain ○ Two Prey ○ Food Only
- ○ Food Loop ○ UFOlogy ○ Two Pred ○ User Set

DO IT! EXIT

Figure 6-5 The Ecology dialog

Keep in mind that Ecology is a *real-time* dialog box, so if you want to apply some changes you must press DO IT! before pressing EXIT.

Eat Values Group

The Eat Values group of the Controls Ecology dialog sets out the Eat Values for each of the possible encounters between a bopper and a differently colored cell of its world. We use three colonies, and we distinguish eight different score colors in the world. Therefore, the Eat Values group takes the form of a three-by-eight table of 24 entries.

The table values can be changed by choosing the radio button next to the value to be changed, and by then choosing the + button or the – button.

Each row of the table corresponds to the Eat Values for one colony. The first row gives the values that members of the Green colony get for eating each of the eight possible score colors. In the same fashion, the second row gives the values that members of the Green colony get for eating each of the eight possible score colors, and the third row gives the values that members of the Blue colony get for eating each of the eight possible score colors.

The eight non-blank score colors are: *Green, Red, Blue, Food, Poison, Wall, Prey Head,* and *Other*. No scores are ever awarded for the blank, or background cells.

If you look closely at the trails of the boppers, you may notice that Green, Red, and Blue come in both faint and strong shades (it helps to use the Lens). The two shades are scored the same.

If a bopper has been assigned a *positive* Eat Value for some other colony's trail cells, then we say that the bopper views that colony as *prey*. If a bopper has been assigned a *negative* Eat Value for the trails of some other colony, then we say that the bopper views that colony as made of *predators*. We do not insist that the predator and prey nomenclature be completely logical; for instance it is possible for colony B to view colony A as prey even though A already views B as prey.

Food, Poison, and Wall are gold, mauve, and gray, respectively.

If you turn off the Body Icons and look closely at the boppers, you will notice that each bopper has a moving dot, or *head*, at its growing end. Occasionally one bopper's head will land on another bopper's head. If the first bopper views the second bopper as *prey*, then the first bopper is awarded the Prey Head Eat Value. If the bopper happens to be a boid, it need only come within the Boid Hit Radius of a prey head to receive the Prey Head Eat Value; Boid Hit Radius being a parameter which is found on the Colonies menu.

The Other score color includes all colors other than the ones I've already mentioned! Other colors arise in two ways: from trail overlaps and from CAs. When two bopper trails cross each other, the colors are combined. That is, a Red and a Blue make a purple (not the same as the Poison mauve), a Red and a Green make a yellow (not the same as the Food gold), a Blue and a Green make an aqua, and a Blue, Red, and Green make a shade of white. These colors are all viewed as Other.

If you have a cellular automaton patch running, the patch can produce a wide range of colors. Some of these colors may be the same as score colors, and will be treated as such, but some of them may also be Other colored.

Note again that the *Boppers* background color (which can be set to either white or black from the Tools Colors popup) does *not* count as Other color. For scoring purposes, the background color is ignored.

You can use the mouse or the arrow key to move among the Ecology radio buttons. Although radio buttons are sometimes used to take actions, in the Ecology dialog they are simply used to highlight or activate different Eat Values. Once you have highlighted the Eat Value you want to change, clicking on the + button increases the highlighted value, and clicking on the − button decreases the highlighted value. The amount of the increase or decrease is always one, except for the Prey Head Eat Values, which change in increments of ten.

Preset Eat Values Group

The *Preset Eat Values* are a group of radio buttons you can choose in order to set the Eat Values to certain standard values. The selections are: *Dog Eat Dog, Food Loop, Food Chain, UFOlogy, Two Prey, Two Pred, Food Only*, and *User Set*.

You cannot directly choose User Set. This selection becomes active after you use the + or − button to directly change one of individual Eat Values.

All the other Preset Eat Values selections assign –1, 0, or 2 to Green, Red, and Blue and the following standard values to the remaining colors: Food = 3, Poison = –2, Wall = 0, Prey Head = 100, and Other = 0. In addition, all the Preset Eat Values selections assign 0 to Green eating Green, 0 to Red eating Red, and 0 to Blue eating Blue.

The motivation behind these standard values is that the boppers will be more likely to move about and interact with other boppers if the net score gain from moving is likely to be positive. Thus, eating a prey trail is worth 2, but encountering a predator trail only costs –1. Food is to be slightly more valuable than prey, and Poison is to be slightly worse than a predator. We give a big reward for encountering a Prey head, and we avoid complicating things further by assigning values of 0 to Wall and Other.

Dog Eat Dog lets each colony view the other two colonies as prey.

Food Chain has Green on the bottom viewing Red as a predator, Red viewing Green as prey and Blue as predator, and Blue viewing Red as predator. You can think of the green boppers as plants, the red boppers as plant-eating animals, and the blue boppers as UFOs that eat the animals.

Food Loop extends the Food Chain settings by bending the food chain around into a cycle, with Green viewing Blue as prey and Blue viewing Green as a predator. Although Food Loop does not easily fit into a logical story about what the boppers are doing, it has the advantage of making every colony's scoring possibilities the same. In this sense, Food Loop is the most symmetric setting.

In *UFOlogy*, the red boppers are again like animals that feed on Green and fear Blue. Here the Blue still feeds on the Red. The difference here is that the Green likes eating both Red and Blue. The story is that the Reds are cows and the Blues are cattle-mutilating flying saucers. The Greens are grass which grows well in the manure of the cattle. And the grass grows *especially* well near the flying saucers. Why? Because the saucers' mighty antigravity drives fix prodigious amounts of nitrogen in the soil!

Two Prey has Blue viewing Green and Red as prey, with both Green and Red viewing Blue as predator.

Two Pred has Red and Blue viewing Green as prey, with Green viewing both Red and Blue as predator.

Food Only sets all colony Eat Values to zero.

User Set is automatically selected whenever you use the + and - buttons to change individual Eat Values by hand.

Colonies Dialog

The *Colonies* dialog, which is shown in Figure 6-6, controls the parameters having to do with the ways in which the individual colonies breed and assign fitness to their members.

The Colonies dialog includes three main groups: the Timed Breeding group, the Hit Breeding group, and the Additional Fitness Measures group.

The Colonies dialog shows the parameter values for one colony at a time. This colony is called the *edit colony*. Each time you click on the Edit Colony radio button, the edit colony changes.

When you have arranged the edit colony's parameters to your liking, you can apply these values by pressing the top gray button on the lower right, which will be labelled DO IT TO GREEN!, DO IT TO RED!, or DO IT TO BLUE!. If you want to apply the edit colony's parameters to *all* the colonies, then press the DO IT TO ALL! button.

Keep in mind that Colonies is a *real-time* dialog box, so that if you want to apply some changes you must press one of the DO IT buttons before pressing EXIT. Note also that if you change the values for one colony and then use the Edit Colony button to view the values for another colony, the changes to the original colony will be lost unless you first press a DO IT button.

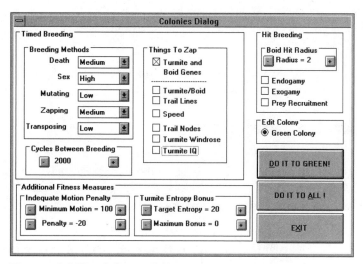

Figure 6-6 The Colonies dialog

Timed Breeding Versus Hit Breeding

Timed Breeding means that after some fixed number of cycles, the colony members undergo a breeding process which changes some of their properties. The fixed number of cycles appears in the Cycles Between Breeding box. If the Cycles Between Breeding shows the phrase, "No Breeding," then the timed breeding process is never performed for that colony.

One *caveat* that should be mentioned here is that Timed Breeding is *suspended* as long as either the Individuals dialog box or the Gene Viewer dialog box is open. The reason for this is that Timed Breeding can greatly change the information that these two dialogs display.

One essential characteristic of the Time Breeding process is that the *population size of the colony does not change*. Timed Breeding simply replaces the existing members of the colony by new members, some of whom will be copies or combinations of the old members.

In addition to Timed Breeding, a colony can change the properties of its members by a *Hit Breeding* process. Hit Breeding can take place whenever two individual boppers' heads come close to each other. Hit Breeding happens sporadically rather than at fixed intervals like Timed Breeding. It is possible to have a colony use *only* Timed Breeding, *only* Hit Breeding, or *both* Timed Breeding and Hit Breeding.

Unlike Timed Breeding, there *is* one kind of Hit Breeding that allows the size of a colony to change. This Hit Breeding method is known as *Prey Recruitment*, and it means that a colony member can force a member of a prey colony to join the colony.

The Timed Breeding Group includes three subgroups: *Breeding Methods*, *Things To Zap*, and *Cycles Between Breeding*.

Breeding Methods Group

There are five Breeding Methods: *Death*, *Sex*, *Mutating*, *Zapping*, and *Transposition*. Each method has a combo box that displays some of the options: None, Low, Medium, High, and Very High. (Refer back to Chapter 3, *Genetic Algorithms,* for more details on breeding methods.)

Death allows the options Low, Medium, or High. Death is an unavoidable prerequisite if evolution is going to happen; so there's no way to have *None*!

The way death works in a bopper colony is that when breeding happens, each bopper has a certain probability of getting to pass one or several copies of itself for the next generation. The boppers with the higher scores have better chances of successfully copying themselves than do the lower-scoring boppers.

We always adjust this process so that a medium scoring bopper is allowed, on the average, to have *one* representative of itself in the next generation—the average-scoring boppers, in other words, don't multiply themselves, nor do they die out.

The best scoring boppers, on the other hand, may be able to pass two versions of themselves to the next generation, while the worst scoring boppers may not survive into the next generation. The net effect is that the best-scoring boppers use up the memory slots of the worst-scoring boppers.

The Low, Medium, High, and Very High Death levels adjust the steepness of the gradient between the worst and best boppers. To be precise, a Low Death level means that the most successful bopper will, on the average, get to pass 1.1 versions of itself to the next generation, while a Medium Death level gives the best bopper an average of 1.3 representatives, a High Death level gives the best bopper an average of 1.6 members of the next generation, and the Very High Death level gives the best bopper an average of 2.0 members in the next generation. These values are on the low side because we work with such low population sizes in *Boppers*, and we do not want the population diversity to get wiped out too quickly.

Note that when *Boppers* decides how many representatives each bopper gets, it is the *relative* numerical values of the scores that matter, rather than the actual numerical values. Thus, at High Death level, the best bopper will get 2.5 times as many representatives as the average bopper irregardless of whether its score is *five* or *five thousand* points higher than the average bopper in its colony.

Sex means that once you have decided which new bopper representatives go into the next generation, you choose pairs from the new group and mate them together. In mating, a crossover is performed on the two boppers' genes as discussed in Chapter 1, *Life and A-Life*. Sex does not change any bopper parameters other than the genes. If the bopper is not a turmite, an extra crossover is performed on the short segment of the bopper's DNA that controls the boid parameters, for otherwise this short segment would usually not get crossed over.

You can set the Sex level at None, meaning that no crossovers are performed. The Low, Medium, High, and Very High levels mean that, respectively, one-quarter, one-half, three-quarters, or *all* of the new boppers perform a crossover with exactly one other bopper.

Mutating means that each of the colony's boppers has some bits of its gene changed at random. Because each bopper's gene is a bitstring of zeroes and ones, a single mutation means choosing one of these bits and flipping its value—changing a zero to a one, or changing a one to a zero.

The Mutation level is managed as a *proportion of bits to be flipped*. The None, Low, Medium, High, and Very High Mutation levels correspond to bitflip proportions of 0.0, 0.0005, 0.001, 0.005, and 0.01. In other words, depending on the mutation level setting, the following ratio of each bopper's genetic bits are flipped: none, one two-thousandth, one thousandth, one two-hundredth, and one hundredth. If the case where the bopper has 16 states, it will have about two thousand bits of DNA, meaning that, depending on whether the mutation level is None, Low, Medium, High, or Very High, the bopper will have 0, 1, 2, 10, or 20 bits flipped. If the bopper has 128 states (the maximum), the number of bits flipped will be, respectively, 0, 8, 16, 80, and 160 each time that the bopper's colony undergoes Timed Breeding.

Zapping is a radical process whereby a bopper is randomized or "zapped," according to which boxes in the Things To Zap group are checked. The Zapping level can be None, Low, Medium, or High.

A Zapping level of Low means that the worst-scoring bopper is zapped with a probability of one-half. Medium Zapping means that the colony's *worst-scoring bopper* is *always* zapped when Timed Breeding takes place; and High Zapping means that the second worst-scoring bopper always gets zapped as well.

Transposing is a process whereby sections of the genetic bitstring are swapped, as discussed in Chapter 1, *Life and A-Life*. The purpose of Zapping is to try something completely new, and the purpose of Transposing is to try to make a good thing better. Accordingly, Transposing is applied to the colony's *best-scoring* bopper.

The Transposing levels are implemented as a probability of doing a transposition on the genome of the best-scoring bopper when Timed Breeding takes place. The Transposing levels None, Low, Medium, and High correspond to these respective probabilities: zero, one-third, two-thirds, and one. More information on the exact nature of transposition appears in the section on the Tools menu Gene Viewer dialog.

For handy reference, the various numbers that regulate the levels of the Timed Breeding Methods are listed in Table 6-1.

Level

	None	Low	Medium	High	Very High
Death	NA	1.1	1.33	1.66	2.0
Sex	0.0	0.25	0.50	0.75	1.0
Mutating	0.0	0.0005	0.001	0.005	0.01
Zapping	0.0	0.5	1.0	2.0	NA
Transposing	0.0	0.33	0.66	1.0	NA

Table 6-1 The numbers behind the Timed Breeding Methods

In consulting Table 6-1, remember that the Death numbers tell how many representatives the colony's most successful member is likely to get in the next generation, the Sex numbers tell what percentage of the new colony members *do it*, the Mutating numbers tell what percentage of the new colony members' bits get flipped, the Zapping numbers tell how many low-scoring members get zapped, and the Transposing numbers give the probability that the best-scoring member will be transposed.

Things To Zap Group

The *Things To Zap* group allows you to control which bopper properties are affected by Zapping. Although the other Breeding Methods only do things to the genetic bitstring of the boppers, the Zapping Method is allowed to change bopper parameters in addition to changing the boppers' genes.

You can check any combination of the Things To Zap selections. The selections are: *Turmite and Boid Genes, Turmite/Boid, Trail Lines, Speed, Trail Nodes, Turmite Windrose,* and *Turmite IQ.*

Turmite and Boid Genes refers to the genetic bitstring that determines the turmite lookup tables as well as the boid motion variables. Generally, you want to keep this one checked.

The remaining Things To Zap selections are all specific parameters that affect bopper behavior independently of the genes. If some of these boxes are checked, you will observe that the behavior and appearance of your boppers changes over time—provided that Zapping is set to Low, Medium, or High, and provided that the Cycles Between Breeding box is not set to No Breeding.

Turmite/Boid refers to the parameter that controls whether a particular bopper acts like a turmite, a boid, a wolf, a beaver, or a dog.

Trail Lines is the parameter that decides whether a bopper draws lines between its successive positions.

Speed is the parameter that controls how far a bopper can move with each step.

Trail Nodes is the parameter that decides if the successive positions of a bopper are drawn as dots or as squares.

Turmite Windrose is the parameter that determines how many different directions a turmite can move in.

Turmite IQ is the parameter that specifies how many internal states a turmite has.

Cycles Between Breeding Group

The Cycles Between Breeding group controls how often a particular colony applies its Breeding Methods. The time is measured in *cycles*, where a cycle is one complete update of all the active boppers. Depending on your machine and on the properties of the world currently being run, *Boppers* might run at anywhere from, say, 5 to 75 cycles per second.

Generally, you want the Cycles Between Breeding to be long enough so that the boppers have enough time to develop a spread in their scores that is based on more than temporary positional advantages. On the other hand, you don't want Cycles Between Breeding to be terribly infrequent, for otherwise evolution happens too slowly. Two thousand is a pretty reasonable number.

The Cycles Between Breeding is decreased or increased by pressing the – and + buttons. If you keep pressing the + button, the phrase "No Breeding" appears, which means that Timed Breeding is now turned off for this colony (provided you press one of the DO IT! buttons).

Hit Breeding Group

Hit Breeding can occur when two boppers' heads are near each other. This breeding method was discussed in some detail in Chapter 5, *Boppers and Their World*.

A turmite bopper is said to *hit* another bopper's head only if the turmite's head is directly on top of the other bopper's head. If a boid bopper's head is within its colony's Boid Hit Radius of another bopper's head it is also said to *hit* the other bopper's head. More precisely, it is necessary for the boid bopper's distance in pixels from the other bopper's head to be *less than* the Boid Hit Radius. If the Boid Hit Radius is one, only a direct hit will do, while a Boid Hit Radius of two, allows a boid to say it has hit a head when the head is really in the pixel next door. Higher Boid Hit Radius values make it easier and easier for a boid to hit another bopper's head.

You can use the - and + buttons to set a colony's Boid Hit Radius to any value between 1 and 10. As just mentioned, a Boid Hit Radius of 1 means that only a direct hit will count.

Remember that a bopper views another bopper as *prey* provided that the other bopper's trails show a positive Eat Value for the bopper on the Controls popup's Ecology dialog.

When a bopper hits another bopper's head and the other bopper is viewed as prey, then the bopper is awarded the Prey Head Eat Value from the Controls popup's Ecology dialog.

The bopper's colony's settings for the three Colonies dialog checkboxes: (Endogamy, Exogamy, and Prey Recruitment) affect the results of a bopper hitting another bopper's head. In discussing these three checkboxes, we assume that the bopper has indeed hit the other bopper's head.

If *Endogamy* is checked for the bopper's colony, and the other bopper is in the same colony, then the two boppers do a crossover on their genomes, replacing their two former genomes by the two crossed-over genomes.

If *Exogamy* is checked for the bopper's colony and the other bopper is in a different colony, then the bopper replaces its genome by a crossover of its genome with the other bopper's genome.

Now, if *Prey Recruitment* is checked and the bopper views the other bopper as prey, then the bopper will recruit the other bopper to its colony. As part of the recruitment process, the bopper copies its parameters onto the other bopper as well. In recruitment, the bopper does *not* copy its genome onto the other bopper—one idea behind recruitment is to try and get some new blood.

What happens when two boppers hit each other, and each views the other as prey, and each has its Prey Recruitment flag on? We flip a virtual coin to decide who gets to recruit whom.

Additional Fitness Measures Group

Thanks to Death, Timed Breeding always has the effect that higher-scoring boppers are more likely to have their information preserved. So how we determine the boppers' scores can have a big effect on their evolution.

So far, we have only talked about boppers changing their scores as a result of eating things. The Additional Fitness Measures group specifies two extra ways of changing a bopper's score: the Inadequate Motion Penalty and the Turmite Entropy Bonus. These two adjustments to boppers' scores are made at the start of the colony's Timed Breeding process.

The Inadequate Motion Penalty specifies a *Penalty* (always zero or negative) that is added to a bopper's score if it has not managed to move a total distance of *Minimum Distance* pixels from the position it was in the last time Timed Breeding took place. The pixel distance is measured in the "taxicab" metric, meaning the horizontal distance plus the vertical distances (plus the depth distance, in the three-dimensional case).

The Inadequate Motion Penalty can be used to penalize boppers that just stay in one place—the ones sometimes called *polygon* boppers. Of course, if you want to be perverse, you can set the Penalty to a positive value, and *reward* do-nothing boppers!

The Turmite Entropy Bonus specifies a *Maximum Bonus*. At breeding time, each bopper receives a bonus anywhere from 0 on up to the Maximum Bonus according to how closely its Entropy matches the *Target Entropy* value. The Turmite Entropy Maximum Bonus is always a *positive* number.

We define a turmite's Entropy to be a quantity that ranges from 0 and 100, and the Target Entropy is always between 0 and 100 as well. The purpose of using the Turmite Entropy Bonus controls is to try and make turmites evolve toward some desired level of Target Entropy.

Individuals Dialog

The *Individuals dialog*, which is shown in Figure 6-7, controls what we called the *Enzyme Parameters* of the individual boppers in Chapter 5, *The Boppers and Their World*. This dialog has two groups: the Scope of Changes Group and the Parameter to Change group.

The Individuals dialog shows the parameter values for one bopper at a time. This bopper is called the *edit bopper*, and its colony is the *edit colony*. If your cursor is in the default arrow-shaped pick cursor mode, you can change the edit bopper by left-clicking on one of the boppers outside the Individuals dialog window. (If the cursor is in some other mode, you can change to pick cursor mode by using the Tools popup's Cursor popup menu to select Pick.)

You use the Individuals dialog to make changes by:

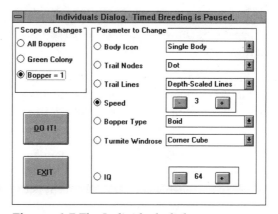

Figure 6-7 The Individuals dialog

1. Choosing a scope for the changes to make

2. Choosing a parameter to change

3. Adjusting the parameter to the desired value

4. Choosing the DO IT! button to change that parameter over the chosen scope

Note that *Boppers* is a real-time dialog, meaning that the changes you make will be implemented as soon as you press the DO IT! button. You need to press the DO IT! button for each parameter change that you want to make. A common mistake is to make several parameter changes in a row, without pressing the DO IT! button after each change.

One thing to remember about the Individuals dialog is that the Timed Breeding process is suspended for as long as the Individuals dialog is left open. This is so that you can use the Individuals dialog in peace without having its values unexpectedly change each time Timed Breeding takes place. So you should make a habit of closing the Individuals dialog when it is not in use so that Timed Breeding can carry out its task of evolution.

Scope of Changes Group

The *Scope of Changes* group contains three radio buttons: All Boppers, [Edit Colony] Colony, and Bopper = [Edit Bopper]. The [Edit Colony] space contains one of the words "Green," "Red," or "Blue", and the [Edit Bopper] space contains a number between 1 and 27. When you open the Individuals dialog, the edit bopper will be the same as the bopper that has the edit icon on screen, and the edit colony will be the same as the edit bopper's colony.

If you repeatedly click the Colony radio button, the edit colony will change. The bopper being shown after you change edit colonies is the highest scoring bopper of the colony.

If you repeatedly click the bopper radio button, the edit bopper will change. The displayed numbers of the boppers normally will *not* be consecutive; they relate to the location of that bopper's data in the program and are of no real significance. As you change the edit bopper, the edit colony changes to match.

When you press DO IT!, the active parameter in the Boppers Parameters group will be changed to the displayed value for the active scope. According to which of the Scope of Changes radio buttons is active, the scope will be either all the boppers, or all the boppers in the edit colony, or the edit bopper only.

Parameter to Change Group

The *Parameter to Change* group contains seven radio buttons with a control group to the right of each button. The buttons are: *Body Icon, Trail Nodes, Trail Lines, Speed, Bopper Type, Turmite Windrose,* and *IQ.*

You can activate a radio button either by choosing it directly, or by choosing its control group. If you press the DO IT! button, the boppers specified by the Scope of Changes group change the activated parameter to the displayed value for that parameter.

Body Icon Group

The *Body Icon* button activates a combo box with the following selections: *No Body, Single Body,* and *Body Trail.*

The *No Body* selection means that the head of the bopper is simply shown as white or black—depending on whether the background color is black or white. The *Single Body* selection means that a moving icon is drawn near the position of the bopper's head. The *Body Trail* selection means that a series of identical icons is drawn for the bopper; one icon at each successive position of its head.

If a Body Trail bopper has had its colony's World Dialog Average Pixels Per Bopper Trail set to Permanent Trail, the Body Trail icons will accumulate indefinitely. Otherwise, the body corresponding to the oldest trail position will be erased each time a new body is added. A picture of a bopper's body trail can be seen in Figure 7-7 in the next chapter.

The presence or absence of body icons does not affect the underlying *Boppers* computation, although the Single Body and the Body Trail options both slow the program down by the same small amount per bopper. The slowdown is due to the time it takes to show a new body bitmap and erase an old one.

The body icons are not drawn inside the active Lens area. When Body Trail boppers are present, scrolling the screen with the *Boppers* window scroll bars will wipe away the Body Trail icons, uncovering the real computation's patterns underneath. When old Body Trail icons are erased, this also wipes away Body Trail icons; giving an effect a bit like a moving eraser.

The body icons are bitmaps that were created with the Windows Paintbrush Accessory. They were drawn by Tom Knight of Wizard, Inc.

Trail Nodes Group

We refer to a bopper's successive positions as *nodes*. At each node, a bopper marks a pixel. A bopper may also draw squares around its nodes, and it may draw lines connecting its nodes.

The boppers receive the appropriate Eat Value for every pixel they draw over, so boppers that make more complicated trails are likely to have wider swings in their score levels.

Also note that a bopper sets its current ReadColorCode not only on the basis of the pixel at the next node, but also on the basis of the pixel colors the bopper draws over. This means that a bopper's behavior will usually change when trail lines and/or node squares are added.

Boppers with complicated trails use up larger amounts of their colony's trail memory resources, so you may want to increase a colony's World dialog Average Pixels Per Bopper Trail values when you make the colony members' trails more complicated.

At each step, every bopper computes whether to mark its trail with light or with dark versions of its colony color, and at each step it makes all its trail marks in the same color.

At any time, a bopper's head is at its *current node*. In addition, a bopper keeps track of its *old node* and its *old old node*—that is, of its most recent and second most recent positions. At each step, a bopper creates its trail markings in the following order: (1) mark a pixel at the old node, (2) draw a square around the old old node, (3) draw a line between the old node and the current node, leaving out the end points. More details on this are in the The "Update Cycle" section of Chapter 5, *Boppers and Their World*.

The *Trail Nodes* button activates a combo box with the following selections: *Dot, Small Squares, Medium Squares*, and *Large Squares*. In each case, a dot is drawn at the bopper's

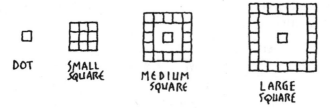

Figure 6-8 The four kinds of Trail Nodes

most recent position. If one of the Squares is selected, a square is drawn around the bopper's next most recent position as well. Depending on whether the Square is Small, Medium, or Large, the radius of the square will be larger, as shown in Figure 6-8.

Trail Lines Group

The *Trail Lines* button has different selections, depending on whether the Controls popup's World dialog Topology group is set to 2 Dimensional or 3 Dimensional.

In the 2 Dimensional case, the selections are *No Lines* and *Thin Lines*. *Thin Lines* means that a one-pixel-wide line is drawn from the bopper's last position to its current position, and *No Lines* means no line is drawn.

In the 3 Dimensional case, the selections are: *No Lines*, *Thin Lines*, *Edged Thin Lines*, *Thick Lines*, and *Depth-Scaled Lines*, as shown in Figure 6-9. The *No Lines* and the *Thin Lines* selections have the same meaning as in the 2 Dimensional case.

The reason for having the additional three-dimensional Trail Lines selections is that when *Boppers* is in 3 Dimensional mode, the markings on the screen are painted in the correct depth order, with the nearer marking being drawn over the more distant markings. This can do a lot to promote the impression that you really are looking in at a three-dimensional scene. The wider the lines are, the easier it is to see which one lies in front of which. The drawback to using wider lines is that it makes *Boppers* run slower.

The *Edged Thin Lines* selection adds an edging of one background-colored pixel to either side of each line for a total line width of three.

The *Thick Lines* selection keeps the two edge pixels and increases the colored line center to a width of three pixels for a total line width of five pixels.

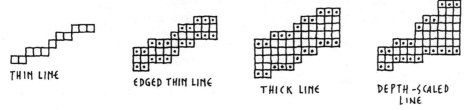

THIN LINE   EDGED THIN LINE   THICK LINE   DEPTH-SCALED LINE

Figure 6-9 The three-dimensional Trail Lines

The *Depth-Scaled Lines* selection lets the width of the lines depend on the distance the bopper is behind the screen: the closer boppers have wider lines. Here the minimum colored line width is one, and the maximum is 17. In each case, a single background pixel edge is added to either side of the lines.

Note that if the World Dialog Topology group is set to Wrapped World, the Depth-Scaled lines will change from thin to thick or thick to thin when the boppers wrap around the depth axis of their world. A peculiarity of the *Boppers* Depth-Scaled Lines algorithm is that the depth-scaled lines have right-angled nicks in them at the positions where the lines change between having a gentle and steep slope—that is, at the positions where the lines pass through having a forty-five degree diagonal slant on the screen.

Although a three-dimensional bopper with a Thin Lines trail will act differently from a bopper with a No Lines trail, the Thin Lines, Edged Thin Lines, Thick Lines, and Depth-Scaled Lines options all *do* give the same behavior. This is because the *Boppers* program stores the records of the additional "edging" pixels so that they are invisible to the boppers.

Speed Group

The *Speed* controls let you press – and + buttons to set the speed anywhere between one and 16. For all boppers, whether turmite or boid, the bopper's steps are multiplied by the speed factor. That is, if at some time a bopper would normally take a step of X horizontal pixels and Y vertical pixels, and if the bopper's speed is S, then the bopper will move S X horizontal pixels and S Y vertical pixels.

Changing a bopper's speed can affect its behavior quite dramatically. If a high speed bopper's Trail Lines option is set to No Lines, the bopper is likely to hop over more marked pixels and interact with its environment a bit less.

One cure for this is to set a high-speed bopper's Trail Lines selection to Thin Lines. When a bopper is drawing lines between nodes it *does* notice whatever intermediary pixels it passes over. Another bonus in using the Thin Lines option for higher-speed boppers is that this makes it easier to see the creatures' motions.

A final observation about speed is that you may want to use the higher speeds if you are using a high-resolution setting of your monitor, for higher speeds tend to generate larger patterns.

Bopper Type Group

There are five kinds of boppers: turmites, boids, wolves, beavers, and dogs. The latter three types are examples of *turboids*, which are combinations of turmite and boid. As a practical matter, turmites run a bit faster than the other types of boppers, especially on machines without math coprocessors. The Boid Hit Radius from the Colonies Dialog Hit Breeding group only applies to non-turmite boppers, and the Colonies Dialog Turmite Entropy Bonus only applies to non-boid boppers. In addition, the following Individuals dialog parameters apply only to non-boids: Turmite Windrose, and Turmite IQ. These "turmite parameters" are described in the following subsection.

Turmite Windrose Group

The *Turmite Windrose* group is a combo box that can be set to 4, 6, 8, 12, 16, 24, 32, 64, or 128. Each number represents a different set of directions that the turmite is allowed to move in, as illustrated in Figure 6-10. In the figure, the black dotted cells indicate the different windrose positions a turmite at the center cell could move to.

Let us think of a *pixel step* as being a horizontal, vertical, or diagonal move of one pixel. Note that within each windrose, every directional move comprises the same number of pixel steps. Therefore, we can speak of the *radius* of each windrose as the number of pixel steps each of that windrose's moves uses. The radii of the various windroses are shown in Table 6-2.

Windrose

	4	8	6	12	16	24	32	64	128
Radius	1	1	2	2	2	3	4	8	16

Table 6-2 Windrose radii in pixel steps

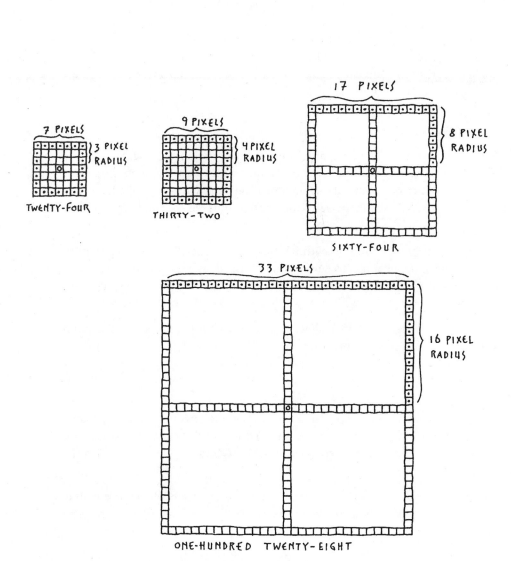

Figure 6-10 The Turmite Windroses

Often the high radii of the higher windroses precludes using them, for if the turmite patterns get too big, they do not fit well into the size of the screen. Unless you are using a very high-resolution monitor, or want boppers that really move around a lot, it's normally best to set the Speed parameter to 1 when using the higher windroses.

On the other hand, if you find yourself using a low radius windrose with a high Speed setting, you might consider lowering the speed and increasing the radius of the windrose. Thus, for instance, using the eight-direction windrose at a speed of three really just picks out eight of the possible moves that can be done on a 24-direction windrose at a speed of one. Your turmites will evolve to act more intelligently if they have more options at their disposal.

IQ Group

The *IQ* group controls how many internal states the bopper uses for turmite motion and for owl motion. Recall that a turmite is like a Turing machine that updates its internal state with each motion. The more states a turmite has access to, the more complicated its behavior can be—thus we use the phrase "IQ" to describe it.

Surprisingly enough, turmites with IQs of even one and two can do fairly intricate things if they happen to have a good set of genes. One approach to evolving a colony of turmites is, in fact, to let them run for a while at a low IQ value, and then later try doubling their IQ. This can be done in several stages.

The – button halves the active IQ value, and the + button doubles it. The minimum IQ is 1 and the maximum is 100.

CAs Popup

As well as having food and poison patches, *Boppers* allows you to have a changing patch that is filled with a cellular automaton, or CA. When a bopper crosses a CA patch, it eats whatever colors it finds there, and it seeds the CA with the trails that it leaves.

If a color found in a CA patch is not the same as any trail color, nor the same color as food, poison, or a wall, then the turmite's score is adjusted by the *other value* that is set on the Controls Ecology dialog. If other value is positive, then a messy CA will act like a source of food.

Running a CA is computationally expensive in direct proportion to the size of the CA patch. If you run a large CA, the program goes slower, with most of the time being spent on the CA and a negligible amount of time being spent on the boppers. So that this is not too boring to watch, *Boppers* updates the boppers several times as often as it updates the CA.

Due to considerations of memory and speed, there is a limit to the sizes of the CA patches *Boppers* allows. Each allowable patch must use at most as many cells as a square patch of 256 by 256 pixels. Patches can, however, be wider or taller than 256 if they are correspondingly shorter or narrower.

The *CAs popup* has 12 selections: CA On, CA Off, Select Rule, Select Palette, Boppers On, CA Wrap, Stretchable CA, Seed the CA, Blank the CA, Resize CA to Window, Less Cells, and More Cells, as shown in Figure 6-11. The following selections are toggle switches that can be either checked or unchecked: CA On, CA Off, Boppers On, CA Wrap, and Stretchable CA. When the CA On selection is not checked, none of the remaining selections do anything.

CA On turns on the CA computation. If you do not notice an effect from this selection, your CA patch is either very small, or it has not been seeded. Try following this selection with a Seed the CA selection.

CA Off turns off the CA computation, if one is active. This selection does not remove the CA patch from the screen. The patch will remain until it is eaten by the boppers or erased by the File Clear Screen selection.

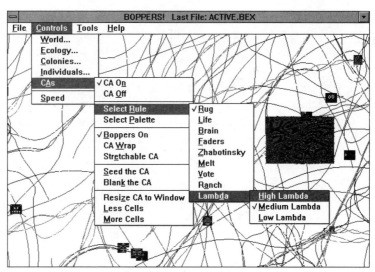

Figure 6-11 The Controls menu with the CAs popup and the Select Rule popup

As a shortcut, all of the remaining CAs popup selections have the side-effect of also turning the CA computation on.

Select Rule opens a secondary popup that lists nine kinds of CAs you can choose from. Their names are: *Rug, Life, Brain, Faders, Zhabotinsky, Melt, Vote, Ranch*, and *Lambda*; a brief explanation of what these rules do can be found in the section on Cellular Automata in Chapter 2, *Computer A-Life*.

The Lambda rule selection leads to a third-level popup that lets you choose High, Medium, or Low lambda values. The meaning of the lambda value is explained in Chapter 2. Each lambda rule is a randomly created rule; you can choose the Select Rule Lambda selection over and over to keep changing this random rule. In order to avoid having to use the popups, there is a control key combination (CONTROL)-(D) that randomizes the lambda rule automatically, as discussed in the section on Control Keys.

Select Palette opens a secondary popup that lists four kinds of palettes you can apply to the CA patch: *Standard, Random, Faders*, and *Melt*. The Standard, Faders, and Melt palettes are all made up of the standard colors used by *Boppers* for trails, poison, and food. The difference is that in the Faders and Melt palettes the higher-index colors are grouped in bands. The Random palette chooses random colors from among the colors that can appear on your Windows display. When you select a CA Rule, *Boppers* automatically selects the palette that makes this rule look the best.

Boppers On is a toggle selection. If it is checked, the boppers are running; if it is not checked, then the boppers are turned off. If you are interested in watching a particular CA run as fast as possible, then you should turn the boppers off. As mentioned above, when both the boppers and a CA patch are running, *Boppers* will perform several updates of the boppers while invisibly working on the update of the CA. Once the entire CA patch is updated, the new patch is copied to the screen. Due to this lack of synchronicity between the boppers and the CAs, bopper trails within the CA patch will sometimes seem to disappear or reappear.

CA Wrap is a toggle selection. If it is checked, the computation of the CA patch wraps from the patch's left to its right and from its top to its bottom. If CA Wrap is not checked, then the CA calculation acts as if the cells at the edge of the patch are frozen in one state. If you have had CA Wrap on for a while and then turn it off, you will sometimes notice that the cells along the edges of the CA patch are fixed at some non-blank values. This can sometimes produce interesting effects.

Stretchable CA is a toggle selection. If it is not checked, then the CA is a patch in the *Boppers* window as usual. If the Stretchable CA selection *is* checked, then the

CA patch is stretched to match the size of the *Boppers* window. For visual clarity, our program requires that each cell of a stretched CA have a whole number of pixels for its vertical and horizontal measurement, so the stretched CA patch will often be smaller than the size of the *Boppers* window. As you drag the lower right-hand corner of the *Boppers* window to resize it, the Stretchable CA patch will keep readjusting itself to take on the largest allowable size. When the CA is in Stretchable CA mode, the updating of the boppers is turned off. The CA runs somewhat slower in Stretchable CA mode. In this mode, no cursor other than the Pick cursor can be used.

Seed the CA is a selection that fills the CA's cells with random values.

Blank the CA sets all the cells in the CA to the blank state. It is interesting to use this option and then wait for boppers to cross the CA patch and kick up activity.

Resize CA to Window changes the dimensions of the CA patch to match the dimensions of the current *Boppers* window, insofar as this is possible given the limitation on the sizes of CA patches previously mentioned. A fast way to adjust the CA patch's size is to take the following steps: resize the *Boppers* window to the intended CA patch size, choose the CAs Resize CA to Window option, and then resize the *Boppers* window to the size you want to view *Boppers* at.

If the total requested patch size is over the limit that *Boppers* can handle, both patch dimensions will be clipped to be less than or equal to 240 pixels. If this produces an unattractive shape, you can attempt to resize the window to a shorter or a narrower shape and try the Resize CA to Window selection again.

Less Cells shrinks the area of the CA patch. If you select this option often enough, the CA reaches the dimensions of 16 by 16 cells.

More Cells increases the area of the CA patch. If you select this option often enough, the CA eventually reaches the size of a square that is 240 pixels on both edges. But until the patch gets too large for *Boppers* to handle, the proportions of the patch will be preserved. Once the patch is too large, it will be clipped in size as discussed under the "Resize CA to Window" section.

Screen shots of CAs can be found in Figure 6-12.

Speed Popup

The Speed popup menu has three selections: Single Step, Slow, and Fast.

When in Single Step mode, the *Boppers* program executes one step of updating the boppers for each time you press a key. Typically, when you are in Single Step mode, you hold the (SPACE) bar down to run the boppers until you want to pause them. In

a

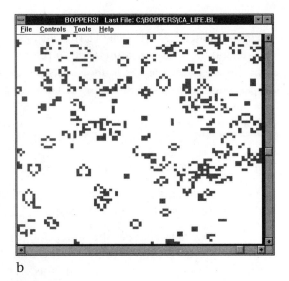

b

c   **Figure 6-12** Some CA samples. (a) Belusov-Zhabotinsky pattern;
(b) a stretchable CA; (c) a Mandala

Single Step mode, the keys still have their customary meanings for use in opening menus and calling Control Key functions.

When in Slow mode, *Boppers* pauses for a slight interval between each update, which makes the boppers move more slowly.

In the default Fast mode, *Boppers* runs as fast as possible.

TOOLS MENU

The Tools menu allows you to enable various methods for directly manipulating the boppers, for getting information about the boppers, and for changing the appearance of the *Boppers* screen.

The Tools menu includes four dialog boxes: Scorebox, Graph, Gene Viewer, and Sound. The menu also has three popups: Background Color, Lens Properties, and Cursors.

Scorebox Dialog

The Scorebox dialog which is shown in Figure 6-13, might more accurately be called a "monolog" box—because it processes very little input from you! Instead of listening for input, the Scorebox tirelessly spews out information about the current scores of the colonies and the edit bopper.

The right half of the *Scorebox* dialog shows the icon of the current edit bopper, along with that bopper's current accumulation of score from Eat Values.

The left half of the Scorebox dialog displays the current running scores of the Green, Red, and Blue colonies next to the *Curr* label. In addition, the most recent colony score averages are displayed in the row labelled *Last*. Fixed icons represent the Green, Red, and Blue colonies.

The running scores of the edit bopper and the Curr row take into account the accumulated *Eat Values* of the boppers. It is only at the end of each breeding period

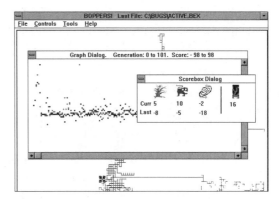

Figure 6-13 The Scorebox dialog and the Graph dialog

that the boppers compute and add in the score adjustments due to the Colonies dialog Inadequate Motion Penalty and Turmite Entropy Bonus groups. This augmented score is called the *full score*.

The effects of the Inadequate Motion Penalty and the Turmite Entropy Bonus groups *are* included in these numbers in the row labelled *Last*. The entries in this row are updated each time the relevant colonies undergo Timed Breeding. If Timed Breeding is turned off for all three colonies, the entries are updated after every thousand steps.

It is often convenient to leave the Scorebox open in a corner of the screen.

Boppers constrains each bopper's score to stay between –32,000 and +32,000. If a bopper reaches a score of 32,000, then further additions to its score will not raise it; similarly once a bopper reaches a score of –32,000, further subtractions will not reduce it.

The upper right-hand corner of the Scorebox window shows the body icon of the edit bopper. You may change this icon without having to close the Scorebox. Simply make sure that the current Cursor mode is the Pick mode, and left-click near the head of the bopper whose score you want to examine.

To close the Scorebox dialog, you may right-click in the dialog box, double-click on the System Menu box in the upper left-hand corner, or rechoose the selection from the Tools menu.

Graph Dialog

The Graph dialog, which is shown with the Scorebox dialog in Figure 6-13, plots the colony scores on the vertical axis against the generation number on the horizontal axis. Each point is plotted as a colored square.

Whenever any colony performs Timed Breeding, the most recent full scores of all three colonies are computed and posted to the Graph dialog. These are the same as the numbers that appear in the second row of the Scorebox dialog.

If Timed Breeding is turned off for all three colonies, the Graph dialog is updated after every thousand steps.

The horizontal axis of the graph starts at the left with the first Timed Breeding after you started up the current run of *Boppers*, and continues out up to one thousand generations to the right. The Graph dialog has room to display 73 generations at a time.

At the initial scale setting, the vertical axis of the graph ranges from the minimum score of –1,000 at the bottom of the window, to 0 at the middle of the window, up to the maximum score of 1,000 at the top of the window. Note that the current visible score range is always displayed in the Graph dialog's caption bar next to the word, *Score*.

To close the Graph dialog, you may right-click in the dialog box, double-click on the System Menu box in the upper left-hand corner, or rechoose the selection from the Tools menu. Note that the Graph dialog has additional controls in the form of *scroll bars*.

The horizontal scroll bar of the Graph dialog moves the dialog box window left and right along the time-line of Timed Breeding generations. The current visible generation range is displayed in the Graph dialog's caption bar next to the word *Generation*. If the last score to be written appears inside the dialog box, the Graph dialog will list that generation value as the high generation range value, which makes it possible for you to know which generation is current. If *Boppers* is run for more than a thousand generations, the Graph data wraps around, and begins writing in new data. The old data is lost.

The vertical scroll bar adjusts the size of the Visible Score Range. If, for instance, all of your data points are clustered near the horizontal zero-score level in the middle of the window, drag the scroll button or click the up arrow on the vertical scroll bar to decrease the Visible Score Range so your data points have a better vertical separation. Different Visible Score Ranges make different kinds of patterns easier to see.

Gene Viewer Dialog

The *Gene Viewer* dialog shows three graphic representations of boppers' genes; see Figure 6-14. The way it works is that a bopper's genome bitstring gets broken into a sequence of 24 bit chunks. Each chunk is represented as a vertical stripe of a certain color, with the color depending on the values of the chunk's 24 bits.

Only as much of the genome as is currently being used by the bopper is shown. Boids use a fairly small amount of genome information, so the stripes in their gene representations are quite wide. This is also the case for turmites that have a low Individuals dialog Turmite IQ setting. But turmites with a higher Turmite IQ have narrower stripes in their gene representations. One way to see this directly is to open the Individuals dialog and the Gene Viewer dialog at the same time, and use the Individuals dialog to vary the Turmite IQ of All Boppers.

The Gene Viewer includes four groups of controls: the *Mother Bopper* group, *Father Bopper* group, the *Child Bopper* group, and the *Breeding Method* group.

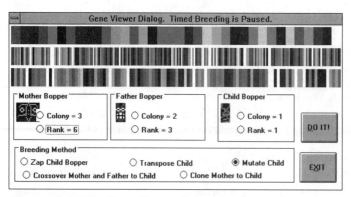

Figure 6-14 The Gene Viewer dialog

The Mother, Father, and Child groups each have a *Colony* radio button and a *Rank* radio button. Repeatedly clicking the Colony buttons changes which colony's boppers are being examined, while clicking the Rank buttons cycles through the boppers in one colony, ranked according to score from best to worst. Note that each of these groups shows an icon of the bopper in question.

One common use for the Gene Viewer is to flip through a colony's different members to see how diverse their genomes are. A key factor in setting a colony's Breeding parameters to good values is the desire to avoid having all of the colony's member boppers end up with identical genomes after only a few generations. On the other hand, if none of a colony's boppers' genomes resemble each other at all, then that colony's Breeding process is probably too random and noisy. See Chapter 5, *The Boppers and Their World,* for more discussion of this issue.

The Breeding Method group has five radio buttons: *Zap Child Bopper, Crossover Mother and Father to Child, Transpose Child, Mutate Child*, and *Clone Mother to Child.*

Depending which Breeding Group radio button is active, pressing the DO IT! button will carry out some kind of breeding action on the genes of the boppers whose genes are displayed. Unlike the results of Timed Breeding, which repeatedly happen every so often, the results of a DO IT! selection happen right away, and only once.

The DO IT! breeding action is immediately reflected in the gene representation and in the real-time behavior of the Child bopper. The genome that used to be in the Child bopper is replaced by the new genome. If you like to be dramatic, you might say that you are killing off the old Child and replacing it with a new

Child that you have just created. But it's more accurate to say that the Child stays the same while you alter its genome.

The Gene Viewer is a useful learning tool for understanding what the Breeding methods do. Note that it is not necessary that the Mother, Father, and Child boppers all be different. You can choose a single bopper for two or even for three of these roles. If, say, the Mother bopper happens to be the same as the Child bopper, the Mother bopper's gene representation will change along with any changes you cause to the Child—here Mother and Child would be two names for the same bopper.

Zap Child Bopper randomizes the genes of the Child Bopper. This happens regardless of whether or not the Colony dialog Things To Zap group is set for the Child Bopper's colony.

Crossover Mother and Father to Child chooses a breakpoint along the Mother and Father's genomes and breaks these genomes into two pieces each. Then either the Mother or the Father's first piece is copied to the Child's first piece, and the other parent's second piece is copied to the Child's second piece. In addition, all of the Child's other bopper parameters are set equal to the Mother's.

If you repeatedly press DO IT! while this button is active, you will see that crossover can happen in various ways. When the Mother and Father have genomes of unequal length, the Child's genome is made the same length as the Mother's.

Transpose Child swaps two bit sequences of the Child's genome. The sequence can be anywhere between four bytes long up to one-eighth the full length in bytes of the Child's genome. For purposes of transposition, the genome is treated as a circular loop, so that if a swap section runs off the end, it wraps around to the beginning.

Mutate Child mutates the Child bopper's genome at the same rate that is required by the Child's colony's mutation level setting on the Controls menu Colony dialog.

Clone Mother to Child copies the Mother's genome to the Child and additionally copies all of the Mother's bopper parameters to the Child.

One thing to remember about the Gene Viewer dialog is that the Timed Breeding process is suspended for as long as the Gene Viewer dialog is left open. This is so you can use the Gene Viewer dialog without having its values unexpectedly change each time Timed Breeding takes place. Another reason is that, if you have the patience, you can organize a custom Timed Breeding by hand, repeatedly using the controls in the Gene Viewer. But normally, you should make a habit of closing the Individuals dialog when it is not in use so that Timed Breeding can carry out its task of evolution.

Sound Dialog

The *Sound* dialog allows you to turn on sounds, some for the standard PC speaker, and some for Windows-compatible sound cards. As shown in Figure 6-15, the Sound dialog includes two groups: the *Sounds On/Off* group and the *Load *.WAV Sound Files* group.

Unlike the other real-time dialogs, the Sound Controls selections take place as soon as you make them. There is no DO IT! button for you to press to make the changes happen. The DONE! button simply closes the dialog.

The idea behind the Sound dialog is that all the sounds you hear are determined by what happens to the edit bopper—the bopper whose body icon has the form of a Maltese cross.

In the *Sounds On/Off* group, you can turn off all the sounds by choosing the No Sounds radio button, or you can choose some combination of sounds from the following: Eating Sounds, Breeding Sounds, State Sounds, and Direction Sounds. Even though there are checkboxes next to them, you cannot activate both State Sounds and Direction Sounds at once.

The Eating and Breeding sounds are made by playing *.WAV files. A *.WAV file is to sound what a bitmap file is to graphics; that is, a *.WAV file is a digitally encoded representation of some sound. Unless you have a Windows-compatible sound card installed for Windows, you will not be able to hear these sounds.

You can use the **.WAV Sound Files* group to load a different *.WAV file for each kind of Eating and Breeding event. We include some *.WAV files on the *Boppers* distribution disk. When you press the *Load Sound File* button, a Windows com-

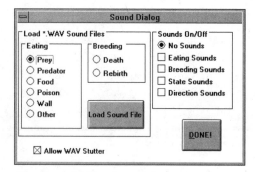

Figure 6-15 The Sound dialog

mon dialog appears for you to load a *.WAV with. The file you load is linked to the event whose radio button is currently active.

The *Eating* sounds correspond to the Eat Values of the pixel colors the edit bopper encounters: Prey, Predator, Food, Poison, Wall, and Other. These sounds can occur quite often.

The *Breeding* sounds are emitted only when Timed Breeding of the edit bopper's colony takes place. Death means that while Timed Breeding takes place the edit bopper learns that it does not get to make a copy of itself to the breeding pool for the next generation. Rebirth means that Timed Breeding is happening and the edit bopper *is* going to contribute at least one version of itself to the next generation.

The *State* and *Direction* sounds are made by sending little beeps to your PC speaker. These sounds can be heard on all machines. The State sound simply changes the pitch of the beep according to the state the bopper is in, while the Direction sound changes the pitch of the beep according to the direction the bopper is moving in.

The *.WAV files you load are permanently noted in Windows configuration, so the same selections will be in effect the next time you run *Boppers*. If *Boppers* is unable to find a requested *.WAV file, it uses one of the standard Windows system sounds instead.

Frequently the sound-triggering events happen too fast for the entire *.WAV file to be played for each event. The *Allow WAV Stutter* checkbox allows you one of two options.

If the Allow WAV Stutter checkbox is *unchecked*, then *Boppers* will reject any request to play a new *.WAV file as long as another *.WAV file is still playing. This means that you will not hear sounds for events that take place while a prior *.WAV file is being played—these sounds get rejected.

If the Allow WAV Stutter checkbox is *checked*, then whenever *Boppers* receives a request to play a *.WAV file, it will stop playing any active *.WAV file and start playing the new *.WAV file. If the sound events happen close together, this produces an overlapped stuttering sound which is quite bizarre. For maximum auditory gnarl, use this option.

Background Color Popup and Screen Capture

This popup lets you choose between having a black background or a white background for the *Boppers* world. The setting you select is saved when you exit the program. (When showing *Boppers* to Mac users, it's a good idea to use the white background, so they feel like they're looking at a Mac!)

A more serious use for the white background is for capturing bitmaps of the screen you later want to print.

To capture a bitmap that is a copy of the currently active *Boppers* window, press
(ALT)-(SHIFT)-(PRINT SCREEN). If all goes well, there will be a slight pause, and then a
copy of the active window will be on the Windows Clipboard. Note that if one
of the *Bopper* dialogs happens to be active (with highlighted caption bar) when
you press (ALT)-(SHIFT)-(PRINT SCREEN), the saved bitmap will just be of this dialog box.

To get the bitmap *off* the Clipboard, open the Windows Paintbrush accessory,
and maximize its size to stretchable CA by pressing the up arrow at the window's upper right-hand corner. Now use the View selection from Paintbrush's
menu bar to turn off the checkmark next to *Tools and Linesize* and to turn off
the checkmark next to *Palette*. Now the Paintbrush canvas is as large as possible.

The final step is to use the Edit selection on the Paintbrush menu bar to select
Paste. A pixel for pixel copy of your *Boppers* screen (including the *Boppers* caption
and menu bar) should appear inside Paintbrush. You can edit this image like
any other bitmap using the Paintbrush tools. Using floodfill, for instance, can
make some odd shapes. To print the image, simply select Print from the
Paintbrush File menu, and select OK in the Print dialog. You don't need to
change any of Paintbrush's Print or Image Size parameters to do this.

If you chose White Background before you saved the *Boppers* screen, then the
printout will look pretty good. If, on the other hand, you saved the image with
a Black Background, then most of the detail will be lost in the inky black background on the paper.

This procedure may not work for every computer and printer configuration, but
it usually works very smoothly. In fact, all the screen dumps in this chapter were
produced by the process just described on an HP Laserjet IIIP printer, with a 486
machine with 12MB of RAM and a 400MB hard disk.

Cursors Popup

The Cursors popup lets you change the appearance and the functionality of the
cursor. The available cursor types are: *Pick*, *Copy*, *Isolate*, *Zap*, *Drag*, and *Lens*. The
currently active cursor type is indicated with a checkmark on the popup, as
shown in Figure 6-16.

The alternative cursors are active only when the cursor is over an uncovered part
of the *Boppers* world. When you move the cursor position out of the *Boppers*
world, the cursor changes back to the standard arrow cursor shape.

For all cursor types except Lens, when you click the mouse with the cursor within the active *Boppers* screen, the program looks for the closest bopper head that

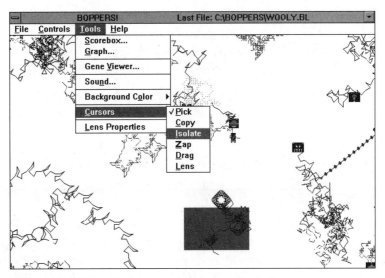

Figure 6-16 The Tools menu with the Cursors Popup

is within a distance of 50 pixels from the cursor position. The exact value of the cursor position is taken to be the location of a special part of the cursor that is called the cursor's *hotspot*.

If some boppers are found within a distance of 50 pixels of the cursor's hotspot, the program makes a beep, and the closest bopper becomes the *edit bopper* and is marked with the *edit bopper icon*, which has the form of a white cross on a red circle. If the cursor is of the type Copy, Isolate, Zap, or Drag, an action involving the edit bopper is now taken.

If you click the mouse and there is no bopper within 50 pixels of the cursor's hotspot, then there is no beep, and no further action is taken. In the following discussion of cursor actions, all the mouse clicks are assumed to be close enough to some bopper to be successful.

The *Pick* cursor is an arrow with the hotspot at its tip, and is used only with the left mouse click. The Pick cursor is used solely for picking different edit boppers. When you use the File Save Bopper selection or the File Load Bopper selection, it is the edit bopper which gets acted on. When the Individuals dialog is open, the edit bopper is the one whose parameters are displayed in the Parameter to Change group.

The *Copy* cursor is a picture of two smiley faces connected by an arrow. The hotspot is in the center of the head of the arrow. The Copy cursor can be used with a left or with a right mouse click. The left-click copies the parameters and genes of the edit bopper to all the other boppers in its colony. That is, the whole colony becomes clones of the edit bopper. The right-click of the Copy cursor copies the parameters and genes of the edit bopper to all the other boppers that are currently moving around in the *Boppers* world. The Copy cursor can be seen in Figure 4-10.

The *Isolate* cursor is a picture of three concentric squares. The hotspot is at the center of the central square. The Isolate cursor can be used with a left or with a right mouse click. The left-click removes all the other boppers except for the edit bopper from the screen, so that you can watch the edit bopper acting alone. This mode of the program is called *isolated mode*. If the program is in isolated mode, a right-click of the cursor restores the original boppers to the screen. The Isolate cursor is visible in Figure 6-17.

When you are in isolated mode, you may want to use the Controls World menu to remove the food and the poison patches, or to lengthen the bopper's trail. If you use the Controls World menu to add some boppers while in isolated mode, then the program stops being in isolated mode and it discards the information that was waiting in the original boppers. In this case, a right-click of the Isolate cursor will no longer have any effect unless the left-click is first used again.

The *Zap* cursor is a picture of a lightning bolt. The hotspot is at the bottom of the bolt. The Zap can be of a lesser or a greater intensity depending on whether you left-click or right-click the mouse. A left-click of the Zap cursor randomizes a bopper's genes. A right-click of the Zap cursor randomizes whatever parameters are checked in the Things To Zap box on the Colony Dialog when it is set to

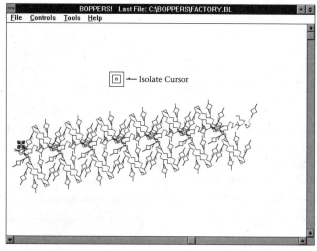

Figure 6-17 The Isolate cursor

show the parameters of the edit bopper's colony. If a bopper is hopelessly boring, a left-click of the Zap cursor will give it a complete new set of genes. A right-click will possibly change some of its Individuals dialog parameters. The Zap cursor appears in Figure 6-18.

The *Drag* cursor is a picture of a hand, with the hotspot at the tip of the pointing finger. If you left-click the Drag cursor, it attaches the edit bopper to the hand, so you can move the bopper with your mouse. This is a particularly interesting thing to do if some of the other boppers are boids (the boids will visibly react to the motions of the edit bopper). With a fine enough touch, you may be able to coax some predator boids into flying circles around a bopper that you drag. When you right-click the Drag cursor, it releases the edit bopper and lets it go back to moving on its own.

As long as you are dragging a bopper around, the Drag cursor executes a *wrap* when you try to drag it across the left edge, the right edge, or the bottom edge of the *Boppers* world. That is, if you drag a bopper off the right, it reappears on the left, and so on. If, while you are dragging a bopper, you move the cursor up across the top edge of the *Boppers* world, the bopper will wait at the top edge for your cursor to reappear.

The *Lens* cursor is the shape of a magnifying glass, with the hotspot at the center of the lens. Clicking the mouse with the Lens cursor active does *not* change the identity of the edit cursor. A left-click of the Lens cursor turns on a square *lens patch* in which the pixels of the *Boppers* world are magnified. Normally, this lens will be centered on the location where the cursor is clicked. A right-click of the Lens cursor turns the lens patch off. Figure 6-19 shows the Lens cursor.

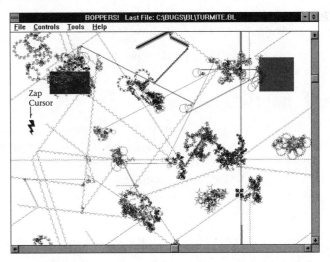

Figure 6-18 The Zap cursor

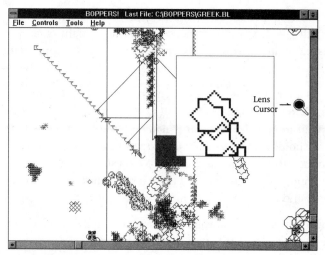

Figure 6-19 The Lens cursor

If you left-click the Lens cursor and the lens patch is already open, the lens patch will move to be centered on the new cursor position. Another way to change what you see through the lens is to scroll the *Boppers* window while the lens patch is open.

The lens patch is always required to lie fully inside the *Boppers* window. If the lens patch would not completely fit on the screen if drawn around the selected position, then the *Boppers* window is scrolled in the appropriate direction. The scrolling amount will not always be enough, but if you repeatedly left-click the lens, the desired location will move into view.

More information about the lens patch is in the following section.

Lens Properties Popup

The *Lens Properties* popup lets you change the size and magnification factor of the square of magnified pixels that we call the *lens patch*. The lens patch is shown in Figure 6-20. There are seven selections: Lens On, Lens Off, Finer Lens Pixels, Coarser Lens Pixels, Smaller Lens, Bigger Lens, and Fullscreen Lens. The Lens Off, Lens On, and Fullscreen Lens selections show checkmarks to indicate whether or not they are active.

Choosing either the Lens On or the Fullscreen Lens option will (1) change the cursor type to Lens and (2) turn on the lens patch. You can turn the lens patch off by choosing the Lens Properties popup Lens Off selection, or by right-

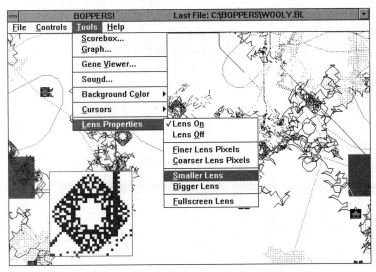

Figure 6-20 The lens patch and the Lens Properties popup

clicking the mouse if the Lens cursor type is active. More information about using the Lens cursor is in the previous section. Figure 6-20 shows a lens patch.

Lens On turns on the lens patch. If this is the first time the lens patch is turned on, it will be located in the center of the *Boppers* window. Otherwise the lens patch will be at the last position where it was shown. If the lens patch would be too small to fit inside the active window, it is drawn at reduced size.

Lens Off turns off the lens patch. If you want to make the cursor stop being the Lens cursor, you need to use the Tools popup's Cursors popup to choose the Pick selection.

Finer Lens Pixels makes the pixel marks in the lens patch smaller. Put differently, this selection makes the lens' magnification power weaker.

Coarser Lens Pixels makes the pixel marks in the lens patch larger. This can be thought of as making the strength of the lens greater.

What lens strengths are available? Well, first lets define what we mean by the lens patch's *lens strength*. If the lens patch's lens strength has some numerical value S, a single pixel in the *Boppers* world is represented by an S by S square of pixels in the lens patch. By this definition, the lens patch can be set to the following five strengths: 2, 3, 4, 8, and 16. The Finer Lens Pixels and Coarser Lens Pixels selections step up and down through these five options, staying put if pushed out to either end.

Smaller Lens and *Bigger Lens* change the length of the edge of the square lens patch. What edge sizes are available? Unless the *Boppers* window is too small, the lens patch starts out with an edge of 200 pixels. The Smaller Lens and Bigger Lens selections change this edge length in steps of 60. Ordinarily, the smallest lens edge is 140, although smaller edges will be drawn if the window is small. The largest allowable lens edge is the shortest measurement (width or height) of the *Boppers* world window.

When you toggle the *Fullscreen Lens* selection to the checked state, the cursor mode is changed to Lens, and a lens patch the size and shape of the *Boppers* world window is turned on. You can right-click to turn the lens patch off, scroll the window to a new position, and left-click to turn the lens back on. You can of course use the Lens Off and the Lens On selections to turn the lens patch off and on as well. Selecting the Fullscreen Lens selection while it is checked will uncheck it, so that now the lens patch will again be a square. Resizing the window also changes the Fullscreen Lens selection to the unchecked state.

HELP MENU

The Help menu has three selections: *Help on Help*, *Help on Boppers*, and *About Boppers*.

The *Help on Help* and *Help on Boppers* selections invoke the Windows Help application. The Help application displays a text file and provides some tools for moving around in the file. You can also use the Help application to print part or all of a help file.

The *Help on Help* information is standard for all Windows programs.

The *Help on Boppers* file consists of the text of this chapter, lightly edited and preceded by a table of contents.

The *About Boppers* dialog displays a slammin' ant and copyright information about the *Boppers* program; see Figure 6-21.

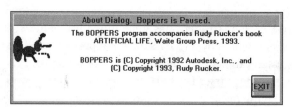

Figure 6-21 The About dialog

CONTROL KEY SHORTCUTS

Boppers includes some control key shortcuts that can be pressed in order to quickly accomplish certain frequently used menu commands. In order to activate the control keys, press (CONTROL) followed by the appropriate letter key for the desired control key shortcut.

In practice, you normally press (CONTROL) and the letter key at the same time, but even if you release (CONTROL) and only then press a letter key, *Boppers* will still attempt to interpret the letter key as a control key. If the letter key pressed is not one of the control key shortcuts listed, then you will need to press (CONTROL) again to make *Boppers* alert for control keys again.

The control key shortcuts are:

(CONTROL)-(B) changes the Controls menu Individuals dialog Body Icons selection for all the active boppers. The first time (CONTROL)-(B) is used in a *Boppers* session, the Body Icons are all set to No Body. Subsequent uses of the (CONTROL)-(B) selection alternate the Body Icons selection between Single Body and No Body. You cannot set the boppers' Body Icons selections to the Body Trail selection by using the (CONTROL)-(B) control key combination.

(CONTROL)-(D) starts a new lambda rule cellular automaton. If a lambda rule CA is already running, this selection changes the particular lambda rule. This is the same as choosing the Controls menu CAs popup Select Rule popup Lambda popup selection for the current Lambda value.

(CONTROL)-(G) randomizes all the active boppers' genes. This has the same effect as the File menu Randomize popup Individuals' Genes selection.

(CONTROL)-(L) changes the Controls menu Individuals dialog Trail Lines selection for all the active boppers. The first time (CONTROL)-(L) is used in a *Boppers* session, the Trail Lines are all set to No Lines. As long as the world is two dimensional, subsequent uses of the (CONTROL)-(L) selection in a *Boppers* session switch back and forth between the No Lines and the Thin Lines selections. When the world is three dimensional, successive uses of the (CONTROL)-(L) combination will cycle through the options Thin Lines, Edged Thin Lines, Thick Lines, and back to No Lines. You cannot set the boppers' Trail Lines selections to the Depth-Scaled Lines selection by using the (CONTROL)-(L) control key combination.

(CONTROL)-(N) changes the Controls menu Individuals dialog Trail Nodes selection for all the active boppers. The first time (CONTROL)-(N) is used in a *Boppers* session, the Trail Nodes are all set to Dot. Subsequent uses of the (CONTROL)-(N) selection in a *Boppers* session cycle the Trail Nodes selection through Small Squares, Medium Squares, back to Dot, and so on.

(CONTROL)-(O) toggles the three-dimensional world display in and out of Stereo Mode. Details on Stereo Mode can be found in the next section.

(CONTROL)-(S) changes the Tools menu Sound dialog Sounds On/Off selections. The first time (CONTROL)-(S) is used in a *Boppers* session, the sounds are set to No Sounds. Subsequent uses of the (CONTROL)-(S) selection alternates between the two alternatives of No Sounds and the combination of Eating Sounds and Breeding Sounds. Note that if you do not have a sound board, these two selections are both silent.

(CONTROL)-(T) changes the Controls menu Individuals dialog Bopper Type selection. The first time (CONTROL)-(T) is used in a *Boppers* session, the active boppers all have their Bopper Type set to turmite. Subsequent uses of the (CONTROL)-(T) selection cycles through the options of Boid, Wolf, Beaver, Dog, Owl, and back to Turmite.

(CONTROL)-(V) randomizes everything. This is the same as the File menu Randomize popup Everything selection. This is a quick way to flip through a lot of different *Boppers* worlds.

(CONTROL)-(Z) clears the screen. This is the same as choosing the File menu Clear Screen selection.

STEREO MODE

The *Boppers* program has a stereo mode for use with three-dimensional worlds. This mode is toggled on and off by using (CONTROL)-(O) (as in stereO) when the world is in three-dimensional mode.

In stereo mode, each colored trail pixel is represented as a pixel pair consisting of a blue pixel and a red pixel, regardless of what color the pixel trail would ordinarily be. The result is that each bopper gets two trails, a blue trail and a red trail. To visually fuse these two trails into a single trail that seems to move about in three dimensions, wear the red and blue glasses included with the *Boppers* program, with the blue lens over your right eye and the red lens over your left eye. This method of achieving an illusion of three dimensionality is known as *anaglyphic stereo*.

To get the effect, keep the spot between your eyes near the axis that runs in through the center of the screen, and move your head forward and backward until the red and blue images fuse. The three-dimensional bopper trails should appear to be floating in front of the screen. You know you have locked in on the effect if moving your head side to side seems to make the image sway.

It is easiest to first lock in on the three-dimensional effect when you are fairly distant from the screen, perhaps five to six feet. You can then move somewhat closer to the screen without losing the effect.

This effect is easier for some people to see than it is for others, but once you get it, it is quite striking. Although throughout Chapter 5, *The Boppers and Their World,* we spoke of the three-dimensional boppers as if they were in a three-dimensional fishtank whose front surface is the computer screen, the technique used in Stereo Mode effectively slides the fishtank out through the screen to sit in front of it, with the back face of the fishtank resting against the computer screen.

Figure 6-22 shows the principle by which the blue and red pixel positions are computed. A 3-D trail point is thought of as being in the space in front of the computer screen; the near region of this space represents points with z coordinates of zero, and the far region represents points with higher z coordinates. The red image of the trail point is drawn where the line from your left eye to the 3D trail point would intersect the screen, and the blue image is drawn where the line from your right eye would intersect the screen.

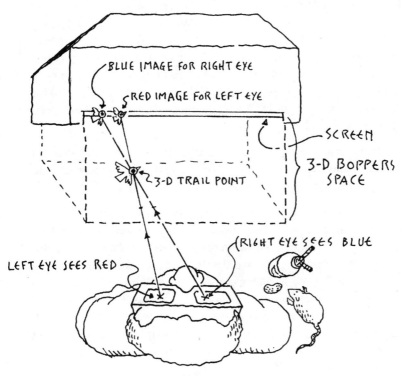

Figure 6-22 Representing a point by a stereo pair

When you enter stereo mode, the *Boppers* world is put into Walled mode, but the Walls are not drawn because the stereo pair images would cut across them.

TROUBLESHOOTING BOPPERS

Boppers is a complicated program that was developed by one person over a period of three years. It is still possible that *Boppers* will occasionally malfunction. There are four types of malfunctions that can happen with a Windows application such as *Boppers:*

1. *Boppers* becomes inconsistent

2. Windows displays an error box

3. Your machine freezes up

4. Windows behaves strangely

A type 1 malfunction is when you notice that some of the values displayed on the *Boppers* dialogs do not make logical sense. There is sometimes a tendency to think a type 1 malfunction has occurred when there is actually a legitimate explanation for the behavior you've seen. For instance, you might exit a dialog without pressing the DO IT! box, and then reenter the dialog and be surprised that the change did not occur. This would be an example of an *illusory* type 1 malfunction. An example of a *true* type 1 malfunction might be if you opened the Gene Viewer Dialog and one of the Colony numbers said 4. This (hypothetical) event would be logically inconsistent, as the only possible *Boppers* colony numbers are 1, 2, and 3.

When a type 2 malfunction occurs, *Boppers* displays an error message, or Windows itself tells you that an error occurred in the *Boppers* application and asks if you want to close the application. You should close the application.

When a type 3 malfunction occurs, *Boppers* stops responding to input. If one of the Menu Bar selections is highlighted, boppers will be paused, so try clicking the cursor in the *Boppers* window to make sure the focus is in *Boppers*. It is also possible that you might think a type 3 malfunction has occurred if you have the World dialog open, for the World dialog pauses *Boppers*. But if you then try to close the World menu and get no response, you really are experiencing a type 3 malfunction. One last thing that might give a false impression of a type 3 malfunction would be if someone has used the Controls popup's Speed popup to set the speed to Single Step. But, again, if you can't get the Controls popup to open, then you really do have a type 3 malfunction.

For a type 3 malfunction, press (CONTROL)-(ALT)-(DEL), and Windows will display a screen asking you if you want to close your malfunctioning application. Press (ENTER), and Windows will close *Boppers*.

A type 4 malfunction may occur after you close *Boppers*, particularly if you closed *Boppers* as a result of a type 2 or a type 3 malfunction. In a type 4 malfunction, the Windows screen looks weird, with inappropriate patches of text and color. This usually means that Windows has run out of System Resources. The best thing to do here is to exit Windows and start a fresh Windows session.

You can use the Windows Program Manager Help menu About selection to display a box that shows the amount of Memory and System Resources available. If System Resources is down below the 20% range, type 4 malfunctions are likely to occur, and you should definitely start a new Windows session.

Boppers uses about 1.5MB of Memory and about 20 percent of the System Resources when it runs. But since Windows itself uses up some RAM, a very minimum of 2MB of RAM is required. When *Boppers* exits normally, it gives back all but about 1 percent of the System Resources it uses. If you repeatedly open and close *Boppers,* or if you exit *Boppers* as a result of a type 2 or type 3 malfunction, then the System Resources can get too low.

Boppers has run on machines with 2MB of RAM and a virtual memory upgrade. Most of the testing of *Boppers* was done at the standard VGA resolution of 640 by 480 pixels. Windows allows you to set the resolution higher if you have SuperVGA video card. Some type 2 malfunctions have occured in the higher resolutions on machines with lower amounts of RAM.

If you find yourself repeatedly getting the same type of malfunction, this means that your *Boppers* keeps loading a bad set of parameters. These bad parameters will be on your disk in the form of one or several files with the name ACTIVE.BEX. When you keep getting repeated malfunctions you need to purge all files named ACTIVE.BEX from the directories of your hard disk. The first place to look is in the C:\BOPPERS directory. Next check in your WINDOWS directory. If you have a disk search program, use it to make sure there are no ACTIVE.BEX files anywhere.

Once you have removed the ACTIVE.BEX files, *Boppers* should start up in a clean, good parameter mode. You know you have started in this mode if the *Boppers* caption bar says START.BL right after startup rather than ACTIVE.BEX.

NOTES AND REFERENCES

- The wrapped three-dimensional mode seems odd at first because there is no way to connect a cube of space like this in ordinary three-dimensional space. In three dimensions, you can wrap a two-dimensional square's edges by gluing left to right to make a cylinder and then gluing top to bottom to make a torus. But if you try this with a three-dimensional cube, you can make a thick torus shell, but then one face of the cube is on the inside of the shell, and the other face is on the outside; and there's no way to glue those two together. Four dimensions are needed to fully glue a cube into a three-dimensional wrapped position! If this bothers you, just suppose that there are matter transmitters connecting the front and back of the wrapped three-dimensional *Boppers* world!

- The choices you make on the File Randomize But Don't Randomize popup are saved in your WIN.INI file as a coded number called "Randomizer Mask," which appears in WIN.INI under the entry [Boppers]. The starting positions of the *Boppers* dialog boxes are stored here as well, as are the names of the *.WAV files you load, as is your preference for White or Black Background. You can edit this information directly with a word processor, although it is always advisable to make a backup copy of WIN.INI before tinkering with it. One false keystroke and your Windows will no longer run until you reinstall it!

Math Alert

The action of the Tools menu Graph dialog's vertical scroll bar is *inverse*, rather than *linear*, which means that the visible score range changes a *lot* for a *small* change near the bottom of the scroll bar, and changes only a *little* for even a *big* change near the top of the scroll bar. You can keep track of this by watching the position of the marker or thumb in the vertical scroll bar. *Boppers* calibrates this scroll bar as having 640 vertical positions.

Now let T stand for the calibrated thumb value, and let R stand for the number such that the caption bar reads:

"Graph Dialog... Score: $- R$ to R"

What is the exact relationship between T and R? The *Boppers* program uses the relationship:

$$R = 32,000 / T$$

Can you guess or calculate the values of R for thumb position 1 (bottom of scroll bar) and for thumb position 640 (top of scroll bar)? To check your answer, open the Graph Dialog and slide vetical scroll bar's thumb first to the bottom and then to the top, looking at the R value listed on the Graph Dialog's caption bar!

7

Examples

This chapter discusses the parameter files that are included on the
Boppers *program disk. All parameter files have the file extension*
*.BL. Load them by using the Files menu's Open popup's Open
Parameters selection, as described in Chapter 4, Installation and
Quick Start, *and in Chapter 6,* Boppers User's Guide. *If the Open*
dialog box does not show a list of *.BL files, try double-clicking on the
name of the BOPPERS directory.

Don't think for a minute that these examples are an exhaustive inventory of possible
kinds of *Boppers* worlds! This handful of examples really only scratches the surface. Go
ahead and start creating and saving parameter files of your own. They take up less
than 1,000 bytes each, actually more like 600 on the average, which means you can fit
over a thousand of them into a megabyte of disk space! Post your *.BL files on the net
and let others download them! They're just plain ASCII text files, by the way.

ALGAE

In ALGAE.BL, all three colonies are made of turmites. The green boppers use a 24-
direction windrose with speed two, and they have an IQ of 1. The other colonies use
12-direction windroses with speed one and have IQs of 64. This means the green
boppers move around much more rapidly. The ecology here is the UFOlogy mode.

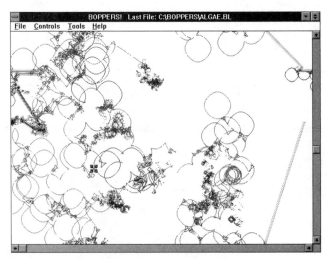

Figure 7-1 ALGAE with a rounded-square turmite

It is worthwhile to use the Files menu's Randomize popup's Individuals' Genes selection (or the (CONTROL)-(G) shortcut for this command) to randomize the genes in ALGAE a few times until you find a certain kind of very exciting behavior in the low-IQ green turmites. The exciting behavior occurs when the greens race around in rounded squares that ricochet into lens-shapes when they bump into things, as shown in Figure 7-1.

BEAVER

In BEAVER.BL, all three colonies are made of beavers. The ecology is Food Loop. The Turmite Windrose and Turmite IQ parameters are checked in the Controls menu's Colonies dialog's Things To Zap box, which means that these parameters undergo zapping and can, therefore, evolve along with the genes. Typical emergent behavior here is that all of the beavers bunch up together in a cluster. When the cluster emerges, use the scroll bars to center it in midscreen.

The cluster will break up if you use the Individuals dialog to change one of the colonies to a different boid or turboid Bopper Type (that is, change one of the colonies to boid, wolf, dog, or owl).

BEAVER3D

BEAVER3D.BL is a 3D version of BEAVER.BL. Note that the thick lines are mostly brightly colored with occasional spots of faint coloring. Whenever a turboid

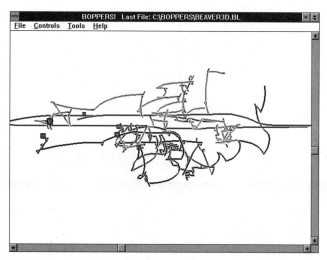

Figure 7-2: A 3D beaver cluster

(such as a beaver) acts like a boid it leaves a bright trail. When it acts like a turmite, it can leave either a bright or a faint trail. Just as in the 2D case, the 3D beavers tend to cluster, as shown in Figure 7-2. As before, you can break the cluster by changing one of the colonies to boids.

BIRDCAGE

BIRDCAGE.BL shows three colonies of three boids each in a Walled three-dimensional world. The Food Loop ecology is in effect.

Try putting other kinds of turboids into the BIRDCAGE. Open the Controls menu's Individuals dialog and check the All Boppers radio button. Now use the Bopper Type combo box to select, say, Owl, and then click the Individuals dialog's DO IT! button to effect the change. Alternatively, you can use the (CONTROL)-(T) shortcut control key combination to change all the Bopper Types. The first time you use this control key, all Bopper Types are set to turmite, and successive presses of (CONTROL)-(T) cycle the boppers through boid, wolf, beaver, dog, owl, back to turmite, and so on.

Another thing to try is to check the Controls menu's Individuals dialog's All Boppers radio button. Then use the Trail Lines combo box to select Edged Thin Lines, Thick Lines, or Depth-Scaled Lines, and press DO IT! to install the selection. You can also use the (CONTROL)-(L) shortcut control key to change the Trail Lines parameter for all the boppers. The first time you press (CONTROL)-(L), all the Trail Lines are set to No Lines, and successive presses cycle through Thin Lines, Edged Thin Lines, Thick Lines, Depth-

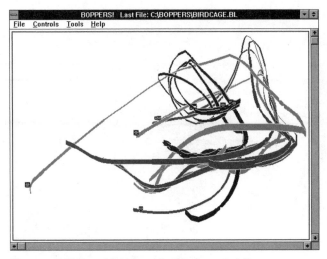

Figure 7-3 Caged boids with depth-scaled lines

Scaled Lines, back to No Lines, and so on. Figure 7-3 shows BIRDCAGE.BL with Depth-Scaled Lines.

You should set the trail lengths to maximum size when using the fancier Trail Line settings. Open the Controls menu's World dialog and click one of the + buttons in the Average Pixel Per Bopper Trail box until the numbers all change to the phrase Permanent Trail. Then use a single click on one of the Average Pixel Per Bopper Trail boxes' - buttons to back down to the largest possible numerical trail length for the current number of boppers. Press DO IT! to accept the change and close the World dialog.

The notes on SPAGGET.BL have a little more information about the Depth-Scaled Lines option and about the meaning of the Permanent Trail setting.

Yet another thing to try with BIRDCAGE is to turn off the cage; that is, choose the Controls menu's World dialog's Wrapped World selection and click the World dialog's DO IT! button.

BOIDWAR

BOIDWAR.BL starts with seven boppers of each color. The red and green boppers are boids, and the blue boppers are turmites. The ecology is set to Dog Eat Dog, meaning that each colony views both other colonies as prey. The red and green colonies have their Prey Recruitment flags set to ON, and the blue colony's Prey Recruitment is set to OFF. This means that when a red or green bopper gets near a member of another colony they try to recruit it.

Because blue boppers do not have their Prey Recruitment turned on, the red and green boppers are free to recruit them. The blue boppers' role here is a bit like the role of the goat tethered in the T. Rex's cage in *Jurassic Park*.

When a red and a green boid get near each other and each wants to recruit the other, *Boppers* uses a random "coin-flip" to decide who wins. When one of the colonies manages to pull ahead, it is likely to take over all the boppers.

BOUNCERS

BOUNCERS.BL is designed to show rapid evolution. The boppers are all six-direction turmites with IQs of two. The death levels are set to Very High, meaning that the most successful bopper in a colony will typically get two copies, and the least successful bopper will get none. The zapping level is set to High, meaning that the lowest two bopper slots get zapped each time.

The ecology is Dog Eat Dog, which means that all other colony trails have positive values. On the Colonies dialog, the Inadequate Motion Penalty is –100 for a motion of less than 40 pixels. The best strategy for getting a high score is for a bopper to move around a lot, bouncing off of all the trails it meets.

With the breeding parameters set as they are, evolution to a reasonable score level happens pretty rapidly.

Once the bouncers are doing well, you can try increasing their IQs a little bit at a time, waiting to let evolution make good use of each new level of IQ before moving further.

CACTUS

CACTUS.BL has nine green turmites and nine red boids. The Ecology is such that the greens like the reds and the reds like the greens, but the greens award negative points to their own trail color.

The typical pattern here is clumps of green with lacy red paths around them. It looks a bit like cactus clumps and desert-rat trails.

If you use the Tools menu's Graph dialog to look at the long-term behavior of the CACTUS world, you will notice that the red dots make a graph that lies above the graph formed by the green dots. The best way to look at this graph is to adjust the vertical scroll bar's slider until the highest red dot is just below the top of the Graph dialog window.

An interesting feature of the red and green graphs is that they tend to build to a certain level, and then crash back to lower levels. The fluctuations of red and green seem to be roughly in synch. The overall pattern is probably chaotic in the sense of seeming almost periodic without actually being predictable.

CA_LIFE

CA_LIFE.BL is a parameter setting in which the bopper activity is turned off. The only activity is that of a maximally sized 255 by 255 cellular automaton patch running the familiar Life rule.

Use the scroll bars to bring the CA patch to the center of the screen. Stuck somewhere on the screen will be all or part of the Maltese cross icon that indicates the location of the edit bopper. Although you don't see the boppers, they are in the background, frozen in place by the fact that the Controls menu's CAs popup's Boppers On selection is not checked. You can repeatedly choose this selection to toggle the boppers on or off.

Try the following steps with CA_LIFE to see the CA run at different sizes. First resize the *Boppers* window to the largest square shape that fits on your screen. Now choose the Controls menu's CAs popup's Stretchable CA selection. This selection has the effect of turning the boppers off, in case they are on. It is possible that you will see no other immediate effect from having chosen this selection. But now try repeatedly choosing the Controls menu's CAs popup's Less Cells selection. The cells of the CA you see should get bigger and bigger, and you should see something like Figure 7-4. You can make the cells smaller again by choosing the More Cells selection.

As long as the Stretchable CA selection is checked, resizing the *Boppers* window can change the appearance of the CA. In terms of speed, visual attractiveness, and scientific meaning, it's a good idea to avoid Stretchable CA window sizes in which the individual cells are shaped like rectangles instead of squares.

Keep in mind that the CA will run slower while the Stretchable CA selection is checked. Toggle the selection back off for greater speed. Note that if you only want to magnify a part of the CA, you can do this by using the Lens cursor.

In resizing the CA, keep in mind that you can shape the CA patch to various small rectangular shapes by sizing the *Boppers* window to the desired shape and by then clicking the Controls menu's CAs popup's Resize CA to Window selection.

Once you have a CA display you like, try using the Controls menu's CAs popup's Select Rule popup to pick all the available rules one after the other. When

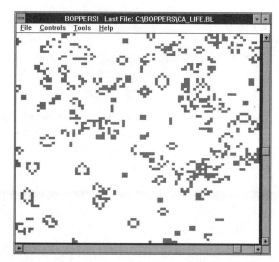

Figure 7-4 The game of life as a stretchable CA

you pick a new rule, it is usually a good idea to pick the Controls menu's CAs popup's Seed the CA selection in order to get the CA going. In the case of the Rug rule, however, it is also interesting to choose the Blank the CA selection, and then to choose the CA Wrap selection so as to toggle off the wrap. A non-wrapping Rug rule will fill the CA patch with something like a mandala, as shown in Figure 7-5.

Figure 7-5 The Rug rule grows a Mandala

CA_STICK

CA_STICK.BL features a long narrow CA patch. As soon as you start this one up, use the *Boppers* window's scroll bars to move the CA patch away from the corner of the screen so it looks cooler, like in Figure 7-6.

The CA is running the Rug rule in wrapped mode. It keeps getting stirred up by the trails of the boppers that pass through it. The Rug rule uses the Standard CA palette, and this palette is made up of the colors of the boppers' trails and of food and poison.

The boppers ecology setting is UFOlogy, which means that the green boppers like every color except poison, so they tend to evolve so as to hang out near the CA patch.

The red boppers are 4-direction turmites with an IQ of three. They tend to evolve to make grids. The green boppers are the same 24-direction guys with IQ 1 and speed 2 that were used in ALGAE.BL. The blue boppers are wolves.

In order to encourage the green and red boppers to move in long, smooth paths, their target entropies are set to zero.

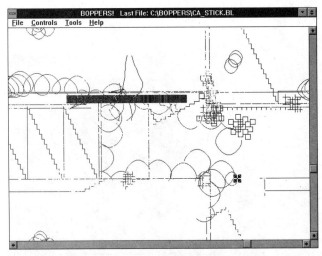

Figure 7-6 The rounded turmites like the CA

CHEESE

CHEESE.BL includes a CA patch set to the Melt rule. The boppers are all 12-direction turmites with speed 3 and IQ 64. The boppers obey the Food Loop ecology.

COLORS

COLORS.BL has three colonies of eight-direction turmites with IQ 64. The green, red, and blue turmites have Trail Nodes set to, respectively, Small Squares, Medium Squares, and Large Squares, and their speeds are set to, respectively, three, five, and six. The speed settings are selected so that the successive nodes of a bopper's trail nest together nicely.

All three colonies have their trail lengths set to Permanent Trail. Over time, many different kinds of colors overlap, and the screen becomes a palimpsest of many colors.

It is interesting to use the Tools menu's Lens Properties popup's Fullscreen Lens selection to be able to see the color patterns in detail. When Fullscreen Lens is active, you can turn it off with a right-click of the mouse, scroll the screen with the scroll bars, and then turn the Fullscreen Lens back on with a left-click of the mouse. While playing with the lens, note that you can also use the Tools menu's Lens Properties popup's Finer Lens Pixels and Coarser Lens Pixels selections to change the effective magnification of the lens. To get rid of the Lens cursor, use the Tools menu's Cursors popup to select the Pick cursor.

If you don't like the messiness that comes with the Permanent Trails, you can open the Controls menu's World dialog, click the three - buttons in the Average Pixels Per Bopper Trail box, and click DO IT!

COWRIB

COWRIB.BL is a setting that was found by using randomization, and a picture of it is in Figure 7-7. When it starts up, the pattern sometimes looks a bit like the half-eaten carcass of a cow, hence the name.

Many interesting patterns arise because some of the red boppers have their Body Icon set to Body Trail, as can be seen in the Controls menu's Individuals dialog. You will notice that the body trail images temporarily disappear if you scroll the screen or if you open a dialog box over them.

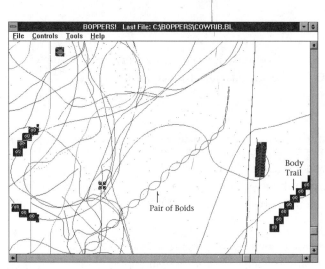

Figure 7-7 A pair of boids in COWRIB.BL

If you want to prevent a rule like this from evolving away from a certain appearance, you can turn breeding off by using the Controls menu's Colonies dialog's Cycles Between Breeding box. To stop, say, the red colony from breeding, click the Edit Colony radio button until it says Red Colony, and then click the + button in the Cycles Between Breeding box until the number changes to the phrase No Breeding, and then click the DO IT TO RED! button. You can repeat this process for the other two colony colors.

Alternatively, you can turn off breeding for all three colonies at once by clicking the + button in the Cycles Between Breeding box until the number changes to the phrase No Breeding, and then clicking the DO IT TO ALL! button. Note, however, that the DO IT TO ALL! button changes *all* of the Colony parameters of all three colonies to match the currently displayed values.

DOG

DOG.BL shows three colonies of four dogs each, using the Food Loop ecology. It takes a while for these boppers to settle down to a clean pattern. This world is also interesting if you use the Controls menu's Individuals dialog to change all the boppers' speeds from two to one, and use the Controls menu's World dialog to change the boppers' average trail lengths from about one thousand to about two thousand.

DOG also looks interesting in 3D, as shown in Figure 7-8. Although this is not too relevant, DOG calls to mind a recent *Peanuts* cartoon in which Snoopy

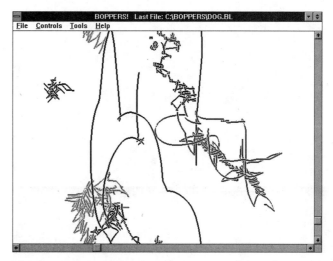

Figure 7-8 A sky full of dogs barking

wishies that dogs could fly. "Imagine a warm summer night," says Snoopy, "with the sky full of dogs barking."

ENTROPY

ENTROPY.BL is a workout for the Controls menu's Colonies dialog's Turmite Entropy Bonus controls. Each colony holds eight 12-direction turmites with IQ 4. All of the eating values on the Controls menu's Ecology dialog are set to zero, so the only way the boppers can get scores is from the Controls menu's Colonies dialog's Additional Fitness Measures. The Inadequate Motion Penalty penalizes boppers that move less than 21 pixels. The Turmite Entropy Bonus sets a Target Entropy of 0 for the green colony, 50 for the red colony, and 100 for the blue colony.

In *Boppers*, entropy is a measure of how randomly distributed is a turmite's series of turns. The Target Entropy is like a percentage between 0 and 100 that measures how close a turmite comes to being maximally random relative the possibilities of its windrose. As this system evolves we expect to see the trails of the green boppers straighten out and form repetitive patterns with only a small number of different kinds of turns. The blue boppers, on the other hand, should evolve into messy, nearly random patterns, while the red should fall somewhere in between. Turmites of three entropy levels are marked in Figure 7-9.

Tweaking the size of the IQ and of the windrose could have an effect here, as could changing the levels in the Breeding Methods box of the Controls menu's Colonies dialog.

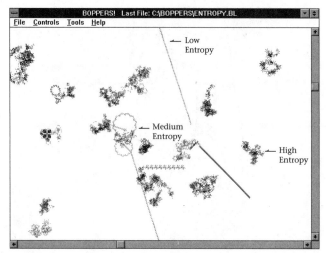

Figure 7-9 Turmites with different levels of Entropy

ESCHER

ESCHER.BL is a three-dimensional world that shows three colonies of four turmites each. On the Controls menu's Individual's dialog, the Speed is set to four
so the boppers make nice big patterns, and the Trail Lines are set to Edged Thin
Lines, so that when lines cross it is easy to see which one is closer to you in the
depth dimension, as suggested by Figure 7-10.

Note that in the Edged Thin Lines mode, there will be pixels covered up by the
lines' edges each time the line turns toward or away from you.

If you want the simulation to run faster, you can switch Trail Lines to Thin
Lines, and if you want the three-dimensional effect to be more dramatic, you
can switch to Thick Lines. The boppers ignore the extra pixels that are laid down
to suggest depth, so changing the Trail Lines parameter should not affect their
behavior.

On the Controls menu's Individuals dialog, the Turmite Windrose parameter is
set to Edge Cube type, which means that the vertical and horizontal motions of
the turmites are parallel to the screen, while the diagonal motions include a
component perpendicular to the screen, as can be checked by looking at Table
7-1. This particular three-dimensional windrose gives a nice effect reminiscent of
some of M.C. Escher's drawings.

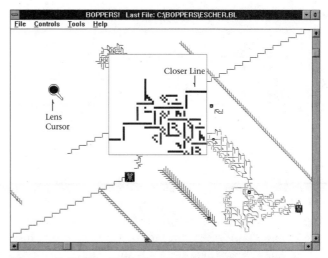

Figure 7-10 The 3D Escher Rule with a lens patch showing a closer line drawn over some more distant lines

Direction

	0	1	2	3	4	5
Change In X	2	1	–1	-2	–1	1
Change In Y	0	–2	–2	0	2	2
Change In Z	0	–1	1	0	1	–1

The Corner Cube Windrose

Direction

	0	1	2	3	4	5
Change In X	2	0	–1	–2	0	1
Change In Y	0	–2	–1	0	2	1
Change In Z	0	0	2	0	0	–2

The Edge Cube Windrose

continued on next page

continued from previous page

Direction

	0	1	2	3	4	5	6	7
Change In X	2	2	0	–2	–2	–2	0	2
Change In Y	0	–2	–2	–2	0	2	2	2
Change In Z	0	–1	0	1	0	1	0	–1

The Lattice Windrose

Table 7-1 The three-dimensional windroses

To get a feel for the other two kinds of three-dimensional turmite windrose, you can try using the Controls menu's Individual's dialog to switch some or all of the Turmite Windrose values to the Corner Cube windrose or the Lattice windrose. The Corner Cube setting is shown in Figure 7-11. To make this picture more striking, the bopper's Speed was increased to 11, and the Trail Lines were set to Thick Lines.

One thing about three-dimensional space is that it is quite rare for two lines in 3D space to cross each other, as opposed to 2D, where almost any two lines will cross. This means that the scores in the Escher world are low, with a significant affect on the scores being contributed by the settings in the Inadequate Motion Penalty box of the Controls menu's Colonies dialog.

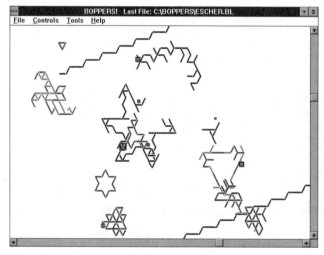

Figure 7-11 A Corner Cube Escher world

EV_SHAPE

In EV_SHAPE.BL, there are three colonies of eight turmites each. If you check the Controls menu's Colonies dialog, you see that each colony includes five of the bopper parameters under Things To Zap. This means that when a bopper is zapped during Timed Breeding, not only are its genes randomized, but five of its bopper parameters are randomized as well. Because the Zapping level is set to High, this means that two boppers in each colony get zapped with each Timed Breeding.

The effect is that the boppers quickly try out various combinations of Speed, Trail Line, Trail Node, Windrose, and IQ.

The ecology setting is Food Loop and there is a negatively weighted Poison Patch present, so it is not always advantageous to eat as much as possible. If you make all the food values positive, then eating as much as possible will indeed be a good idea, and you will soon see the world evolving toward all boppers having lines and large nodes.

To set all food values to positive, open the Controls menu's Ecology dialog and click the Dog Eat Dog radio button. This sets all the trail color values to positive. Now click the first radio button in the column under the Poison label on the Ecology dialog. Click the Ecology dialog's + button three times to change the first Poison value from –2 to 1. Now click the second radio button in the column under the Poison label and click the + button three times; and then do the same thing for the third radio button under Poison. Now click the Ecology dialog's DO IT! button to incorporate this change. Now click the Ecology dialog's EXIT button to close the dialog. If you want to save these settings for future use, click the File menu's Save popup's Save Params selection, type in the file name EATSHAPE, and then press (ENTER).

EATSHAPE.BL should make a parameter setting that is fairly certain to produce a triumphantly upward-sloping graph to view in the Tools menu's Graph dialog. The original EV_SHAPE, on the other hand, is more likely to produce a graph that fluctuates chaotically, like most of the other *Boppers* graphs.

FACTORY

FACTORY.BL has three colonies, each with a Controls menu Individuals dialog Speed of four and Turmite Windrose of twelve. Each colony has a Controls menu World dialog Average Pixels Per Bopper Trail setting of about 1,800. The Food Loop ecology is in effect, so each bopper is presented with the same kind of world situation.

The difference between the colonies is that the green boppers have an IQ of 4, the red boppers have an IQ of 16, and the blue boppers have an IQ of 64. You can watch to

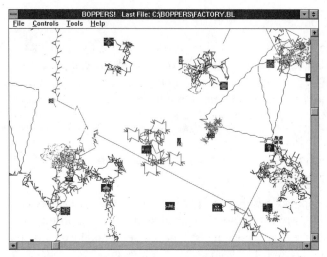

Figure 7-12 Busy Boppers in the factory

see which IQ usually does best. The bopper drawing the bow-tie shapes in the middle of Figure 7-12 is a red one.

For simple eyeball kicks, you can use the Controls menu's Individuals dialog to click the All Bopper radio button, and then set the IQ to some low value like four or two and click DO IT! Lower IQs tend to give simpler, more machine-like patterns.

Once you find some boppers that look interesting, use the Tools menu's Cursor popup to select the Isolate cursor, and left-click on a bopper to see the pattern it draws when its all alone, as in Figure 7-13.

The bopper in Figure 7-13 was saved as the PROTEIN.BOP file using the File menu's Open popup's Save Individual selection. The PROTEIN.BOP file is on the *Boppers* disk and you can load it onto one of your boppers by using the File menu's Open popup's Open Individual selection. Once you have it, you can try isolating it. Note that it may not always make the same pattern as in Figure 7-13, as the pattern depends on what state the bopper is in when you isolate it.

FATBIRDS

FATBIRDS.BL shows three colonies of four three-dimensional boids in a wrapped world. The Trail Lines setting is Thick Lines. Look at the notes on BIRDCAGE.BL for some suggestions of things to do with this world.

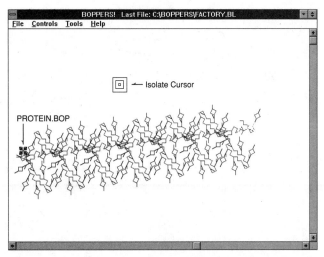

Figure 7-13 An Isolated Bopper Called PROTEIN.BOP

Note that while BIRDCAGE has nine boppers, FATBIRDS has 12 boppers, which makes it run a bit slower. But larger flock sizes make for more interesting behaviors. You might even try increasing the sizes of the flocks, or you might get rid of the blue boids and just increase the sizes of the red and the green flocks.

One of the most interesting of boid behaviors is when one boid flies in a helical, or corkscrew-shaped, path around the path of another boid. Try randomizing the genes a few times with the control key shortcut (CONTROL)-(G), and sooner or later you're likely to spot a helix, which can sometimes be more regular than the skinny double helix in Figure 7-14. Setting the Speeds of the three colonies to different values may help promote helices.

FISHTANK

FISHTANK.BL shows a walled world of two-dimensional boids. Note that sometimes a boid gets stuck next to a wall, but when another boid flies near it, the influence of the other boid will free up the stuck boid.

The Food Loop ecology is active, meaning that the greens chase blues and flee reds, the reds chase greens and flee blues, and the blues chase reds and flee greens.

For each step that a boid is near a wall, the boid always receives a score value equal to the Controls menu's Ecology dialog Wall setting for that boid's colony color. If you highlight the Wall values and decrease them with the - button on the Ecology dialog

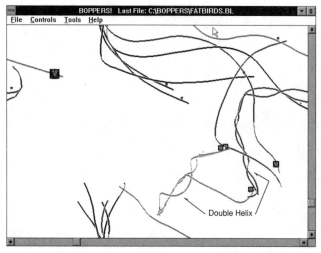

Figure 7-14 Two double helices of boids

and then press the Ecology DO IT! button to install these values, the boids will be penalized for staying near the walls, which means that they should evolve to try and avoid them.

GNAT

GNAT.BL shows a three-dimensional world of boids that have a Controls menu Individual's dialog Trail Line setting of Dot. This means that these boids move around quite rapidly...like gnats. As in FISHTANK, the Food Loop ecology is active.

GNATLINE

GNATLINE.BL is the same as GNAT.BL, except with a Controls menu Individual's dialog Trail Line setting of Edged Thin Lines.

GREEK

GREEK.BL shows three colonies of seven turmites each. All the turmites have the Controls menu's Individuals dialog Trail Lines set to Thin Lines, Speed set to four and Turmite Windrose set to eight. This creates patterns that look a bit like Greek letters, or perhaps Martian or Egyptian (see Figure 7-15). This is a good world in which to play with the Isolate cursor, left-clicking it on individuals to see what they do in a world of their own. Some get stuck, some repeat, some make irregularly expanding patterns, and some go fully chaotic.

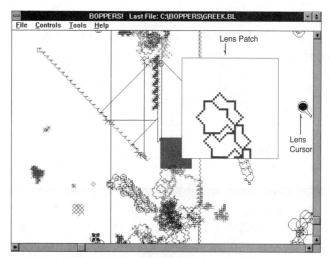

Figure 7-15 Turmite hieroglyphs

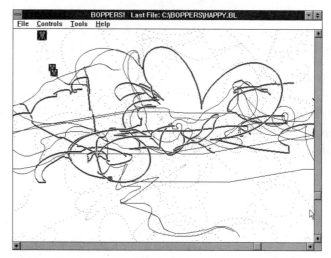

Figure 7-16 Gnarliness is happiness

HAPPY

HAPPY.BL is a randomly created three-dimensional parameter setting. It got its name because the boppers look excited and happy in this world (see Figure 7-16).

The Timed Breeding has been turned off for HAPPY, using the process described in the note on the COWRIB parameter file.

Note that loading a parameter file such as HAPPY.BL does not change the genes of the boppers. And often a rule like this will look better with different gene settings. Most of our parameter files include the ability to evolve their own parameters. But evolution can involve the change of bopper parameters, which is something you don't want to happen to a serendipitously discovered parameter setting like HAPPY.BL.

Instead of using evolution to change a non-breeding rule such as HAPPY.BL, you can simply press (CONTROL)-(G) to randomize the genes, and then (CONTROL)-(Z) to clear the screen so you can more readily see the effect of the new genes.

If you find a gene setting that you simply can't stand to lose, save the configuration as an experiment file, perhaps as HAPPYME.BEX. If you later reload the HAPPYME.BEX experiment file, you'll get back the same parameters *and* the same genes.

To save an experiment file, choose the File menu's Save popup's Save Experiment selection. This opens the Save As dialog box. Type in the file name you want to use and press (ENTER).

HERD

HERD.BL is a two-dimensional boid world, so named because earth-bound creatures form herds in somewhat the same way flying creatures form flocks. You can try changing the creatures from boids to owls. Open the Controls menu's Individual dialog, click the All Boppers radio button, select Owl from the combo box next to Bopper Type, and click the DO IT! and then the EXIT buttons of the Individuals dialog.

HOLE

HOLE.BL is another randomly arrived at parameter setting. This setting includes a large cellular automaton patch running the Zhabotinsky rule. If you start Hole up with a black background and then use the Tools menu's Background Color popup to select a white background, the CA looks like a dark square *hole* in the white world, as shown in Figure 7-17.

Because the Controls menu's CAs popup's CA Wrap selection is not checked, patterns can build up inside the edges of the CA patch. If you use the Controls menu's CAs popup's CA Rule popup to select Melt, the patch will end up being mostly blank, and more hole-like.

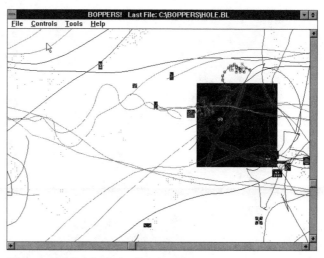

Figure 7-17 A hole in the world

HUNT

HUNT.BL is similar to BOIDWAR.BL in that all the colonies have the Controls menu's Colonies dialog's Prey Recruitment flag checked. Instead of being boids and turmites, however, the boppers are all wolves.

The ecology is such that green views nobody as prey, the reds view only green as prey, and the blues view only green as prey. The upshot is that the red and green compete for recruiting the blue boppers. To keep the evolution going, you need to step in every so often and use the Controls menu's World dialog to put back some blue boppers.

JINGLE

JINGLE.BL has three colonies of five boppers each. The green boppers are owls, the reds are beavers, and the blues are wolves. The name JINGLE comes from the sound a Sound Blaster makes if you use the Tools menu's Sound Dialog to set the Prey *.WAV file to the standard Windows 3.1 file CHIMES.WAV.

LAMBDA

In the LAMBDA.BL world, a CA patch is set to the Lambda rule type. Try using the (CONTROL)-(D) combination repeatedly to get different randomized Lambda rules.

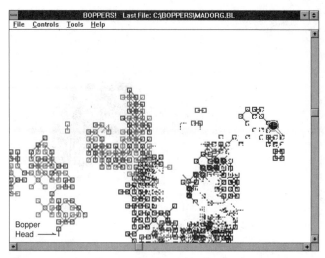

Figure 7-18 Fullscreen Lens view of a mad org chart

MADORG

MADORG.BL consists of three colonies of five turmites each. The Controls menu's Individuals dialog has Trail Nodes set to Medium Squares, Trail Lines set to Thin Lines, Speed set to seven, and Turmite Windrose set to eight.

The turmites create patterns that look like boxes connected by lines, similar to the kind of organization charts or "org charts" that administrators in large businesses enjoy endlessly drawing up. The name "MADORG" stands for "mad org charts."

If an administrator catches you playing with *Boppers* on the job, try winning him or her over by demonstrating MADORG.BL. Say that you're investigating artificial life methods of designing new methods of bureaucratic organization!

Figure 7-18 shows a Fullscreen Lens view of MADORG. The Fullscreen Lens option can be turned on by using the Tools menu's Lens popup. In the lower left of the figure, you can see the head end of a turmite. Note that, as was discussed in the Draw Trail Shapes section of Chapter 5, *The Boppers and Their World,* a turmite with Thin Line trail and Square nodes draws the line ahead of the square.

MAZE

MAZE.BL shows a maze pattern that consists of a gray spiral of walls around a central glob of food. The ecology setting is Dog Eat Dog, so the boppers like

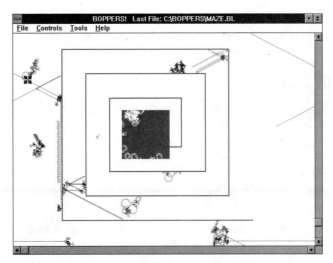

Figure 7-19 Who nibbled the treasure at the center of the maze?

everything. They do, however, have an Inadequate Motion Penalty set, so if they get stuck against a wall they will receive a negative score.

If you want to start off all the boppers outside the maze, open the Controls menu's World dialog and click on the Maze selection to turn off the checkbox, and then click DO IT! Then reopen the Controls menu's World dialog and click on the Maze selection to turn on the checkbox and click DO IT! again. You'll get a new maze, with all the boppers starting off outside of it. In Figure 7-19, some bopper found its way to the food at the center, but it wasn't smart enough to stay there.

MAZE uses three colonies of six turmites each, each with Speed one and with Turmite Windrose 12. Note that if you use non-turmite boppers, or turmites with higher windroses, the maze's walls will not be respected.

MIXHERD

MIXHERD.BL is similar to HERD.BL, except that here the blue boppers are turmites instead of boids.

OWL

OWL.BL shows a two-dimensional world with three colonies of five owls each. The owls have an IQ of eight each. Generally, evolution works better with lower IQs, simply because using high IQs means that the search space is very large, which lowers the odds of the genetic algorithm finding high-scoring genes.

REDFOOD

REDFOOD.BL has the most boppers possible: 27 of them, all turmites. Twenty-four are green, and three are red. The Dog Eat Dog ecology is active, meaning that red likes green and green likes red.

All the boppers have Speed one. The green boppers use a Turmite Windrose of 12, while the red boppers have a Turmite Windrose of 16. In general the 12-direction windrose seems to give the nicest patterns.

The fact that there are so many green boppers gives them a good chance of being able to evolve well. In the Controls menu's Colonies dialog, the green colony's Breeding Methods are set to try and take advantage of the large population.

In particular, a Very High level of Death is used, meaning that the most successful green boppers are likely to get two representatives in the next generation, while the least successful are likely to get no representatives. A Transposing level of High is set, meaning that the highest scoring bopper will always get its genes transposed—this is to try and avoid a premature convergence of the boppers to all resemble one individual.

SCRIBBLE

SCRIBBLE.BL is a walled two-dimensional world with a Dog Eat Dog ecology that has been modified to give the walls a negative score value—this punishes boppers who get stuck near a wall.

There are five boppers of each color. Each bopper is a turmite with a 128-direction windrose and an IQ of 100. Evolution is unlikely to occur rapidly here because of the high IQ, but the scribbles are interesting to look at. To avoid having the colonies converge to uniform behavior, the Death level is set to Low and the Zapping level is set to High.

A good way to see a lot of different scribbles is to keep using the (CONTROL)-(G) combination to randomize the genes. It is also interesting to try slightly longer trail lengths.

SMELLY

SMELLY.BL tries to get an interaction going between the boppers and a large CA patch which is running the Melt rule. When you start SMELLY up, use the scroll bars to move the CA patch to the middle of the screen. Then use the Controls menu's CAs popup's Blank the CA selection to empty out the CA patch.

When the boppers move across the CA patch, they leave trails like the scent trails of ants. The Melt rule of the CA acts like physical diffusion: the markings left by the boppers spread out and then dissipate like *smells*.

Note that because CA Wrap is on, a smell can run off one side of the CA patch and come back on the other side. If you don't like this, then toggle the Controls menu's CAs popup's CA Wrap selection off.

You can experiment to try and find the kinds of boppers that interact the most interestingly with the Melt patch. Making the boppers' trails longer as in Figure 7-20 makes it easier to see where they have been.

SPAGGET

SPAGGET.BL shows three colonies of four boids each in three dimensions, using the Food Loop ecology. Two things make this world special: first, the boids use the Trail Lines setting Depth-Scaled Lines, and second, the Average Pixels Per Bopper Trail is set to Permanent Trail.

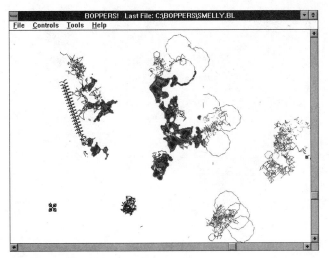

Figure 7-20 Smelly turmite trails

The Depth-Scaled Lines are thinner or thicker according to whether the bopper is nearer or farther from the surface of the screen. Note that some of the fatter lines have chunks missing from them when they turn, this is an artifact of the particular algorithm that *Boppers* uses for drawing thick lines.

Using Depth-Scaled Lines normally makes for a slow simulation because of the work of erasing these fat lines as the trail tidies itself up. But in the Permanent Trail mode there are no old trail markings to erase. An additional aspect of using the Permanent Trail mode is that the program makes no effort to sort the pixels in the right order—the new pixels are always written over the old ones. But the picture is cool (see Figure 7-21).

To see the Depth-Scaled Lines being drawn correctly, open the Controls menu's World dialog, give a single click to one of the - buttons in the Average Pixels Per Bopper Trail box, and then click DO IT! Now *Boppers* carefully decides for each pixel if it should be in front of or behind the preexisting pixels.

If you next use the World dialog to change from walled world to wrapped world, you will notice that sometimes a fat line changes abruptly to a thin line, and vice versa. This happens when the boppers wrap around in the third depth dimension: from the front of the space to the back of the space and vice versa.

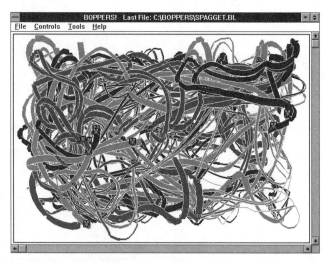

Figure 7-21 A nice plate of SPAGGET

SPARROWS

SPARROWS.BL shows three colonies of five boppers each in a two-dimensional world with food. The ecology is almost like Food Loop, except that the blue boppers do not give a negative weight to the green trail cells.

The green, red, and blue colonies consist, respectively, of owls, beavers, and wolves. Remember that the wolves act like boids except when they hit positively weighted pixels, in which case they act like turmites. The blues view the red trails and the food patch as positive, so the result is that they tend to hang out in these regions. Blues that are in blank regions tend to flock with the other blues, who are likely to be munching on positive food, which means that the blues tend to circle around to join the other blues that are in the red regions or in the food patch, as shown in Figure 7-22. The way the blues circle around to join each other is reminiscent of feeding sparrows, hence the name for this parameter file.

To see the blues cluster more dramatically around the food, you might try using the Controls menu's World dialog to shorten the Average Pixels Per Bopper trail length for the red colony.

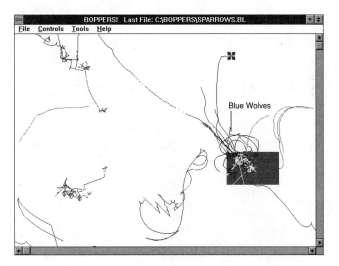

Figure 7-22 The blue wolves cluster around the food patch

SPRING

In SPRING.BL, the green, red, and blue colonies consist, respectively, of turmites, wolves, and boids. The Food Loop ecology is in effect.

With certain gene settings, some of the blue boppers will fly a series of circles around each other or around a red bopper. This is the two-dimensional analog of a three-dimensional helix, and it makes a pattern that looks a bit like a bedspring, hence the name for this parameter file.

SQUIRM

SQUIRM.BL shows an all turmite world. The turmites all have Turmite Windrose 12, Speed 3, and IQ 64. They make paths that look sort of like spiky squirmy worms.

The Controls menu's World dialog's Average Pixels Per Bopper Trail are around three or four hundred here; you might try making these numbers larger.

START

START.BL is a parameter setting that is hardcoded into the BOPPERS.EXE program. If you start *Boppers* in the absence of an ACTIVE.BEX file, *Boppers* will always enter the START.BL parameter setting and write a fresh copy of this parameter file to the disk.

START has six boppers of each color, all with trail length of about 1,400, and all with Speed 1, Turmite Windrose 12, and IQ 64.

The Controls menu's Colony dialog has the Cycles Between Breeding set to 800, and the Breeding Methods box has a Death level of Very High. The effect is that each bopper colony tends to converge fairly rapidly on a single kind of behavior.

STEREO

STEREO.BL shows a 3D world of boids with long thin trails that you can observe in stereo mode. After loading this parameter file, press the control key combination (CONTROL)-(O) to toggle on the stereo mode. (The key is the letter O, and not the numeral zero.) Move your head nearer and farther from the screen until the patterns appear to float in front of the screen. Eventually, you should see something like a big tangle of wire.

In getting the effect, try and keep your eyes centered near the line that goes perpendicularly through the center of the screen. Often, it is easiest to first lock in on the three-dimensional effect when you are about five to six feet from the screen.

The stereo mode works with the different kinds of bopper Types and Trail Line types. It can, however, be a bit confusing when you put the world into wrapped mode—although this is worth trying when you want to look at turmites, as turmites tend to get stuck against the walls of the walled world.

Note that when you enter Stereo mode, the world is automatically put into Walled mode until you change it with the World menu. Because the pairs of stereo lines would eat into the gray walls, the walls are not drawn on the screen when in Stereo mode. There is no provision for making the body icons stereo, so it is usually better to turn them off when in Stereo mode.

SURFIN

SURFIN.BL tries to develop an interaction between the boppers and a CA patch. The CA rule is the Zhabotinsky rule, which generates spiral waves. In the best of all possible situations, the bopper would evolve to learn how to move along with the Zhabotinsky waves like little surfers, hence the name of this parameter file.

TERRA

TERRA.BL is a randomly discovered parameter setting that looks cool. Note that the Controls menu's Colonies dialog has a lot of things checked in each colony's Things To Zap box, which means that the appearance of the boppers changes pretty frequently. Thus, in Figure 7-23, some of the boppers have started to use Square Trail Nodes.

TILEBOID

TILEBOID.BL shows a two-dimensional walled world. The ecology is the Food Loop ecology, but with the Wall values set to negative one. The boids are set to have the Controls menu's Individuals dialog's Trail Nodes set to Small Squares, and with Trail Lines set to No Lines. This means that the bopper leave trails of small squares or tiles.

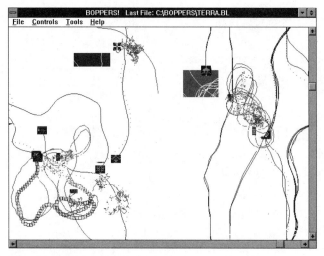

Figure 7-23 TERRA with Trail Node evolution

You can use the Controls menu's World dialog to check the Wrapped World radio button so that the boids don't have to deal with walls. You might also open the Controls menu's Individuals dialog, click the All Boppers radio button, change the Speed to two, and click DO IT! If the pattern gets too tangled, you may want to use the Controls menu's World dialog to decrease the Average Pixels Per Bopper trail values.

TILES

TILES.BL is similar to the COLORS.BL parameter file in that it consists of turmite boppers with Permanent Trail settings in the Controls menu's World dialog's Average Pixels Per Bopper box. Unlike COLORS, all the Trail Nodes are of the same type in TILES: Small Squares.

TURMITE

TURMITE.BL was the starting point of the creation of the *Boppers* program, which was originally created as a way to view turmites.

There are eight turmites of each color, with all trail lengths set to the maximum value. The symmetrical Food Loop ecology is in effect. The Turmite Windroses are set to the attractive value of 12. The IQs are set to the maximum value of 100, so that the most intricate kinds of behavior are likely to appear. Food and Poison patches are present to give the turmites more things to interact with. The

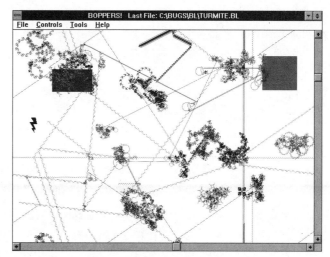

Figure 7-24: Turmites with the Zap cursor

Controls menu's Colonies dialog has Minimum Motion set to 100, with a severe low motion penalty of negative 400—there's no punishment too severe for a lazy turmite! Another good way to stir up activity is to randomize the genes of idle turmites by left-clicking them with the Zap cursor, which is what was done for Figure 7-24.

The Cycles Between Breeding is set to 2,000, which gives the boppers plenty of time to undergo a variety of different encounters and develop a meaningful score.

It is uncertain whether good evolution happens in TURMITE; it might be better to start with a very low IQ, let behavior for that IQ evolve, increase the IQ and let good behavior evolve for that level, and so on. This scheme has never been properly tested. You try it! Leave TURMITE.BL running in your office overnight, and in the morning save it as an experiment file, say TURM_MY.BEX. Then reload TURM_MY.BEX before you leave in the evening, save it again in the morning, and so on. Maybe use an IQ of 1 the first day, and increase the IQ every day after that. It could lead to some awesome turmites.

You can keep a rough eye on how evolution is progressing both by looking at the Tools menu's Graph dialog, and by using the Tools menu's Gene Viewer dialog to see how diverse the different colonies gene pools are. If you get a feeling that the Colony dialog's Breeding Methods parameters are not optimal, then change them! There's no reason to believe that the current Breeding Methods settings are in fact optimal.

If you and a friend both get involved in evolving better boppers, you can run the boppers head-to-head against each other. To do this, save your best bopper as, say BEST_ME.BOP. This is done by choosing the File menu's Save popup's Save Individual selection, which opens up a Save As command dialog box. Your friend saves his or her best bopper as, say, BEST_YF.BOP. Then you put the two *.BOP files on the same machine and bring up *Boppers* with TURMITE.BL running.

Now you click one of the green boppers to make it the edit bopper, and use the File menu's Open popup's Open Individual option to load BEST_ME.BOP onto the edit bopper. Use the Tools menu's Cursors popup to change the cursor to the Copy type, and left-click on your edit bopper. This copies BEST_ME.BOP onto all the green boppers.

Now your friend clicks on a red bopper to make it the edit bopper, and uses the same procedure to put the BEST_YF.BOP genes onto all the red boppers.

To make the experiment repeatable, you might want to put some standard DUMMY.BOP gene onto all the blue boppers. For a strictly repeatable contest, open the Controls menu's Colonies dialog and change all the Cycles Between Breeding values to No Breeding.

Because TURMITE.BL uses the Food Loop ecology, the situation between red and green is not symmetrical. So you might want to have your contest in two rounds: in the first round you occupy green and your friend occupies red, while in the second round you occupy red and your friend occupies green. Alternatively, you might evolve your boppers in a world with a Dog Eat Dog ecology, where red and green are scored in the same way.

UFO

UFO.BL uses the UFOlogy ecology. The green, red, and blue boppers are, respectively, turmites, dogs, and wolves. As mentioned before, the story that goes with the UFOlogy ecology is that the greens are like grass, the reds are like cows, and the blues are like cattle-eating saucers. The grass likes both cows and saucers because the cows fertilize the soil with manure, and the saucer drives fix nitrogen in the soil.

You might try increasing the Average Pixels Per Bopper values to fill up the screen with more color.

VENUS

VENUS.BL is a randomly found three-dimensional parameter setting that looks cool. Other randomly found settings are COWRIB, HAPPY, HOLE, and TERRA; see the notes on these for suggestions about things to do.

WINBLU

WINBLU.BL shows a two-dimensional world with five boppers in each colony. The green, red, and blue boppers are, respectively, owls, beavers, and wolves. The Food Chain ecology is active, meaning that green fears red, red likes green and fears blue, and blue likes red. This world has good, lively action.

WOLF

WOLF.BL shows three colonies of four wolves each. There is a Food patch present. It's a joy to watch the wolves rip into the food patch. The ecology is like the Food Loop ecology except that the wolves get extra high rewards for eating their prey's trail colors.

WOOLY

WOOLY.BL is a turmite world. The green, red, and blue boppers have Turmite Windroses of, respectively, 8, 64, and 16. The overall effect looks kind of wooly, hence the name.

ZHABOBUG

ZHABOBUG.BL is similar to the SURFIN.BL parameter setting. Here the CA patch is a bit smaller, and it has the Controls menu's CAs popup's CA Wrap selection toggled off.

NOTES AND REFERENCES

- Because the *.BL, *.BEX, and *.BOP files are ASCII text files, it is in principle possible for you to edit them directly and, thereby, get low-level control over the boppers.

  So that you can figure out which numbers mean what in these files, the source code for the functions that write and read these files is included in the document file LOADSAVE.DOC. LOADSAVE.DOC also includes the code for the DNA_to_RNA function which converts the boppers' DNA into parameter settings.

  Be warned that directly editing a *.BL, *.BEX, or *.BOP file and then trying to load it will cause *Boppers* to crash if you have changed some of the numbers to inappropriate values or if you have added any extraneous characters to the file. This kind of low-level tinkering is only a job for the truly comitted computer fanatic! But don't worry, most of the things you might want to do to your parameter files can be done safely and easily simply by using the *Boppers* menus to adjust the current file and then saving it.

8

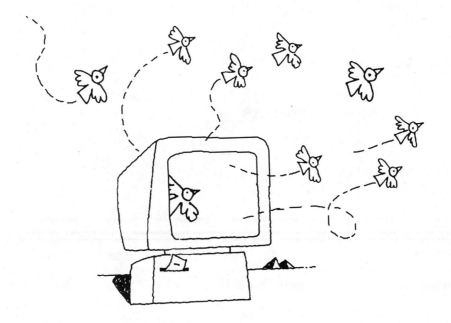

Onward!

Thus ends this phase of my ongoing obsession with artificial life. The Boppers *program is in your hands now, and I hope that you can use it to push the frontiers of this exciting new science another notch forward. And even if you don't get around to pushing the frontiers of science forward, I hope you have a lot of fun playing with* Boppers.

A good way to play with the program is to take a randomly generated configuration, or some existing parameter file, and start changing things. Let the program evolve a bit, and then look at what is happening. Inevitably you will find some of the boppers more interesting and attractive than others. Try and change the program parameters so that more of the interesting kinds of boppers evolve, or use the Copy cursor to make some or all of the boppers act just like the interesting ones. Then let things evolve some more....

If you always save your current genes and parameter settings as the ACTIVE.BEX file, you can go on evolving and tweaking your little world of boppers over many sessions. The longer the program runs, the richer the information in the genes of the boppers should become.

On the scientific front, some things that remain to be tried are

- Very long runs of bopper worlds
- The controlled breeding of selected individual boppers that have been saved as *.BOP files

- Experiments with the Endogamy and Exogamy options

- Comparisons of different settings of Timed Breeding parameters

As well as providing a richer understanding of artificial life and of genetic algorithms, *Boppers* can also give you insight into the nature of computation and into the grouping patterns of living things. After using the program for a while, you may find that you have an altered perception of such things as plant ecologies, flocks of birds, and even groups of people.

A mundane but exciting application of the program is to produce really striking graphics. As described in the Background Color Popup and Screen Capture section of Chapter 6, *Boppers User's Guide,* it is quite easy to capture and print images of the boppers. Another interesting use for the program might be to couple it to a computer projector and use *Boppers* to create real-time lightshows for music performances, including raves, rock shows, string quartets, jazz, or anything.

Have fun using *Boppers*, and if you discover something you'd like to share, write me a letter c/o Waite Group Press.

Index

worm worlds, 54
worms, 44-45
wrapped worlds, 119-120, 193, 238
WriteColor variable, 135, 145, 150, 151
WriteColorTable array, 134, 137, 142-143
writing data, 38-39

Y

Yukawa, Max, 30

Z

ZapLevel parameter, 175, 202
zapping
    for boppers, 175-176, 202
    generic, 17-18
    options for, 203-204
ZHABOBUG.BL, 273
Zhabotinsky CA rule, 83, 269

Books have a substantial influence on the destruction of the forests of the Earth. For example, it takes 17 trees to produce one ton of paper. A first printing of 30,000 copies of a typical 480-page book consumes 108,000 pounds of paper which will require 918 trees!

Waite Group Press™ is against the clear-cutting of forests and supports reforestation of the Pacific Northwest of the United States and Canada, where most of this paper comes from. As a publisher with several hundred thousand books sold each year, we feel an obligation to give back to the planet. We will, therefore, support and contribute a percentage of our proceeds to organizations which seek to preserve the forests of planet Earth.

WALKTHROUGHS AND FLYBYS CD

Phil Shatz

Fly around buildings before they exist, tour the inner workings of imaginary machines, and play electronic music while watching the motion of atoms. Welcome to the world of animated PC demos, a new area of technology and design that relies on high-powered PCs, an assortment of graphics animation software, a Sound Blaster board, and some special tricks. The **Walkthroughs and Flybys CD** presents breathtaking computer animation and music including over 300 megabytes of Autodesk 3D studio movies.

ISBN: 1-878739-40-9, 128 pages, 1-CD-ROM, $29.95, Available now

MAKING MOVIES ON YOUR PC

David Mason and Alexander Enzmann

Flex your imagination and direct animated movies! You'll get everything you need in this book/disk package to create fantastic rotating television logos, MTV-style action-clips, eye-boggling flybys and walkthroughs, or just about any movie effect you can dream up. The disks include the POLYRAY ray tracer for creating photorealistic images, and DTA, Dave's Targa Animator, the standard for converting ray-traced images to FLI movies. You'll also get ready-to-run example movies and explanations. No need to draw precise locations of objects and shadows—the included programs make realistic animation a snap; programming skills aren't required.

ISBN: 1-878739-41-7, 200 pages, 2-5.25" disks, $34.95, Available now

VIRTUAL REALITY PLAYHOUSE

Nick Lavroff

Jack-in to the world of Virtual Reality with this playful new book and disk package. Virtual Reality is a new interactive technology which creates the convincing illusion that you are completely immersed in worlds existing only inside your computer. **Virtual Reality Playhouse** lets you enter those worlds and even create your own personal digital dimension. Expand the parameters of your mind as you move rapidly from an introduction of Virtual Reality's basic concepts to visual explorations illustrating real-life applications. Demo programs include a 3-D simulation that puts you inside a robot which travels through a computer-generated city. Or, you can play a game in a 3-D room that can be tilted, spun, and twisted in near impossible ways. Put on the enclosed 3-D glasses and jump right into any one of 8 startling VR simulations. There are even plans for building your own LCD shuttering VR glasses and PowerGlove to manipulate objects in a VR world. For MS/PC DOS machines.

ISBN 1-878739-19-0, 146 pages, 1 3.5" disk, 3-D Glasses, $23.95 Available now

Send for our unique catalog to get more information about these books, as well as our outstanding and award-winning titles, including:

Image Lab: This unique book/disk set is a complete PC-based "digital darkroom" that covers virtually all areas of graphic processing and manipulation.

Multimedia Creations: Whether novice or professional, you can jump into multimedia with **Multimedia Creations** and its powerful built-in GRASP program and utilities. Create interactive educational games, multimedia kiosks, digital real-time movies, and music videos.

Virtual Reality Creations: Use this book, along with the included REND386 software and Fresnel viewers, to build virtual worlds—limited only by your imagination.

Nanotechnology Playhouse: Learn about building objects, machines, devices of all kinds, one atom at a time. Comes with multimedia demos to give you a taste of tomorrow.

Fractals for Windows: Create new fractals and control over 85 different fractal types with a zoom box, menus, and a mouse! Comes with WinFract, a powerful Windows version of Fractint for DOS, this package is faster than lightning at computing mind-bending fractals.

Falcon 3: The Complete Handbook: Master the skies and catch the thrill of flight with over 30 custom missions, a full-featured demo, and two hot utilities.

Master C: Let the PC Teach You C and **Master C++: Let the PC Teach You Object-Oriented Programming:** Both book/disk software packages turn your computer into an infinitely patient C and C++ professor.

LIMITED WARRANTY

The following warranties shall be effective for 90 days from the date of purchase: (i) The Waite Group, Inc. warrants the enclosed disk to be free of defects in materials and workmanship under normal use; and (ii) The Waite Group, Inc. warrants that the programs, unless modified by the purchaser, will substantially perform the functions described in the documentation provided by The Waite Group, Inc. when operated on the designated hardware and operating system. The Waite Group, Inc. does not warrant that the programs will meet purchaser's requirements or that operation of a program will be uninterrupted or error-free. The program warranty does not cover any program that has been altered or changed in any way by anyone other than The Waite Group, Inc. The Waite Group, Inc. is not responsible for problems caused by changes in the operating characteristics of computer hardware or computer operating systems that are made after the release of the programs, nor for problems in the interaction of the programs with each other or other software.

THESE WARRANTIES ARE EXCLUSIVE AND IN LIEU OF ALL OTHER WARRANTIES OF MERCHANTABILITY OR FITNESS FOR A PARTICULAR PURPOSE OR OF ANY OTHER WARRANTY, WHETHER EXPRESS OR IMPLIED.

EXCLUSIVE REMEDY

The Waite Group, Inc. will replace any defective disk without charge if the defective disk is returned to The Waite Group, Inc. within 90 days from date of purchase.

This is Purchaser's sole and exclusive remedy for any breach of warranty or claim for contract, tort, or damages.

LIMITATION OF LIABILITY

THE WAITE GROUP, INC. AND THE AUTHORS OF THE PROGRAMS SHALL NOT IN ANY CASE BE LIABLE FOR SPECIAL, INCIDENTAL, CONSEQUENTIAL, INDIRECT, OR OTHER SIMILAR DAMAGES ARISING FROM ANY BREACH OF THESE WARRANTIES EVEN IF THE WAITE GROUP, INC. OR ITS AGENT HAS BEEN ADVISED OF THE POSSIBILITY OF SUCH DAMAGES.

THE LIABILITY FOR DAMAGES OF THE WAITE GROUP, INC. AND THE AUTHORS OF THE PROGRAMS UNDER THIS AGREEMENT SHALL IN NO EVENT EXCEED THE PURCHASE PRICE PAID.

COMPLETE AGREEMENT

This Agreement constitutes the complete agreement between The Waite Group, Inc. and the authors of the programs, and you, the purchaser.

Some states do not allow the exclusion or limitation of implied warranties or liability for incidental or consequential damages, so the above exclusions or limitations may not apply to you. This limited warranty gives you specific legal rights; you may have others, which vary from state to state.

SATISFACTION REPORT CARD

Please fill out this card if you want to know of future updates to
Artificial Life Lab, or to receive our catalog.

Company Name:

Division/Department: **Mail Stop:**

Last Name: **First Name:**   **Middle Initial:**

Street Address:

City: **State:**   **Zip:**

Daytime telephone: (   )

Date product was acquired: Month   Day   Year   Your Occupation:

Overall, how would you rate *Artificial Life Lab?*
☐ Excellent   ☐ Very Good   ☐ Good
☐ Fair   ☐ Below Average ☐ Poor

What did you like MOST about this book?

What did you like LEAST about this book?

Please describe any problems you may have encountered while installing or using *Boppers:*

How did you use this book (problem-solver, tutorial, reference...)?

What is your level of computer expertise?
☐ New   ☐ Dabbler   ☐ Hacker
☐ Power User   ☐ Programmer   ☐ Experienced Professional

What computer languages are you familiar with?

Please describe your computer hardware:
Computer _____ Hard disk _____
5.25" disk drives _____ 3.5" disk drives _____
Video card _____ Monitor _____
Printer _____ Peripherals _____
Sound Board _____ CD ROM _____

Where did you buy this book?
☐ Bookstore (name): _____
☐ Discount store (name): _____
☐ Computer store (name): _____
☐ Catalog (name): _____
☐ Direct from WGP   ☐ Other _____

What price did you pay for this book? _____

What influenced your purchase of this book?
☐ Recommendation   ☐ Advertisement
☐ Magazine review   ☐ Store display
☐ Mailing   ☐ Book's format
☐ Reputation of Waite Group Press ☐ Other

How many computer books do you buy each year? _____

How many other Waite Group books do you own? _____

What is your favorite Waite Group book? _____

Is there any program or subject you would like to see Waite Group Press cover in a similar approach? _____

Additional comments? _____

☐ **Check here for a free Waite Group catalog**

Waite Group Press, Inc.

Attention: *Artificial Life Lab*

200 Tamal Plaza

Corte Madera, CA 94925

- **FOLD HERE** -